Cadenus
&
Swift's Most Valuable Friend

Cadenus
&
Swift's Most Valuable Friend

Two books on Jonathan Swift
by Sybil le Brocquy

Reissued with two images by Louis le Brocquy
and an introduction by Andrew Carpenter

THE LILLIPUT PRESS
DUBLIN

Cadenus & Swift's Most Valuable Friend first published 2003 by

THE LILLIPUT PRESS LTD
62–63 Sitric Road, Arbour Hill,
Dublin 7, Ireland
www.lilliputpress.ie

Frontispiece: 'Image of Swift', from a watercolour by
Louis le Brocquy

Cadenus first published 1962 and
Swift's Most Valuable Friend first published 1968 by

THE DOLMEN PRESS
23 Upper Mount Street
Dublin 2, Ireland

A CIP record for this title is available
from The British Library.

1 3 5 7 9 10 8 6 4 2

ISBN 1 84351 017 0

The Lilliput Press receives financial assistance from
An Chomhairle Ealaíon / The Arts Council of Ireland.

Printed in Ireland by ßetaprint of Dublin

Contents

Preface

Sybil le Brocquy (1892-1973) was a remarkable Irishwoman – one whose enthusiasm for life, for literature and for the arts in general was a source of inspiration to all those with whom she came into contact. Although she had many interests, the life and work of Jonathan Swift was one of those nearest her heart. During the 1940s and 50s, Sybil collected books by and about Swift and became an acknowledged expert on his life and work, concentrating much of her energy on the task of determining the precise nature of Swift's relationship with the two women in his life, Esther Johnson (Stella) and Esther Van Homrigh (Vanessa). In the 1960s, she put her knowledge to use and wrote or edited four books on Swift and his relationships: *Cadenus: a reassessment in the light of new evidence of the relationships between Swift, Stella and Vanessa* (1962), a play entitled *A View on Vanessa* (1967), *Stella's Birthdays* (a selection of poems by Swift and Stella with a commentary and notes which also appeared in 1967), and *Swift's Most Valuable Friend* (1968). The present volume, which contains the texts of the first and the last of Sybil's books on Swift, is designed to bring to a new generation of readers the fruits of her researches into a subject which fascinated her and to which she devoted much energy during the last twenty years of her life. *Cadenus* is primarily concerned with the relationship between Swift and Vanessa, and *Swift's Most Valuable Friend* with that between Swift and Stella. All four of Sybil's books on Swift were printed and published in Dublin by Liam Miller's Dolmen Press.

A note on the text

Cadenus and *Swift's Most Valuable Friend* are here reissued exactly as they appeared in the first Dolmen Press editions except that the illustrations in *Cadenus* are reproduced on text paper. Modern scholarship would present quotations, bibliographies and footnotes in different format from those employed here, and would put greater emphasis on textual accuracy than Liam Miller demanded of his authors in the 1960s. If a new edition of these books were called for, editorial amendments could be undertaken, the bibliographies updated, and account taken of recent scholarship. However, the books as they stand reflect, in a unique way, a vanished world where an enthusiastic and dedicated person from outside the academy could expect books of speculation and commentary on a figure such as Swift to be reviewed at the highest international level. For this reason, it has been decided to reissue them unaltered. The reader who wishes to gain access to the latest work on Swift is directed to the annual journal *Swift Studies* or to the extensive Swift bibliographies on the internet.

It is important to note, however, that the texts of Swift's correspondence, poems or prose, as included in the original Dolmen Press editions of Sybil le Brocquy's books and as reproduced here, were modernized and amended in various ways by Sybil or her publisher. As a result, they should not be relied on as accurate texts for quotation. The passages quoted by Sybil may be found in the correct form in the following standard editions: *The Correspondence of Jonathan Swift*, ed. Harold Williams, 5 vols (Oxford, 1963-72); *The Correspondence of Jonathan Swift, D. D.*, ed. David Woolley, (Frankfurt am Main, 1999 - in progress); *The Prose Works of Jonathan Swift*, eds. Herbert Davis et al, 16 vols (Oxford, 1939-68); *The Poems of Jonathan Swift*, ed. Harold Williams, 2nd ed., 3 vols (Oxford, 1958).

The main players in these books

Jonathan Swift; born 30 November 1667 in Dublin, his father (also named Jonathan Swift) probably having died in March or April of that year; educated at Kilkenny College (1673-82) and Trinity College Dublin (1682-9); acts as secretary to Sir William Temple at Moor Park Surrey for various periods between 1689 and 1699 where he becomes tutor to the young Esther Johnson (Stella), daughter of Temple's housekeeper; 1695, ordained priest into the Church of Ireland; 1704-13, intermittent visits to England where he becomes an ally of the Tory ministry and meets Esther Van Homrigh (Vanessa); 1710-13 sends daily journal from London to Stella (who, with Dingley has moved to Dublin); 1713, appointed Dean of St Patrick's Dublin; 1714, returns to Ireland on the death of Queen Anne and the fall of the Tory ministry and is followed (in November) by Vanessa; 1723, death of Vanessa; 1726, publication of *Gulliver's Travels*; 1728, death of Stella; 1735, publication of Swift's *Collected Works* in Dublin; 19 October 1745, death.

Esther Johnson, 'Stella'; born 1681, daughter of the housekeeper in Sir William Temple's house in Surrey; meets Swift in 1689, he becomes her tutor during the 1690s; moves to Dublin with her companion, Rebecca Dingley, on Swift's advice, in 1701; joint recipient (with Dingley) of the letters known as the *Journal to Stella* 1710-13; suffers increasing ill-health from about 1722 and dies in January 1728.

Rebecca Dingley; born *c.* 1665, a distant relative of the Temple family; becomes Stella's companion and moves to Dublin with her in 1701; joint recipient of the *Journal to Stella*; remains a spinster and dies in 1743.

Esther Van Homrigh, 'Vanessa'; born in Dublin 1687/8, the daughter of a wealthy Dutch merchant; 1707 (after the death of her father) moves, with her mother, brother and sister, to London and meets (or re-encounters) Swift who visits the Van Homrigh house regularly and becomes an intimate of the family; 1711, is said to have marriage 'in prospect', presumably to Swift; 1714, after the death of her mother, moves to Ireland, to which Swift has just returned; sends Swift many tempestuous and passionate letters before her death in 1723. Believed by Sybil le Brocquy to have borne Swift a son in 1714.

Introduction

Generations of readers have been drawn to the commanding figure of Jonathan Swift, not simply because he wrote *Gulliver's Travels* and *A Modest Proposal* or because of his 'savage indignation' and his powerful satire, or because he was the famous Dean of St Patrick's Cathedral Dublin, but because of the fascinating, unsolved mysteries of his private life. Swift himself was well aware that people could not resist speculating about him, and warned Vanessa Van Homrigh (Vanessa) of '... the Tattle of this nasty Town (Dublin)' in December 1714; his death in 1745 did nothing to dampen interest in the questions which had been so often asked during his life: Was the Dean the illegitimate son of Sir William (or of Sir John) Temple? Was he married to Esther Johnson (Stella)? If he did not marry Stella, why not? What was his relationship with the passionate, stormy Vanessa? How could a clergyman love two women at once? Did these two women meet each other? Why did Vanessa cut him out of her will? These, and many other questions, have echoed around the books, articles and conversations on Swift for two hundred and fifty years, sometimes raised by those who investigate his life as an aid to understanding of his work, sometimes by the merely curious.

Yet Swift's serious biographers – particularly those who have earned their livings as academics or ecclesiastics – have been remarkably disinclined to comment on persistent rumours that he was illegitimate, and equally unwilling to address problems associated with his relationships with Stella and Vanessa. Rumours of his illegitimacy are normally dismissed as idle speculation for which no factual evidence exists, and the business of Swift, Stella and Vanessa as being irrelevant to his great writings. There are excellent editions of the significant texts – the *Journal to Stella* and the poems which passed between Swift and Stella, on the one side, the long poem entitled 'Cadenus and Vanessa' and more than forty letters between Swift and Vanessa on the other – but surprisingly little mention of this material. Clearly, this is uncomfortable territory for many commentators: Swift was an unmarried clergyman, yet he loved, and was loved by, two women at the same time – albeit in very different ways. It easier to write about Swift as Sir William Temple's secretary, as the propagandist of the Tory ministry, as the most powerful satirist of his age, as the friend of Pope, as the Irish patriot or as the Dean of St Patrick's than as a man in love, or as a man loved by two women. Still, his fraternal or avuncular relationship with Stella is less painful to write about than his puzzling, stormy relationship with Vanessa – a beautiful, passionate woman twenty years his junior: it is the dangerous Vanessa whom Swift's staid biographers have tried to push to the sidelines. As Sybil le Brocquy put it neatly in *Cadenus*:

> At an early stage, biographers took sides in the implied rivalry between Stella and Vanessa, with the unfortunate result that Vanessa's denigration was regarded as essential to Stella's glorification. (page 8)

Sybil's aim, in both her main books on Swift, was to bring new light to bear on the relationship between Swift and the women in his life, and to facilitate a more sympathetic assessment of them, particularly of Vanessa. *Cadenus* was designed for this purpose. But Sybil also wanted to scrutinize Swift's relationship with Stella and, in her other major work on Swift, *Swift's Most Valuable Friend*, she used the text of the notes Swift wrote on Stella at the time of her death as the basis for a compassionate account of this relationship. The result is two remarkable books, driven by sympathetic and intuitive inquiry, which made an important contribution to Swift studies when they appeared in the 1960s and which still remain significant for all those interested in Swift's life and works.

The context

Though Sybil le Brocquy was widely acknowledged to be an expert on Swift and his work by the time she wrote *Cadenus* in 1962, she knew that the theories she was putting forward about Swift and the women in his life would not be popular with the Swift establishment of the day. She had seen the reviews which had greeted Denis Johnston's *In Search of Swift* in 1959; Johnston, a good friend of Sybil, had spent many years searching for information which would help him prove that Swift was the illegitimate son of Sir John Temple. He had scoured legal and parish records and put together a fascinating work which read almost like a detective story. His main conclusion was that Swift could not marry Stella because she was his niece – he being the illegitimate son of Sir John Temple and Stella the illegitimate daughter of Sir John's son, Sir William Temple.

The Swift establishment, however, did not want, in public at least, to be convinced by, or even to entertain Johnston's theories. The reviews of his book were almost universally damning, much to Johnston's disappointment. For most established Swiftians of the day – even Irvin Ehrenpreis who was at work on his massive biography of Swift – there was no need to question the received truth about Swift's parentage. Speculation that Swift was a Temple was unhelpful and might even undermine the basis on which some of their work on Swift was based. However, Sybil knew that, in private, these Swift experts were considerably more rattled by Johnston's book than they were prepared to admit in public, and that their personal views were far less resolute than they seemed to be. Loosely inserted in her own copy of Johnston's *In Search of Swift*, Sybil kept copies of a series of fascinating letters which passed between the leading Swiftians at the time of Johnston's book.

It is clear from this correspondence that some of them, at least, seem to have been uncomfortable about their ostrich-like attitude to this side of Swift. When he received *In Search of Swift* for review, Herbert Davis, the editor of Swift's prose works, wrote to Sir Harold Williams, the editor of Swift's poetry and the *Journal to Stella*, as follows:

> … I am also reviewing Denis Johnston … and it is certainly not easy. I found it I must say very easy to read, though of course knowing what was coming. There is of course no evidence whatever for his main suggestion that Sir John Temple was Swift's father, no more than there is for the suggestion that Stella was Sir William Temple's daughter.
>
> But I do not think it is so easy to demolish some of the facts that he puts forward about the family of Swifts in Dublin, on the evidence of the parish records and the Black Book. Here again of course he has not been able to prove the main point on which his case rests, that is that Swift's father, that is his mother's husband, died at the end of January [1667]. But I think he does succeed in putting some very awkward questions, which are not at all easy to answer. And I am not sure that Ehrenpreis, who was spending a lot of time in his investigations of the family of Swift's mother and her Leicester connections, will be able to deal with them all either. But as to Swift's genius, Johnston evidently thinks it is easier to believe in it if we knew that he was indeed connected with such a brilliant family as the Temples.
>
> What I can never understand is why his mother abandoned him. And who did pay for his education?
>
> I have always shied away from these biographical problems and I am afraid that I have never quite made up my mind about some of them … [1]

This fascinating letter helps us put Sybil le Brocquy's work on Swift into perspective. Like Denis Johnston, Sybil was convinced that the scholars and academics of the 'establishment' had overlooked vital clues in their assessment of Swift's life, and had failed to address important issues. When

1. Letter from Herbert Davis to Sir Harold Williams, 29 October 1959.

these previously unknown or undervalued facts were brought into the light, Sybil (like Denis Johnston) believed that a fuller and more truthful portrait of Swift could be painted. Where Denis Johnston was determined to unearth every scrap of information on Swift's parentage and establish whether Jonathan Swift Senior could possibly have fathered the Dean, Sybil wanted to show that Swift's relationships with Vanessa and Stella could be reassessed once certain documents were revealed. Her work, like that of Johnston, was a work of detection and explanation. Both writers believed that their discoveries would cast new light on rumours which had been around for two hundred years.

The problem was that, though the establishment itself was aware of its failure to investigate these sides of Swift's life, it could not afford to acknowledge the failure in public. The books in which Denis Johnston and Sybil aired their theories were reviewed in leading newspapers and journals, but in such a way that they were made to seem peripheral to mainstream Swift scholarship – at least in the reviews written by top Swift scholars. It was not hard to suggest that the speculations in these books were not really significant since the books were written by amateur scholars rather than professionals and published not by university presses but by small firms based in Dublin.[2]

Sir Harold Williams's review of *In Search of Swift* in *The Library Review* dismissed the book out of hand. He began by describing it as 'This strange volume …', and went on to characterize its author as one who manipulated evidence to suit his purpose, and who was guilty of 'deliberate misinterpretation'. Johnston was a man who belittled 'the genius and

2. Neither Liam Miller of the Dolmen Press nor Allen Figgis (the publisher of Johnston's book) required authors to follow scholarly stylebooks or to consult *Hart's Rules for Compositors*: as a result, both authors quoted texts in unconventional ways and neither book reproduced texts accurately. This made it easy for a scholarly reviewer to pick holes in work produced to different standards from those of a university press, and to imply that it belonged at the margins of commentary on Swift.

power of Swift's writings' in 'chapter after chapter'. He had failed to produce 'convincing evidence' and had merely 'resuscitated a legend'. Herbert Davis was a little less harsh in the *Review of English Studies*. Though he had admitted in private that he could not 'quite make up his mind' about some of the biographical problems connected with Swift, Davis's review of Johnston's book dismissed Johnston magisterially as if he were an undergraduate who had submitted a paper of only Beta quality for a second year assignment. Here are some examples of his patronizing comments: 'Mr Johnston should be careful in challenging ...', 'Mr Johnston has been indiscreet enough to provide us with ...', 'He wastes our time and seems to wish to arouse our suspicions ...', 'He does not take the trouble to inform us whether ...'.[3] Towards the end of his review, Davis did, however, acknowledge that 'Mr Johnston has succeeded in showing what doubtful evidence has been accepted by many of Swift's biographers as a basis for our knowledge of important matters connected with Swift's family, birth and early life,' and complimented Johnston on 'excellent detective work'. In general, however, it is clear that Sybil le Brocquy knew, when she began work on Swift, that she was venturing into difficult terrain.

Cadenus

Like Denis Johnston, Sybil le Brocquy was a born detective and, also like Denis Johnston, she was not afraid to tread on academic toes. She had been interested in Swift for many years before she put pen to paper to write *Cadenus*. Late in the 1950s, she came across the Family Petition made by the Van Homrigh family to the House of Lords in 1711 and recognized the significance of one particular phrase in it. The document describes Vanessa as one who has 'marriage in prospect' and, as Sybil correctly deduced, this clearly suggests that Swift intended to marry Vanessa in 1711 – a like-

3. *Review of English Studies*

ly enough direction for the relationship to take, since everyone expected his powerful Tory friends to provide an English bishopric for him very shortly. Both Swift and the Van Homrigh family intended, at this point, to remain in England for the rest of their lives.

Unfortunately, however, things did not turn out like this and, as Sybil's story unfolds, the tragic consequences of Swift's appointment to the deanery of St Patrick's Dublin becomes increasingly clear. His enforced return to Dublin brought him back to the city in which Stella – whom Swift has known since his days at Moor Park and to whom he had been acting as guardian for the last ten years – now lived with her companion, Rebecca Dingley. When Vanessa arrived in Ireland in 1714, she, Swift and Stella – three players in an unfolding tragedy – were all on the same stage.

As Sybil put together the various pieces of the human jigsaw, she began to realize the significance of various previously overlooked small pieces. There were mysterious mentions of a boy in Swift's letters to Vanessa, in Swift's poems and in Stella's will, as well as a mysterious entry in the burial register of St Patrick's Cathedral. All became clear to her, and Sybil proposed her startling theory that Swift had become Vanessa's lover in London during the years 1711-14, that he had had a child by her and that the boy, Bryan McLoughlin, had been brought to Ireland. Further, Sybil suggested that, when Vanessa knew she was dying in the 1720s, she approached Stella asking her to act as guardian to Swift's son, that Stella agreed and took him into her house, that she had left the boy a legacy in her will and that, on the boy's death, he had been buried in St Patrick's Cathedral. This was, in brief, the bombshell which Sybil detonated in *Cadenus*.

Austin Clarke was quite correct when he prophesied dryly in his *Irish Times* review of *Cadenus* that, 'The book should provoke controversy.' Predictably, the Swift establishment closed ranks against the book and most managed to avoid reviewing it; other reviewers (many of them not well-disposed to the stuffier heights of academe) expressed ill-disguised glee at the arrival of a volume whose author was perceived as a lively iconoclastic bull having a field day in the stuffy and pedantic china shop of Swift scholarship. The reviewer in *The Sunday Telegraph* suggested that 'If Mrs Le Brocquy is right, every book about Swift will now be wrong,' and *The Times* expressed the view that 'Sybil Le Brocquy may well have penetrated the Dean's secret where professionals have not – a view which did not go down well, one presumes, with the 'professionals'. One of the few Swiftians to comment on the book was the veteran Emil Pons who wrote of Sybil: 'She has, I believe, succeeded at last in discovering the truth, by her sympathy and intelligent intuition, where documentary research and cold deduction alone have failed.' The phrase 'cold deduction' can not have delighted Sir Harold Williams, Herbert Davis or, indeed, the younger Irvin Ehrenpreis.

For the ordinary reader, however, *Cadenus* was a delight – a lively, enjoyable account of a remarkable group of people, written with lightness of touch and deftness of expression. The book was widely appreciated for its real understanding of Swift and his age, and for its sympathy and compassion for the human predicament in which Swift, Stella and Vanessa found themselves. Sybil's extraordinary empathy with Vanessa's suffering, in particular, emerges clearly from her comments on the documents reproduced.

The problem with the book – and indeed with Sybil's theory – is that the key letter upon which it is founded is more ambiguous than Sybil considered it to be. This is a letter from Swift to Vanessa, which though undated, Sybil assigned to 1720; it refers to the rumours abounding in Dublin about a relationship between Swift and Vanessa, that he was 'in love' with her and 'that little master and I visited' her 'and that the A-B did so'. As Sybil says: 'The question naturally arises, who was "little master"' (page 64). She goes on: 'If Vanessa had had a son about October 1714, … he would now be about five or six years old,' and draws the conclusion that this son, Bryan McLoughlin, was indeed the child of Swift and Vanessa.

There are several difficulties with Sybil's interpretation of this letter. The first lies in its date. The ordering of letters between Swift and Vanessa is a problem which has exercised editors of his correspondence ever since the full cache of letters between the two became available in Martin Freeman's *Vanessa and her Correspondence with Jonathan Swift: the letters edited for the first time from the originals* in 1921. Freeman dates the letter '[? end of 1714]'; Harold Williams, in his 1963 edition of Swift's correspondence, dates it '[27 December 1714]' and David Woolley in his 2001 edition of the correspondence dates it '[December 1714]'. Though, as the square brackets show, no editor is prepared to be definitive about the date, none of them suggests a date later than December 1714 for the letter. Woolley defends his dating by noting that the letter contains the phrase 'I beg you to be easy', which is echoed in Vanessa's letter to Swift dated December 1714 where she writes: 'You bid me be easy.' Woolley takes the second letter (dated 'December 1714') to be a direct response to the undated one. In her copy of Freeman's book, Sybil put a question mark above the date 1714 and wrote in the margin '1720?'. Unfortunately, she gave no evidence there or elsewhere to support a date of 1720.

If the letter was written in 1714 – and there seems to be no evidence that it was not – then Sybil's theory that 'little master' refers to a son born to Swift and Vanessa in October 1714 can not be correct. Swift's first letter to Vanessa after she arrived in Ireland in November 1714 refers to the journey as 'full of fatigues' and makes comparisons between the air and the walks in Dublin and London: there is no mention of a baby or anything which might be taken to refer to one. Nor is there any evidence that Vanessa left a baby behind her in London.

In addition, it is hard to accept that Vanessa could have given the name 'Bryan McLoughlin' to a child born to her in London while she still expected to marry Swift and to stay in England all her days. It seems, on balance, much more likely that the name belonged to an unfortunate Irish child – one of the hundreds abandoned in the streets of Dublin every year – whom Stella had taken into her house and supported, as she says in her will, 'on charity'.

Another difficulty arises in the letter assigned to 1720 by Sybil. Though it is certainly not clear who or what is referred to by the phrase 'little master', that phrase is followed by another odd one, 'the A-B'. Most commentators have assumed that this referred to Archbishop King but Sybil herself, in her copy of Freeman's *Vanessa and her Correspondence*, wrote:

'The 'A-B' was obviously one of Swift's many nicknames for somebody, since visits from the Archbishop, Dr King, could not possibly cause 'the tattle of this nasty town' – a phrase used later in the letter.[4]

If 'the A-B' is a nickname for someone, then it seems highly likely that 'little master' is another of the same type – as fancifully ironic as 'the A-B', perhaps. It seems unwise to interpret the words as literally as Sybil does.

The status of the letter itself is hard to assess. It tells a story which Sybil herself admits she finds it impossible to believe. Swift asserted that he had been told the gossip about himself and Vanessa by 'a woman who does business for me'; as Sybil writes: 'No woman or man, from the Archbishop down, would have dared, or been permitted, to repeat such tittle-tattle to the Dean of St Patrick's. It is an incredible story' (page 63). It is simply not possible to read as much into this phrase in this context, in a letter written in 1714, as Sybil did in *Cadenus*.

To point out this error of interpretation on Sybil's part is not, in any way, to detract from the importance or value of the book as a whole. Throughout the text, Sybil's sharp, detective eye recognizes the significance of words and phrases in the various documents she reproduces and provides ingenious, sometimes witty, usually convincing explanations. Her handling of the events surrounding the deaths of both Vanessa and Stella is sensitive and sympathetic, though she does – here as elsewhere – give more credence to the world of rumour than do most biographers of Swift. Finally, the book contains most useful appendixes in which Sybil repro-

4. See also *Swift's Most Valuable Friend* p. 90.

duces the wills of Vanessa, her mother and her brother, among other key documents. Bruce Arnold's recent unearthing of the will of Bartholomew Van Homrigh himself, in an article in *Swift Studies*, seems to complete the documentation of the Van Homrigh family.[5]

Swift's Most Valuable Friend

Though *Swift's Most Valuable Friend* is a slighter work than *Cadenus* and not based on any documentary discovery, it represents, nevertheless, an original contribution to Swift studies. It consists of a reprinting of portions of Swift's 'On the death of Mrs Johnson' interspersed with illuminating commentary in which Sybil used to the full her considerable knowledge of Swift and his work.

If the earlier book had tried to be fair to Vanessa, this book pays honour to Stella, but Sybil does not shrink, once again, from addressing the awkward questions which arise in dealing with Stella's life. On page 85 she writes that Swift 'almost certainly intended to marry Stella soon after he persuaded the Ladies (i.e. Stella and Dingley) to move to Dublin' but goes on to explain that he must have become aware of the fact that (as Denis Johnston suggested) he and Stella were blood relations and that such an alliance was impossible. Elsewhere in the book, she highlights inconsistencies and contradictions in Swift's versions of events, and between his accounts and those of his contemporaries. Throughout, she remains sympathetic to human frailty and ready to recognize and applaud actions which demonstrate courage and a sense of honour.

Swift's Most Valuable Friend is a more slow-paced book than *Cadenus*, an extended meditation on friendship and its responsibilities rather than a detective story; for though, as Sybil shows, Swift clearly loved Stella, his

5. Bruce Arnold, '"A Protestant Purchaser": Bartholomew Van Homrigh, merchant adventurer', *Swift Studies* 15 (2000), 42-50. For the text of the will, see pp. 47-50.

love was more fraternal or avuncular than passionate, and the relationship Sybil describes was one of easy familiar friendship rather than of ecstatic discovery. Swift described himself as one who had 'the happiness of [Stella's] friendship' (quoted on page 55) and Stella as his 'most valuable friend'. Despite the many unhappinesses which it chronicles – the greatest of which is Swift's misery at the death of Stella – this book is an account of as serene a relationship as Swift ever experienced.

Yet throughout both works, Sybil le Brocquy was acutely aware that the figures she was considering – particularly the figure of Swift himself – were destined to play out a tragedy. It is characteristic of Sybil's view of Swift as a whole that the epilogue she wrote for *Swift's Most Valuable Friend* should be a compassionate and sombre summary of the miseries of the Dean's last years. As she put it in her very last sentence: 'Few tragedies are not diminished by comparison with that of Jonathan Swift, Dean of St Patrick's Cathedral Church, Dublin.'

SYBIL LE BROCQUY

CADENUS

A reassessment in the light of new evidence of
the relationships between
SWIFT, STELLA *and* VANESSA

Dublin
THE DOLMEN PRESS

To

A. Le B.

Sincere thanks are due to

The Very Reverend Dr. Armstrong, Dean of St. Patrick's, Dublin, *for permission to photograph the entry in the Cathedral Records;*
The Reverend A. Lister, *for permission to photograph the entry in the Records of the Church of St. Andrew, Northborough, England.*
Mr. P. I. King, M.A., Archivist, *Northamptonshire Record Office, England.*
Mr. G. M. Kirkwood, *Literary Department, Principal Probate Registry, Somerset House, London;*
The National Library of Ireland, *for permission to publish portion of Peter Partinton's letter;*
Miss M. Pollard, *Marsh's Library, Dublin;*
Mr. D. Englefield, M.A., *Library of the House of Commons, London;*
Louis le Brocquy
for their most generous help.

Preface

THE recent discovery of the Petition of the Van Homrigh family to "*The Right Honble the Lords Spiritual & Temporal*" and of the Judges' Opinion offered to that august body has given an opportunity for a reconsideration of the much-debated relationship between Jonathan Swift and Esther Van Homrigh.

To those critics who insist that the private life of a great writer should be left in decent obscurity, the reply must be that, in this case, there has been from the beginning no reluctance to speculate, and indeed to dogmatise freely about the ties which bound together Swift, Esther Johnson and Esther Van Homrigh.

A great deal of evidence has been given about the characters of both women; many unfavourable judgements have been passed on the younger. But, for some curious reason, Swift's own testimony about his relationship with that unhappy girl has been almost entirely ignored. The kindest picture presented has been that of a reluctant man pursued by a determined young woman, from whom he did his utmost to escape, without being too unkind to her frailty. His letters, particularly his later ones, give not the slightest support to such a theory, unless on the assumption that Swift was a hypocrite and a liar.

Such evidence as still exists in their obviously mutilated correspondence would seem to show that this extraordinary, thwarted man loved deeply, over many years, an intelligent, attractive, frustrated girl. Because no conjecture offered so far gives any plausible explanation of the tragic events which submerged Dean Swift and these two unhappy women, it is permissible to put forward yet another, in the light of new evidence.

Contents

Illustrations

I

Vanity makes terrible devastation in the female breast . . .
Vanessa was exceedingly vain . . . fond of dress . . . im-
patient to be admired; very romantic in her turn of mind;
superior in her own opinion, to all her sex: full of pertness,
gaiety and pride . . . far from being either beautiful or
genteel . . . happy in the thoughts of being reputed Swift's
concubine, but still aiming and intending to be his wife. . . .
Thus perished at Selbridge, under all the agonies of despair,
Mrs. Esther Vanhomrigh, a miserable example of an ill-
spent life, fantastic wit, visionary schemes and female weak-
ness.

> *Remarks on the Life and Writings of Dr. J. Swift:*
> *Orrery, 1752*

I have been assured that Miss Vanhomrigh was, in her
general Converse with the World, as far from encouraging
any Stile of Address inconsistent with the Rules of Honour
and Good-breeding as any Woman alive. Neither can it be
said, if any Conclusions can be drawn from her Appearance
and Behaviour in Ireland, that she was either a vain Woman
or fond of Dress . . . . Her only Misfortune was that she
had a Passion for Doctor Swift. Thus died at Celbridge,
worthy of a happier Fate, the celebrated Mrs. Esther Van-
homrigh, a Martyr to Love and Constancy.

> *An Essay upon the Life, Writings and Character of*
> *Dr. Jonathan Swift: Deane Swift, 1755.**

Deane Swift was a first cousin once removed of Jonathan
Swift.

TO these two very different descriptions of Esther Van Homrigh must be added a third, from a person who, over many years, knew her far better than anyone else:

Il n'y a point de merite, ni aucun preuve de mon bon goût, de trouver en vous tout ce que la Nature a donne á un mortel, je veux dire l'honneur, la vertue, le bon sens, l'esprit, la douceur, l'agrement et la fermité d'ame. Mais en vous cachant comme vous faites, le monde ne vous connait pas, et vous perdez l'eloge des millions de gens. Depuis que j'avois l'honneur de vous connoitre, j'ay toujours remarquè que, ni en conversation particuliere ni en general, aucun mot a eschappè de votre bouche, qui pouvoit etre mieux exprimé; et je vous jure qu'en faisant la plus severe critique, je ne pouvois jamais trouver aucun defaut, ni en vos actions ni en vos paroles. La coquetrie, l'affectation, la pruderie sont des imperfections que vous n'avez jamais connu. Et, avec tout cela, croyez vous qu'il est possible de ne vous estimer au dessus du reste du genre humain? Quelle bestes en juppes sont les plus excellentes de celles que je vois semèes dans le monde au prix de vous. En les voyant, en les entendant, je dis cent fois le jour, Ne parle, ne regarde, ne pense, ne fait rien comme ces miserables. Sont ce du meme sexe, du meme espece de creatures? Quelle cruautè, de faire mepriser, autant de gens, qui sans songer de vous seroient assès supportable.

When Jonathan Swift wrote these words to *Madam Hester Vanhumri*, on the 12th May 1719, he had known her intimately for at least eleven years; neither Lord Orrery nor Deane Swift had ever met her.

How well did Swift know this young woman, whom he could assure, after many years of acquaintance, that her perfections made all other women appear, by contrast, as *brutes in petticoats?* The answer to that question is clearly given in the letters they wrote to one another. Their story begins in 1707.

When the Rev. Dr. Swift was travelling from Dublin to London, in December 1707, he broke the tiresome journey in an inn at Dunstable, and there he almost certainly met Mrs. Van Homrigh who, with her young family, was also on her way to London, having decided that the social life of that great capital offered greater advantages than the smaller one of Dublin. She was a pleasant, irresponsible, light-hearted woman, the youngish widow of Bartholomew Van Homrigh, a Dutch gentleman who had come to Dublin from Amsterdam some time before the Revolution of 1687. How long before is not known, but it must have been a considerable time for him to have acquired the Freedom of Dublin and to have become an important citizen by 1685, when his name appears as a member of the Dublin Corporation and one of a small group appointed to supervise the building of the Tholsel. By 1688, he had become an Alderman, and his infant daughter, Esther, was therefore eligible for the Freedom of the City in the Spring of that year.

The Van Homrigh family — so they consistently spelled their name on official occasions — not unnaturally threw in their lot with the Dutch King, and fled to join his forces. In 1689, Alderman Van Homrigh *having unlawfully absented himself from the business of the City and gone to England*, was removed from the Dublin Corporation roll.

During the Revolution, Bartholomew Van Homrigh played an important part, acting as Commissary-General to the Williamite army. After King William's victory, Van Homrigh returned to Dublin, and in 1691 was reinstated as

3

Alderman and appointed a Sheriff of the City; later he became Chief Commissioner of Irish Revenue and Member of Parliament for Londonderry. In 1697 he was elected Lord Mayor of Dublin. During his term of office, street-lighting was first introduced there.

But for these bare outlines, little is known of this Dutch gentleman except that he was father of a famous daughter, but in 1698 he was left a small legacy by Sir William Molyneux, which bears eloquent testimony to his worth. Sir William, (who was described by the great John Locke as *that thinking gentleman, whom I am proud to call my friend*) bequeathed money for mourning rings to four only of his many close associates: the Rev. Dr. Smythe, Dean of St. Patrick's, Dublin; Bishop St. George Ashe; John Locke and Bartholomew Van Homrigh. Sir Thomas Molyneux, renowned philosopher and scientist, with his friends was responsible for the foundation of what is now the Royal Dublin Society. It would seem that Bartholomew Van Homrigh was a remarkable person, as well as being a prosperous citizen. When he died, in 1703, he was probably still a young man.

His widow was the daughter of John Stone, who like Van Homrigh had been a Commissioner of Revenue in Ireland. Lord Orrery's description of Mrs. Van Homrigh's *mean birth* is as inaccurate as his account of her daughter, Esther. Both in Dublin and in London, the Van Homrigh family moved in the higher ranks of society.

The decision to move to London was probably the result of many considerations. Mrs. Van Homrigh was extremely hospitable and fond of society; she intended sending both her sons to an English university. According to the records of Christ Church, Oxford, the elder matriculated there on the 15th April 1708, at the age of fifteen. She hoped that her well-dowered girls would make suitable marriages in London society. She may well have planned some comfortable alliance for herself — Dublin gossip had already been whispering of a romance with Sir William Robinson, her late husband's colleague. In the great world of London, opportunities for a gay life were much wider than in Ireland. The Van Homrighs were already on an excellent footing with the families of such nobility as the Marquess of Kildare, the Earl of Athlone — godfather to her son, Ginkell — and the Duke of Ormond. They would also have met visiting English notabilities at Dublin Castle, and Mrs. Van Homrigh would certainly not have forgotten the very signal honours paid to her late husband — and, possibly, to herself — during a visit to the Court of William and Mary, and also the fact that that parsimonious King had given the very considerable sum of £770 for a Mayoral chain to grace the inauguration of Bartholomew Van Homrigh as Lord Mayor of Dublin. (The gold chain with the imposing medallion was not, unfortunately, ready in time for that occasion, but has ever since lent magnificence to his successors in office). The future must have seemed very bright to Mrs. Van Homrigh as she rested in a Dunstable inn, after a very stormy passage across the Irish Sea.

That meeting of the Van Homrigh family and Dr. Swift, a poor Irish clergyman, is the first important milestone in the story of Swift and Vanessa, as young Miss Esther was to be known in the not so distant future. Five years later he wrote to her mother:

I could not see any marks in the chimney at Dunstable of the coffey Hessy spilt there.

It would seem that the stay in the Dunstable inn, long or short, was sufficient to admit Swift into a warm friendship with the family, with whom he may well have had some previous acquaintance when he was Chaplain to Lord Berkeley and to Lord Pembroke during their terms of office in

Dublin. A few weeks later, Mrs. Van Homrigh had set up her hospitable home in London, and Swift was already involved in the humorous bullying which was always so dear to him; the *Decree for concluding the Treaty between Dr. Swift and Mrs. Long,* that cousin of the Van Homrighs who was a famous Toast, and, as such, had claimed exemption from the Doctor's rule that, *all persons whatsoever shall make advances to him, as he pleases to demand.* This pleasantry, which refers to *Mrs. Van Homrigh and her fair daughter, Hessy,* purports to be the work of young Ginkell and is one of the boy's few appearances in the story.

The easy friendship between Swift and the Van Homrighs continued during his considerable stay in London. There, he was working on behalf of the Church of Ireland to obtain the remission of the First Fruits, a concession made to the Church of England, some years previously, by the Queen. After his return to Dublin in June 1709, his own records show that letters passed between himself, the mother and the elder daughter, but the letters did not survive. When he returned again to London, in September 1710, (after a short interval, during which Ginkell was dying) the Van Homrigh household rapidly became Swift's home from home. The *Journal to Stella* begins reporting dinners at *Mrs. Van's* with increasing regularity and invariable excuses — *It was such dismal weather I could not stir further,* or *out of mere listlessness, dine there often, as I did today.*

By the end of the year, Stella (Esther Johnson) in Dublin, had obviously become suspicious of danger in London, and had made some slighting reference to the Van Homrighs' social circle. To which Swift replied:

Sir Andrew Fountaine and I dined by invitation with Mrs. Van Homrigh. You say they are of no consequence; why they keep as good female company as I do male. I see all the drabs of quality at this end of the

6

town with them. I saw the two Lady Bettys there this afternoon.

As Stella presumably knew, the two ladies were the daughter of the Duke of Ormond and the daughter of the Earl of Berkeley. Later, he cannot resist reporting to the rank-conscious Stella:

Went to Mrs. Van Homrigh's; and there was Sir Andrew Fountaine at Ombre with Lady Ashburnham, Lady Frederick Schomberg and Lady Betty Butler.

Another time he tells her that he had dined with the Van Homrighs and that later they had all gone to spend the evening with the Duchess of Ormond.

These entries offer an opportunity for some assessment of the atmosphere of the Van Homrigh home; and it may be usefully noted that Sir Andrew Fountaine, whose constant visits to that ménage are reported in the *Journal to Stella*, was a young man of considerable importance. He had graduated brilliantly at Oxford, and he was already a recognised authority on a wide range of subjects, which included Anglo-Saxon coinage, painting, porcelain and music. Sir Andrew was a wealthy young man, owner of a fine Norfolk estate, and unmarried. According to his close friend, Leibnitz, *his wit and good looks made much noise* in the European courts which he visited. He was a distinguished diplomatist, in whom Queen Anne had sufficient confidence to entrust him with a delicate mission to the court of Hanover, where her distasteful relatives waited, with ill-concealed impatience, for the throne of England.

He had probably made the acquaintance of the Van Homrigh family in Dublin some years previously, when his friend, the Earl of Pembroke, was appointed Viceroy of Ireland, and brought Sir Andrew with him in his entourage.

It is certainly a tribute to the Van Homrigh family that this distinguished young man should have become a close friend and constant visitor. The same is true of another remarkable man, Erasmus Lewis, who was also on terms of close intimacy. Like Sir Andrew, Lewis was a brilliant young man, who had spent much time travelling abroad and had served as Secretary to the Embassies in Paris and Brussels, before being appointed Under-Secretary of State under the Earl of Dartmouth. Swift made constant use of his good offices for the forwarding and receiving of letters, and he was a confidant in the Swift-Vanessa correspondence; her bequest to him in her will proves that her friendship and gratitude lasted to the very end of her life. That Erasmus Lewis, friend of Prior, Arbuthnot, Gay and Pope, was also on intimate terms with the Van Homrigh family is a tribute to them and their circle of friends. The atmosphere must have been a congenial one to have attracted, amongst others, such men as Swift, Fountaine and Lewis, as well as Charles Ford, who was described as *the best lay-scholar of his time and nation.*

As to their female friends, Swift himself tells Stella, *the drabs of quality* formed their intimate circle.

Unless one relies on the evidence of the type of people who frequented the Van Homrigh home, there is little to help any estimation of the family. Even in the case of its most famous member, the only direct evidence is that of Swift. But the abhorrence of this near-vacuum has produced much unfortunate conjecture, which has studiously ignored the plain evidence of Swift's letters to her.

At an early stage, biographers *took sides* in the implied rivalry between Stella and Vanessa, with the unfortunate result that Vanessa's denigration was regarded as essential to Stella's glorification. After Stella's death, Swift left a fairly detailed description of her character and personal appearance. All that he definitely tells about Vanessa's looks is that her eyes were *not* black.

There exist a number of portraits labelled *Esther Johnson,* or *Esther Van Homrigh;* unfortunately, there is no unanimity in the labels, nor, indeed, any certainty that either young woman is the subject of any of the pictures. One drawing of Esther Johnson exists, done by her friend Archdeacon Parnell; it appears in the Faulkner edition of Swift's works, published in Dublin in 1768, when some of her friends were still alive to confirm or repudiate its likeness. It may well be an authentic portrait, but it bears no resemblance to any of the other alleged portraits.

Of Esther Van Homrigh, there remains not even a pencil sketch which can be relied on to show what she looked like; there is not even a grave, where a tombstone might offer a silent testimony of her last resting-place. Everything seems to have conspired to hide all traces of the unhappy girl who, according to Swift, made all other women appear *like brutes in petticoats.* But *his* evidence has been almost totally ignored, or else completely mis-interpreted.

By May 1711 Swift has the use of a room of his own at *Mrs. Van's* where he keeps his *best gown and periwig to put on when I come to town and be a spark.* It must have been with very mixed feelings that Stella read:

> *I got little MD's letter, No. 15, and I read it in a closet they lend me at Mrs. Van's.*

Since he had informed MD (his code name for Esther Johnson and Rebecca Dingley) that he changed his wig and gown twice daily, the ladies in Dublin must have realised that he was a constant visitor at the *Van's.*

It is very significant that Swift's garrulous *Journal to Stella* contains only three allusions to *Mrs. Van's* daughter. One such entry, dated February 1710-11, throws a melancholy shadow of future events:

> *Her eldest daughter is come of age and going to Ireland to look after her fortune and get it into her own hands.*

9

The first existing letter from Swift to Esther Van Homrigh (*little Missessy*) is dated 18th December 1711. It is a covering letter for her eye alone, enclosing *a starched letter* to herself for display to her family and a long letter, which he asked Esther to forward to her cousin, Mrs. Long.

I have writ three or four lies in as many lines. Pray seal up this letter to Mrs. Long, and let no one read it but yourself. I suppose this packet will lie two or three hours, till you awake. And pray, let the outside starched letter to you be seen, after you have sealed that to Mrs. Long. See what art people must use, though they mean ever so well. Now are you and Puppy lying at your ease without dreaming anything of all this. Adieu, till we meet over a pot of coffee or an orange in the Sluttery, which I have so often found to be the most agreeable chamber in the world.

In the enclosed letter to Anne Long which *Missessy* is bidden to read, he humorously lists Esther's faults, but states, *I think there is not a better girl on earth. I have a mighty friendship for her.* The *starched* letter, written to be produced for the family, no longer exists; so it is not possible to know whether the *three or four lies* appear in it, or whether the criticisms he makes of Esther in the letter to her cousin are referred to. The *starched letter* is the first of many precautions taken by Swift to guard his correspondence from prying eyes; they range from the use of cyphers to the use of Latin and his curious French.

This year is one of the greatest importance in the relationship between Swift and Esther Van Homrigh. In his *Journal to Stella* he records, on the 4th February, 1711-12:

I was this morning soliciting at the House of Commons' door for Mr. Vesey, a son of the Archbishop of Tuam, who petitioned for a Bill to relieve him of some difficulty about his estate. I secured him above fifty members.

He does *not* tell Stella that, a couple of weeks previously, the Van Homrigh family had petitioned the House of Lords for a similar private bill, to enable them to dispose of their Irish estate, since

> *all the parties concerned in Interest in the same are now residing and intend to make their residence in England, and are therefore desireous that the said Premises may be sold and the Produce thereof brought into this Kingdom, which will be more beneficial for all the Parties concerned,*

to quote from the opinion of the learned judges, appointed by the Lords to advise them on the Petition.

Swift, at this time, was visiting the Van Homrigh family at least twice daily, frequenting the Sluttery, which he described as *the most agreeable chamber in the world*. On the 14th January, one week before the Petition was presented, Swift dined with Mrs. Van Homrigh and, next night, he had a very prolonged meeting with Sir William Robinson, one of the closest friends of the family, who for many years had been trying to unravel Bartholomew Van Homrigh's tangled affairs. A few weeks later, Swift records in his *Journal to Stella 7th March. I was today at the House of Lords about a friend's Bill.*

His omission of the friend's name is highly significant. It is straining all probability to believe that this influential man, who was so actively interesting himself in Mr. Vesey's private Bill, was not also doing his utmost to help his close friend, Mrs. Van Homrigh, to get a similar private Bill through the House of Lords. It is, therefore, extremely significant to read in this Petition, which is signed by the four surviving members of the family:

> *The said Ginkell is since dead, and Hester the daughter is now come to age and in prospect of marriage; but cannot receive her portion by reason the same Bartholomew, her brother, being only of the age of 19 years.*

The date of this Petition is 22nd January 1711-12. If at that time Esther Van Homrigh had any *prospect of marriage* it could only have been with Swift, who certainly advised and probably drew up the Petition for her mother. Lest there be any lingering doubt that he was intimately concerned with the proceedings, there is his letter to Esther, dated August 1722, in which he reminds her, eleven years later,

You were once a better solicitor, when you could contrive to make others desire your consent to an Act of Parliament against their own interest, to advance yours.

This Petition has been inexplicably overlooked by the host of interested persons, who have speculated about the baffling relationship between Swift and Esther Van Homrigh. It gives an entirely new starting point if it be conceded that, in the year 1711, Swift was regarded by Mrs. Van Homrigh as being betrothed to her elder daughter, who was then just under twenty-three, Swift being forty-four. Because he was extremely inaccurate about ages—and many other things ––or because of the demands of rhyme, Swift immortalised this period with the lines, in *Cadenus and Vanessa*,

> *Vanessa, not in years a score*
> *Dreams of a Gown of forty four.*

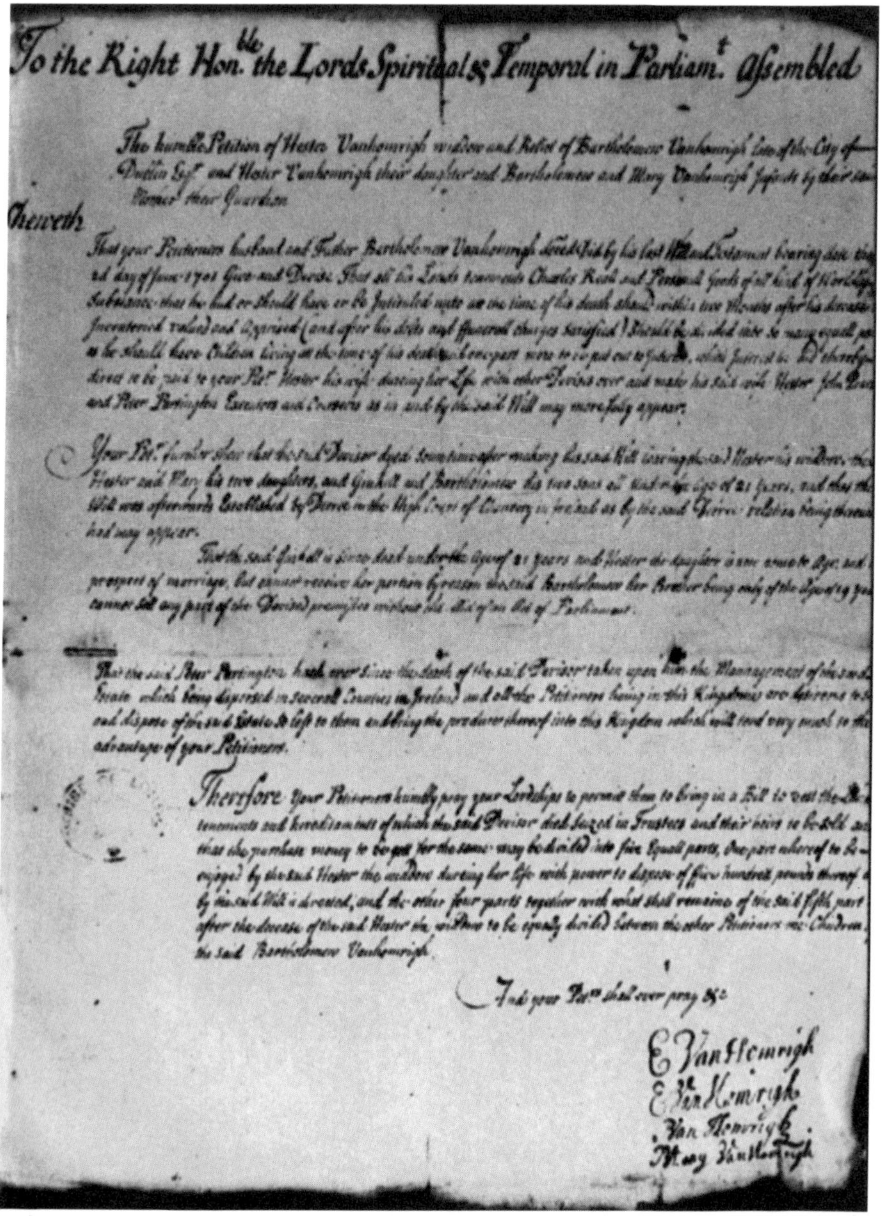

PLATE I   The Van Homrigh Petition.

II

AT this point it is useful to consider the circumstances of Swift's public life, which had so much bearing upon his private world. In the portrait painted by Jervas, immediately after Swift's return to London in 1710, he sits proudly, in the splendour of *my best gown and periwig, to put on when I come to town and be a spark,* the very picture of clerical confidence and decent gravity. Indeed, the forceful dignity of the pose would merit those more lavish episcopal trimmings which Swift had then every reason to expect. His Whig friends, as he reported immediately in the Journal, *were ravished to see me, and would lay hold of me as a twig, while they are drowning.*

Politically, the Whigs *were* drowning, through the hushed, back-stairs diplomacy of the humble Mrs. Masham, who had meekly supplanted the masterful Duchess of Marlborough in Queen Anne's simple affections. Swift, thoroughly resentful of the failure of the Whig lords to obtain him any reward for his services, was now not unwilling to acknowledge in the newly victorious Tory party, the true protectors of the Church and State. The Tories had the good sense to recognise, immediately, the deadly value of Swift's pen; and so a new alliance was born and, in 1710, he had once again bright prospects of rapid preferment.

Considering the acuteness of Swift's judgement in most things, it is a mystery that he apparently never realised until the very end that, whether Whig or Tory were in power, he was completely barred from any clerical appointment which required the Queen's consent. His early masterpiece, *The Tale of a Tub,* had profoundly shocked Queen Anne, one of whose characteristics was a deep and very genuine piety, combined with a dogged devotion to the Church of England. Theologically, she was her father's daughter, in reverse; where he was fanatically devoted to the Church of Rome, she was equally dedicated to the Church of England. Anyone who could treat that Church with irreverent levity, as Swift had done, was a blasphemer, or an atheist and totally unfitted for clerical office. Indeed, Queen Anne carried her convictions so far that, in spite of her passion for listening to sermons, she never once permitted that very distinguished clergyman to preach before her. Over years, Swift haunted the Court—at St. James, Windsor, Kensington, Richmond— where he was on intimate terms of friendship with the most powerful men and women surrounding the Queen; but his friends were never sufficiently powerful to overcome the Queen's distaste, and Swift was never permitted to make his bow to her. Since Queen Anne held all important clerical appointments firmly in her poor, gouty hands, Swift's chances of preferment were negligible, although he could not or would not recognise that unpalatable fact.

To return to January 1711-12, when the Van Homrigh Petition was drafted, Swift was almost at the peak of his career, the object of flattery, both social and political. He was, it is true, often hard-up, but money could always be borrowed by a man of his position so apparently marked out for imminent preferment. He and his Irish serving-man moved lodgings fairly frequently; he was a welcome visitor at the dining tables of the great and boasted that he scarcely ever had a meal at home. He had also the use of a room in Mrs. Van Homrigh's ever-hospitable establishment, presumably that *Sluttery, which I have so often found to be the most agreeable Chamber in the World*, where he savoured *Mishessy's* sugared oranges and coffee. But for increasing *giddy spells* and a deafness in his left ear (which he shared with his good friend the Lord Treasurer), all was exceedingly well with Dr. Jonathan Swift.

Mrs. Van Homrigh's affairs were not nearly so satisfactory, although there is no reason to suppose that she confided the full extent of her embarrassments to her good friend, the Doctor. Already, on 5th October 1709, her finances were in a precarious condition. In a letter of that date from Peter Partinton,[1] one of the co-executors of her husband's will, he refuses to honour a bill she has drawn for £100, and he begs her to curtail her expenditure. It was a *cri du coeur* across the Irish Sea:

> *Where this money is to be found, God Almighty only knows. If you doe, for God's sake, in your next tell me and upon the Worde of a Christian, noe Stone shall be left unturned nor noe Pains thought too much to serve you and yours. Could you sende me a Pattent to coyne Money and Bullion enough, I would sitt up Night and Day to serve you. But since you cannot doe it, you must not expect I will throw myself in Jayl for another's Debt.*

That Mrs. Van Homrigh should find herself in trouble after a couple of years in London society is not surprising, if it be remembered that her husband's estate had been left in great confusion at his death and that his affairs were still unsettled. What is much more surprising is to find that her sons, Ginkell and Bartholomew—aged, respectively, about fifteen and sixteen—were in considerable trouble, financial and otherwise. In the same letter, Mr. Partinton writes:

> *I am exceedingly concerned at the Relation you give about Mr. Ginkell and his late proceedings. I pray God Almighty to open his eyes and convince him of the Wrong he has both done himself and the Reflections he has caste upon the whole Family.*

(Whatever Mr. Ginkell's *late proceedings* may have been, he had little time left to *caste Reflections* upon himself or the Family; according to the burial register of St. James's

---

[1] A.L.S. National Library of Ireland.

Church, London, *Gingell Van Homeridge Gent* was buried there on 8th October, 1710, almost exactly a year later.) Mr. Partinton adds:

> *You may depende upon it, Mr. Barty's Crime is an extraordinary Waisting of Money occationed by keeping bad Company and striving to imitate others that are far above him . . . . . I find all Persons gives mee the deafe Ear, Mr. Ginkell nor Mr. Barty will not confine themselves within their allowance that is judged sufficient to them and Madm. Van Homrigh still goes along the olde Roade, never considering the Reckoning at last that must be made.*

Mr. Partinton ends by protesting his extreme, and, under the circumstances, not unnatural anxiety to be finished with the Van Homrigh business affairs. Yet, fourteen years later, when Esther died, he was still deeply involved. Later still, her heirs, Dr. Berkeley and Mr. Marshall, were vainly struggling to wind up the Van Homrigh estate, which Mr. Partinton had been handling for nearly quarter of a century. As an executor, he would appear to have been very unlucky, over-conscientious, or extremely incompetent. Nor did the difficulties die with him. In a letter from Dr. Berkeley to Mr. Prior, dated 1725, he implores:

> *In God's sake adjust, finish, conclude anyway with Partinton; for at the rate we have gone on these two years, we may go on twenty!*

Evidently Mr. Partinton junior was as difficult to deal with as his late father had been.

The picture of Mrs. Van Homrigh which emerges from Mr. Partinton's despairing letter gives little hope of any real reformation and so, a couple of years later, he is found agreeing to the petition of the family to *the Right Hon.ble the Lords Spiritual and Temporal in Parliament assembled* for a Private Bill, to enable them to dispose of their properties which *lye dispersed in several Counties of the Kingdom of Ireland.*

16

It is an interesting sidelight on the times that the original will of Bartholomew Van Homrigh could not safely be sent from Dublin *by reason of the danger of the Seas*, and Mr. Partinton had to send a certified copy to the House of Lords in London. This copy, unfortunately, cannot now be traced, and the original will was destroyed, with so many other valuable documents, in the holocaust of the Record Office in Dublin in 1922.

Whether any of their Irish property was actually realised, after the English House of Lords passed the Bill, it is not possible to discover. Certainly, the fine mansion at Celbridge and the Dublin house in Turnstile Alley were still owned by Esther during her lifetime. Her brother, Bartholomew, died in 1715 in his property in Co. Cork.

There is no way of knowing how much Swift really knew about the Van Homrighs' affairs when the Petition was being drawn up. On paper, the property was impressive. Bartholomew Van Homrigh's estate is variously estimated up to £20,000. According to Betham's Genealogical Abstracts, each daughter became entitled to £250 a year, on attaining majority or on marriage. Ginkell was already dead in 1711, when the Petition to the House of Lords was drawn up, so, according to the will, the estate was to be divided into four parts, the widow having a life interest in one part. She was also given power to bequeath £500 of the capital as she wished. This power she duly exercised in her will, put into probate in February 1713-14—a document which also seems to have escaped notice.

It would appear then that the two Van Homrigh daughters and their brother would be entitled to about £5,000 apiece, if the property could be realised; they would also be entitled to share the further £5,000 on Mrs. Van Homrigh's death. (Mrs. Van Homrigh died early in 1713-14, Barthlomew died in 1715, leaving his estate to his sisters for their lives. Mary Van Homrigh died in 1720, bequeathing everything to Esther, so that—in theory—she was mistress of the entire Van Homrigh fortune at her death in 1723.)

In 1711, the value of money was enormously higher than today. Swift's mother is said to have lived *and wanted for nothing* on an annuity of £20. Swift, in his Journal, records the difficulty his cousin had in living on £18 a year. So that Esther Van Homrigh, either with an income of £250 a year, or a fortune of £5,000, was a reasonably wealthy young woman, sufficiently well endowed to be a suitable wife for a prospective Dean, or even a Bishop, in England.

The two significant words are *prospective* and *England*. Swift was a man with an overweening sense of his own dignity and independence, fostered, perhaps, by his years of dependence and enforced humility as a member of Sir William Temple's household. Under no circumstances would he have consented to figure as the poor suitor of a rich girl; he would certainly have insisted that the betrothal be kept absolutely secret between Esther, her mother and himself until such a time as he had been appointed to his Deanery or Bishopric, in England. But England it had to be; firstly, because to Swift England was home and Ireland bitter exile, and secondly, because *the Ladies* were living in Dublin.

III

THE Ladies, Esther Johnson and Rebecca Dingley, (both by eighteenth century usage enjoying an honorary *Mrs.*) were two Englishwomen, whom Swift had encouraged to come to live near him in Dublin in 1701, some ten years previously. Esther had then been about twenty and her companion some fifteen years older.

Both during her lifetime and afterwards, gossip persistently whispered that Esther Johnson was the illegitimate child of Sir William Temple; and rumour was considerably stimulated when, at his death, he left her land in Ireland worth more than £1,000. The fact that she is described in the will as *servant of my sister Giffard* may well have been an embarrassment to her, but did nothing to allay gossip. Sir William also left £20 to her widowed mother, who had been, and remained for many years, a serving-woman to Lady Giffard, who was virtual head of her brother's household at Moor Park. When the Temple household there was broken up by Sir William Temple's death, Esther Johnson, on Swift's advice, arrived in Dublin accompanied by Rebecca Dingley. As Denis Johnston points out in his penetrating and excellent study, *In Search of Swift*, it is very curious that this other lady, who was a close relative of the Temples, should have been willing to come to Ireland as an attendant-chaperone to the child of her cousin's serving-woman.

Many years later, immediately after Esther Johnson's death, Swift wrote a moving description of her many excellences: her kindness, her courage, her beauty, her wit. During her lifetime we get glimpses of her character in the poems he wrote and the allusions to her in letters. But the clearest picture of these two women and their relationship to Swift is found in the misnamed *Journal to Stella*, which covers the

19

years he spent in London between September 1710 and June 1713. Over most of those years, he wrote almost daily, reporting his private and public activities, his hopes and fears, his illnesses, almost everything which concerned him—with one notable exception. Only once does he actually refer to Esther Johnson's namesake, Esther Van Homrigh.

About this time, Swift wrote the much discussed poem [1]*Cadenus & Vanessa*, and it will be convenient to anticipate its appearance and to refer to this second Esther, from now on, by the name he then gave her, and under which she has reached a tragic fame.

When Thomas Sheridan in 1784 edited the *Journal*, the letters appeared for the first time consecutively and in correct order. But, by giving a misleading title, he helped to deepen the mystery of Swift's relationship to Esther Johnson. It is, therefore, important to remember that, in no sense were they love letters, written to *Stella*—for the greater number were addressed to Mrs. Dingley and the contents were invariably intended to be read by both ladies. The name *Stella* was not used by Swift until nine years later. The Ladies, in reply, wrote joint letters to Swift. Every letter he wrote was addressed to MD, and Swift very clearly explains the initials:

18*th Feb.* 1710-11 . . . . *certain ladies of Presto's acquaintance* . . . . . *are called, in a certain language, our little MD.*

The exact significance of the initials is a matter for speculation, but *my dears* has been suggested. Occasionally the initials DD appear, which may well stand for *dear Dingley*; sometimes *ppt* refers to Esther, and it has been suggested, may represent *poppet*, a popular term of endearment. The use of *Presto* for PDFR is another change made by the first editor. Presto was a name given to Swift by the Italian Duchess of Shrewsbury, who couldn't manage the English version.

---

[1] See Appendix IX, page 156.

Again, there has been much guesswork as to the significance of PDFR, and some agreement that it stands for *poor dear foolish rogue*. Like the *little language* which Swift often makes use of in the letters, no certain translation is now possible. Occasionally, he combines all three in PMD, as in the following:

> *I believe there has not been one moment since we parted, wherein a letter was not upon the road, going or coming, to or from PMD. If the Queen knew, she would give us a pension; for we bring good luck to their post-boys and their packet.*

His own explanation of the *Journal* is given later on:

> *23rd October 1710 . . . . . I know it is neither wit nor diversion to tell you every day where I dine, neither do I write it to fill my letter; but I fancy I shall, some time or other, have the curiosity of seeing some particulars how I passed my life, when I was absent from MD this time . . . . I am weary of friends, and friendships are all monsters but MD's.*

One of the many odd circumstances in the relation of Swift and these two women—now aged thirty and fortyfive—is that he took such extraordinary precautions never, so far as is known, to see either of them alone. He would seem to have carried this so far as never to have written them anything except a joint letter. The *Journal* is full of passages such as:

> *I wish my dearest pretty Dingley and Stella a happy New Year.*
> *Goodnight my own two dearest MD.*
> *January 16th 1710-11. Farewell, dearest beloved MD, and love from Presto, who has not had one happy day since he left you, as hope saved. It is the last sally I will ever make, but I hope it will turn to some account. I have done more for these, and I think they are more honest than the*

last, however, I will not be disappointed. I would make MD and me easy, and I never desired more.

The *they* above refers to his new friends in the Tory party who, he hoped, would prove *more honest* in rewarding his political services than the Whigs had been. It is informative to expand the initials, so that the sentence reads—

I would make Esther Johnson, Rebecca Dingley and me easy, and I never desired more.

Again, soon after he writes:

My new friends are very kind and I have promises enough but I do not count on them . . . . . However, we will see what may be done, and, if nothing at all, I shall not be disappointed; although perhaps MD may, and then I shall be sorrier for their sakes than my own.

The stress is always on his desire to make their circumstances easier. He was already making them an annual allowance. Had his letters protested his desire to improve the circumstances of either lady, it might have been construed into matrimonial intentions; but since both were always linked in any future prospects, he was perfectly safe. So far as Esther Johnson was concerned, on paper or off, Swift was invariably the soul of discretion.

What then was his attitude towards this young woman whom he had known intimately since he taught little Esther Johnson her early lessons at Moor Park? Years later, Swift wrote these lines to her:

Thou, Stella, wert no longer young
When first my harp for thee was strung
Without one word of Cupid's darts,
Of killing eyes, or bleeding hearts;
With friendship and esteem possest
I ne'er admitted Love a guest.

Into the company of *friendship and esteem*, he may never have admitted *Love*, in the usual sense of the word, but it is impossible to read the *Journal* without becoming aware of the deep affection which warms it. Swift's attitude is that of an extremely affectionate, rather humorous uncle towards a favourite and favoured niece. The letters are full of loving banter, *saucy jades, lazy sluttikins, blundering goose-caps, dearest sauce-faces.* He constantly corrects her spelling blunders—sixteen in one letter—twits her about the Dublin circle of card-playing nonentities; he scolds her for forgetting his messages; boasts of his personal successes, of his familiarity with the great. He addresses the pair, oddly, as *Sirrahs, lads, dear brave boys.* He does little shopping commissions for them in London, buys spectacles, chocolate, tobacco for snuff, aprons, tea. He reports on the weather:

> *5th October* 1711. *To-day it grows bloody cold.*

But, above all, and in almost every letter, he is concerned about Esther Johnson's health. After her death, he wrote:

> *She was sickly from childhood to about fifteen, when she grew into perfect health.*

She certainly did not enjoy perfect health during the years 1710-1713. The symptoms of her illness recur so frequently in the *Journal* that it is of interest to list some of them. A few weeks after his arrival in London he writes:

> *3rd October* 1710. *This morning Stella's sister came to see me . . . she gave me a bottle of palsy-water and desired that I would send it by the first convenience . . . She promises a quart bottle of the same.*

A fortnight later:

> *I got MD's fourth letter, at the Coffee-house today. God Almighty bless poor Stella and her eyes and head. What shall we do to cure them, poor dear life? Your disorders*

*are a pull-back for your good qualities. Would to Heaven
I were this minute shaving your poor dear head, either
here or there. Pray do not write, nor read this letter, nor
anything else.*

And a few weeks later:

*I saw your mother and made her give me a pint of palsy-
water . . . and sent it to Mr. Smith, who goes tomorrow
for Ireland.
Poor Stella's eyes. God bless them and send them better.
Pray spare them.*

Months later:

*Is Stella well enough to go to Church, pray? No numbing
left? No darkness in your eyes?*

A year later he remarks:

*I hoped Stella would have done with her illness but I
think we both have the faculty never to part with a disorder for ever.*

Meanwhile, the Ladies tried that great Eighteenth century cure-all, the Spa, and had drunk the waters at Wexford
and Templeoge, as well as making many country visits in
search of better health. Swift writes to them to Wexford:

*Don't think of reading or writing until your eyes are well,
and long well. God be thanked the ugly numbing is gone
. . . Why do you write, Sirrah Stella, when you find
your eyes so weak that you cannot see?*

And, finally, when in February 1712 he is developing
shingles in London, he writes:

*The pain has left my shoulder and crept to my neck and
collar-bone. It makes me think of poor Stella's blade-
bone . . . dogs gnawing.*

Shortly after his arrival in London he records:

Sir Andrew Fountaine has been very ill . . . The nurse

asked me whether I thought it possible he could live, for the doctors said not. I said I believed that he would live; for I found the seeds of life in him, which I observe seldom fail. And I found them in poor dearest Stella, when she was ill many years ago.

This, presumably, was the serious illness which Swift says she suffered before she was fifteen, and of which it seems she had nearly died. It is tempting to diagnose that illness from her reported symptoms — severe headaches, constant eye trouble, numbness and acute pain in her neck and shoulder. All these symptons are associated with the after-effects of a facial palsy which with eighteenth century treatments would almost certainly leave behind such long-lasting disabilities.

So that Esther Johnson, living a quiet life in Dublin's Cathedral world, a delicate woman in her early thirties, may well have suffered too from the growing certainty that Swift was in constant contact with a vital, attractive young lady, many years her junior, who inhabited the gay world of London. *The danger of the seas* might interfere with the safe passage of Bartholomew Van Homrigh's will, but it certainly would not stop the passage of gossip between London and Dublin. Apart from Swift's treasured and warmly affectionate relationship with Esther Johnson, (a relationship which obviously quite gladly included her friend and companion Rebecca Dingley) and his knowledge that his marriage with another woman would have disastrous reactions on that relationship, it must also have been obvious to him that the consequences of such a marriage would be extremely damaging to himself, in Ireland.

When first the Ladies came to make their home in Dublin, as Swift relates, their appearance was highly suspect in that social group which revolved around the two Cathedrals. (Dublin is probably the only city which, for curious reasons, has two Protestant Cathedrals within a stone's throw of one another.) But their circumspect and exemplary behaviour gradually won them a very high place in the affectionate regard of the host of Anglo-Irish divines who filled the leading clerical positions in eighteenth century Dublin; and the Ladies were also welcome guests in the homes of some of the leading citizens. For more than ten years, those friends had taken it more or less for granted that Doctor Swift, in his own good time and when his income warranted it, would marry the charming young woman, whom he had persuaded to come to live in Dublin. Ranged behind the claims of Esther Johnson was a very solid group who, from the Archbishop of Dublin down, would have been scandalised at any suggestion that Swift would marry anyone else. All hope of Irish promotion would, at the very least, have been seriously jeopardised and many of his friendships would have been broken. Had Swift wished to marry in Ireland, he had only one choice: the pleasant young woman who had waited, in patient dignity, for ten years.

So that if Swift *had* proposed marriage to Vanessa he must have done so in the certainty that, henceforth, his living was to be in England. He may well have indulged in wishful thinking, to blur the outlines of an unpleasant picture. Ambition is a conjurer that can produce almost limitless *rabbits* to suit the Act, and Swift was an extremely ambitious man. With greater revenues at his disposal (he may well have reasoned) he could make a far larger allowance to *dearest MD*, so making their lives more easeful . . . . After all, they had obviously learned to live very pleasantly without him, owing to his lengthy absence from Dublin . . . There would, undoubtedly, be a painful interlude, but there was no real reason why the old, affectionate correspondence should not eventually be re-established between Dublin and London . . . And, if not, a powerful Churchman, living in England among his own peers, would find eventual compensation for the loss of the old affection in the new, passionate devotion of a most attractive, well-dowered young wife . . .

Swift must have been well aware that there was no possibility of the Ladies returning to England. Like so many English people, they had become *more Irish than the Irish themselves*. As Swift tells us, Stella *loved Ireland much better than the generality of those who owe both their birth and riches to it*. There was also the important consideration that, whereas in Ireland Esther Johnson had won for herself a very definite and dignified place in a pleasant society, in her native England she was at a serious social disadvantage. Her mother was still a serving-woman, employed in Lady Giffard's household at £12 a year; her only sister was married to a man who could do no better, with Swift's influence behind him, than a lowly job in the Salt Office, with a salary of £40. Esther Johnson's only social asset in England was the doubtful one of her rumoured illegitimate connection with the Temple family. So that in 1711 there was no question of her returning to London; and at that time there seemed even less chance that Vanessa would ever leave it for Ireland. The scene was set and the choice was Swift's. He was the uneasy base of a triangle whose sides were equal and opposite.

IV

AT the end of March 1712, Swift had a very severe attack of shingles, and he describes the agonies he endured in great detail in the *Journal*. Swift was a very sick man, and it was several months before he had completely recovered. The kindly Mrs. Van Homrigh and her family would have been assiduous in their attentions to the suffering man, and may well have moved him to their own lodgings. Severe shingles is not a disease to be borne in solitude. About this time, too, Swift seems to have dismissed his servant, Patrick, whom he had brought from Dublin and who was devoted to Mrs. Dingley. It is significant, too, that at this time, the daily *Journal* to MD ceases. Occasional letters, with long intervals, took its place. Perhaps Swift's conscience smote him when he wrote, on 15th Sept. 1712, after an interval of five weeks:

> *I was never so long without writing to MD as now since I left them, nor ever will again while I am able to write.*

The letter ends:

> *Love PDFR who loves MD above all things. Farewell dearest, ten thousand times dearest MD.*

But there is another interval of three weeks until the next letter, and the long gaps continue. The Ladies must have wondered . . .

On 1st August, 1712, just six months after the Petition had been presented and a couple of months after the private Bill had been passed, Swift wrote the second existing letter to Vanessa. He writes from Windsor, where he has been staying:

> . . . . *I am so weary of this place that I am resolved to leave it in two days, and not return in three weeks. I will come as early on Monday as I can find opportunity and will take a little Grubstreet lodging, pretty near where I did before and dine with you thrice a week; and will tell you a thousand secrets, provided you will have no quarrels with me. Don't remember me to Moll, but humble service to your Mother.*

Moll, of whom the jocose remark is made, was Vanessa's delicate fifteen-year old sister, Mary, to whom Swift used to *tell stories and bring sugar-plums.* Presumably he made his visit to London, as the next letter, written from Windsor suggests that the Van Homrigh family visit that town:

> . . . . *for four or five days. Five pounds will maintain you and pay your coach backwards and forwards . . . . I will steal to town, one of these days, and catch you napping. I desire you and Moll will walk as often as you can in the Park, and do not sit moping at home, so that you can neither work nor read, nor play, nor care for company. I long to drink a dish of coffee in the Sluttery, and hear you dun me for secrets and: Drink your coffee—why don't you drink your coffee?*

Ten years later, Swift was still reproaching her for moping and lack of social interests. In his absence, life stood still for Vanessa.

Soon after, Swift is back in London, and there is no need for further letters since he was presumably, according to his promise, dining with the Van Homrighs *thrice a week* and relaxing in the pleasant atmosphere of the Sluttery, which he had *so often found to be the most agreeable chamber in the world.*

The political whirlpool, of which Queen Anne's court was the muddy vortex, is not of importance here, except in so far as it affected the private life of Swift. The ever-widening rift between the Tory leaders, which Swift worked so feverishly to mend, made it tragically obvious that their Ministry could not possibly survive much longer. The nation's uneasiness about the childless Queen's failing health—public Funds rose or fell with every new batch of rumours—was enormously increased by the uncertainty of the Succession. English eyes were fixed, in hope or fear, on the unsavoury Court in Hanover, or on the romantic Stuarts in their sad, shabby exile. Never a strong woman, Queen Anne's health was obviously declining rapidly. Rumour buzzed like a bluebottle fly. Swift records in the *Journal* on 9th October 1712:

I asked . . . . . Lady Masham, seriously whether the Queen were at all inclined to dropsy . . . . She assured me that she was not. So did her physician, Arbuthnot, who always attends her. Yet these devils have spread that she has holes in her legs and runs at her navel and I know not what.

Nevertheless, Swift must have realised that the reign was drawing to a close; that the Tory Ministry was fast losing its cohesion and therefore its power; and that he, himself, through his political activities, had made so many bitter enemies amongst his former friends, the Whigs, that with the fall of the Tories he would lose all chance of preferment and, very possibly, his liberty itself. During the previous year, various English Bishoprics and Deaneries had been awarded to him—by rumour. In cold fact, Swift was still the same poor rector of a poor Irish parish, who had arrived in London in 1710.

In the middle of April 1713, the omission of his name from a new list of clerical appointments brought things to a head. On 13th April, he writes in the *Journal*:

I bid Mr. Lewis tell the Lord Treasurer that I take nothing ill of him but his not giving me timely notice, as he had promised to do, if he found the Queen would do nothing for me . . . . I told the Lord Treasurer I had nothing to do but go to Ireland immediately, for I could not, with any reputation, stay longer here, unless I had something honourable immediately given me . . . . . I told the Duke of Ormond my intentions. He is content Sterne should be a Bishop, and I have St. Patrick's.

The Queen's closest friend, Lady Masham, wept openly at the prospect of losing him to faraway Dublin, and did her utmost to persuade her royal mistress to make Swift a Prebend of Windsor. But Anne remained adamant. She probably salved her conscience for Swift's appointment as Dean of St. Patrick's, by the fact that that Deanery was in the gift of the Duke of Ormond.

Swift was deeply humiliated by the whole transaction.

The Lord Treasurer said he would not be satisfied, but that I must be a prebendary of Windsor. Thus he perplexes things . . . . I confess, as much as I love England, I am so angry at this treatment that, if I had my choice, I would rather have St. Patrick's . . . . Neither can I feel joy at passing my days in Ireland; and I confess I thought the Ministry would not let me go,

he wrote to MD.

But the Tory Ministry *did* let him go, Lord Oxford and Lord Bolingbroke being too occupied with their private feuds to realise how little they could afford to lose his services, at so critical a time.

The Duke of Ormond is to send over an order, making me Dean of St. Patrick's . . . . I suppose MD is malicious enough to be glad and rather have it than Wells.

He adds, perhaps with a touch of malice himself:

They expect me to pass next Winter here.

31

It was then more than three months since the Ladies had written to him, as Swift had complained. Something had stopped the busy pens. The intimation that he only intended spending a few months in Ireland can have done little to improve relations. As it happened, he only stayed in Ireland about ten weeks.

He left London on the 31st May, and that night, from his first stopping place, he wrote to Vanessa,

I promised to write to you; and I have to let you know that it is impossible for anyone to have more acknowledgements at heart, for all your kindness & generosity to me. I hope this journey will restore my health: I will ride but little every day, and I will write a common letter to you all from some of my stages, but directed to you ... Pray be merry, and eat and walk and be good and send me your commands . . . . I have hardly time to put pen to paper, but I would make good my promise. Pray God preserve you and make you happy and easy—and so adieu, brat.

Swift's last letter to the Ladies had been written more than a fortnight earlier; nor did they hear from him again until a week later, when the *Journal* ends, on the 6th June, at Chester.

He arrived in Dublin, some days later, to find himself in a hostile Whig community. On the day of his installation, a scurrilous verse was nailed to the door of his Cathedral. It was an open secret that it was the work of the Dean of Killala.

To-day, this Temple* gets a Dean,
Of parts and fame uncommon;

---

*As the "poet" was a bitter enemy of Swift, rumours of whose Temple paternity were already in circulation, this description of the church may not have been accidental!

Used both to pray, and to profane,
To serve both God & Mammon . . . .
This Place he got by wit and rhyme,
And many ways most odd;
And might a Bishop be in time,
Did he believe in God . . . .
Look down, St. Patrick, look, we pray
On thine own Church and Steeple;
Convert thy Dean on this great Day,
Or else, God help the People.

Swift was installed in his Deanery — the bitter-tanged fruit of his long political labours—and fled from Dublin to his country parish. In a letter to Vanessa from Laracor, dated the 8th July 1713, he describes his misery:

I stayed but a fortnight in Dublin, very sick; and returned not one visit of a hundred that were made me, but all to the Dean, and none to the Doctor. I am riding here for life, and think I am something better, and hate the thoughts of Dublin, and prefer a field-bed and an earthen floor before the great house there, which they say is mine. I had your last spleenatic letter. I told you when I left England I would endeavour to forget everything there and would write as seldom as I could . . . . I design to pass the greatest part of the time I stay in Ireland here in the cabin where I am now writing, neither will I leave the Kingdom till I am sent for; and if they have no further service for me I will never see England again. At my first coming I thought I should have died with discontent, and was horribly melancholy while they were installing me: but it began to wear off and change to dullness . . . . I must go to take my bitter draught to cure my head, which is really spoilt by the bitter draughts the public hath given me . . . . .

33

His black cloud of misery does not appear to have been much lightened by MD's presence. His accounts show that he spent less than twelve shillings on meals with them.

Swift had arranged to return to London before the winter, and Vanessa was, naturally, aware of the fact, but not prepared to be forgotten in the interval. In spite of his apparent prohibition, she had written four times before he replied from Laracor. Their mutual good friend, Erasmus Lewis, provided the cover. One of these letters ends:

> *I am impatient to the last degree to hear how you are. I hope I shall soon have you here.*

The next:

> *Pray let me hear from you soon, which will be an inexpressible joy to her that is always—*

Presumably in accordance with Swift's desire for caution, Vanessa signed none of her letters. He can have needed no signature to recognise the possessive love of the girl, who so confidently was counting the days till his return. She had not long to wait. At the end of August, Dean Swift left Ireland, and early in September was back in the whirling activities of London. The warmth of his welcome, both private and public, must have been singularly comforting after the bleak and hostile weeks in Ireland.

V

PROVERBIALLY, distance makes hearts grow fonder, and much wisdom is crystallised in these old sayings. It requires no vivid imagination to picture Vanessa's welcome. To Mrs. Van Homrigh the Dean was her daughter's accepted suitor, even if, for his own good reasons, the engagement still had to be kept secret. In spite of the new powers conferred by the Act of Parliament, little progress had been made in straightening out the Van Homrigh financial muddle; and there was no immediate prospect of Vanessa's dowry becoming available, in spite of the girl's distracted struggles with Mr. Partinton. Mrs. Van Homrigh would thoroughly sympathise with Swift's refusal to regard the Deanery of St. Patrick's as anything but a stepping-stone to his real aim: an appointment in England, worthy of his powers. Mrs. Van Homrigh had removed herself and her family from the Kingdom of Ireland; as stated in the *Petition*, they were *now residing and intended to make their residence in England.* She would have thoroughly agreed with the letter Swift wrote, before going to Dublin to take over his Deanery:

I am condemned to live again in Ireland, and all the Court and Ministry did for me was to let me choose my station in the country where I am banished.

Nor were Swift's hopes of an English appointment oversanguine. After all, the Bishop of Bristol had been made Lord Privy Seal, and Swift's good friend, Prior, had been appointed a Plenipotentiary to negotiate the Peace of Utrecht. A similar diplomatic appointment might well advance Swift's reputation so far that his claims to higher clerical honours could scarcely be refused, even by *the royal*

35

Prude — as Swift had described the Queen, somewhat unwisely, in a recent publication.

It is clear that the Dean returned to London with renewed zest for power and privilege, and that he soon established himself in higher favour than ever with the Tory Lords. By the end of 1713, he was again their chief adviser and pamphleteer.

No letters exist between Swift and Vanessa during those nine months—presumably, there was no need for them. Of their relationship, nothing can be said with certainty. The only clue to the situation is in the Burial Register of St. James's Church. Piccadilly.

10*th February* 1713-14, *Hester Van Homry.*

In her will, which has also been overlooked, Mrs. Van Homrigh states that she is *sick and weak in body, but (praise be to God for it) of sound and disposing mind and memory.* The will is dated the 16th January, 1713-14, and was put into probate on the 11th February following. She appointed her daughter, Esther, sole executrix, and left her, amongst other items, her diamond necklace and earrings, her wedding-ring, a ruby and diamond ring, as well as her *fur-tippett.* To her daughter, Mary, she bequeathed her pearl necklace and earrings, her cornelian and diamond ring and other valuables. Mrs. Van Homrigh also exercised the right she was given in her husband's will to leave £500 as she wished. She divided this sum, equally, between her three children on condition that her debts be paid. She also left her son, Bartholomew, *my silver dressing-plate, gold seal and large silver medal.*

From her statement that she was *sick and weak in body* in January, it seems probable that she may have been ill for some time. (So many of her family died young that it is possible they all had tuberculosis: her husband died in

1703-4, presumably still a young man; Ginkell died in 1710, aged about sixteen; Mary, after years of illness, died in 1720, aged about twenty-four and Bartholomew died in 1715, aged about twenty-two.)

Curiously enough, Dean Swift, in his letters to Ireland, appears to have made no reference whatever to the death of this lady, well known in Dublin society. In her will, she asks to be buried *in a decent but very private manner;* it is not known whether discretion prevented Dean Swift's attendance on the 10th February, at St. James's Church, when the kindly Mrs. Van Homrigh was buried near her wayward boy, Ginkell. Seven years later, when Mary Van Homrigh died after a long illness in Ireland he wrote to the distracted Vanessa:

. . . . For God's sake get your friends about you, to advise and to order everything in the forms. It is all you have to do. I want comfort myself in this case and can give little. Time alone must give it to you. Nothing is now your part but decency . . . .

It is to be hoped that on the death of Mrs. Van Homrigh, Swift did not leave her daughters entirely to the good offices of their friends.

Swift was now at the pinnacle of his political career, cherished and flattered by the Tories and correspondingly loathed and feared by the Whigs. His recommendation was sufficient to job-seekers, high and low; but he was curiously ineffective for himself. He had been promised £1,000 to pay his out-of-pocket expenses in connection with his installation as Dean of St. Patrick's, and he had asked for the appointment of Historiographer. He got neither, to his justifiable indignation.

The intrigues around the obviously dying Queen became more and more frantic. The Whigs, their eyes firmly fixed on Hanover, were arrogantly sure of an early victory and openly vowing vengeance on their enemies, amongst whom Swift stood prominently. The times were dangerous, and he recognised that he could no longer hope to control the suicidal progress of the Tory Ministry. By the end of May, against the advice and pleadings of his friends, Swift left London for a quiet Berkshire village, there to await events.

VI

My informant was Richard Brennan, he is at present a bellringer in St. Patrick's and in a state of penury. (Such should not be the case, the servant in whose arms Swift breathed his last, and who attended him during the six years immediately preceding his death.) My informer, who is still living in Dublin, told me that when he was at school there was a boy boarded with the Master who was commonly reported to be the Dean's son by Mrs. Johnson. He added that the boy strongly resembled the Dean in his complexion, that he dined constantly at the Deanery on Sunday, and that when the other boys were driven out of the deanery yard, he was suffered to remain there and divert himself. This boy survived Mrs. Johnson by a year or two at most.

Monck Berkeley's *Literary Relics* Jan. 1789.

I received your letter when some company was with me on Saturday night; and it put me in such confusion that I could not tell what to do. I here send you the paper you left me. This morning a woman, who does business for me, told me she heard I was in love with one—naming you, and twenty particulars, that little master and I visited you, and that the A-B did so; and that you had an abundance of wit, etc. I ever feared the tattle of this nasty town and told you so; and that was the reason why I said to you long ago that I would see you seldom when you were in Ireland. And I must beg you to be easy if, for some time, I visit you seldomer, and not in so particular a manner. I will see you at the latter end of the week—if possible. These

39

are accidents in life that are necessary and must be sub-
mitted to; and tattle, by the help of discretion, will wear
off.

Swift to Vanessa, undated

I bequeath to Bryan MᶜLoghlin (a child who now lives
with me and whom I keep on charity) twenty five pounds,
to bind him an apprentice, as my executors and the sur-
vivors of them shall think fit.

Extract from the Will of Esther Johnson. 1727

SINCE the letters, which over years passed between
Swift and Vanessa, provide the bulk of the evidence
available for any assessment of their relationship, a
short account of the subsequent history of this correspondence
may be useful here.

In June 1723, Vanessa on her deathbed is believed to
have given instructions for the publication of the letters and
other papers, to one of her heirs, Robert Marshall, a young
law-student. As she was an indefatigible letter-writer, it is
extremely probable that she would have put such important
instructions in writing, and it is very significant that no such
document ever appeared in public, so that it is impossible to
know whether her last wish was to embarrass and injure the
man whom she had loved so deeply for sixteen years, or
whether she believed the publication of her papers necessary
to clear her memory of some grave imputation. The absence
of any written instructions from Vanessa, together with the
obvious removal of many of her carefully numbered letters,
gives ample reason to believe that her papers were rigorously
censored.

Her heirs and executors were the famous Dr. Berkeley—
who could not remember ever having met her—and young
Marshall, who may have been some distant connection.

Pleasantly surprised and grateful for their large and totally unexpected legacies, they arranged for the publication. According to Sheridan, writing in 1784, the manuscripts were *put to the press, and some progress made in the letters, when Dr. Sheridan getting intelligence of it . . . . . applied so effectively to the executors that the printed copy was cancelled, but the originals still remained in their hands.* One curious feature is that Dr. Berkeley (who was friendly to Swift) several times assured the Dean's very close friend Dr. Delany that the manuscripts contained *nothing which would either do honour to her character, or bring the least reflections upon Cadenus.* Either Dr. Berkeley had already carelessly edited the papers, suppressing anything he thought damaging to Swift, or else he had left the matter to young Mr. Marshall, who, not being so friendly to the Dean, was less careful about what went to the printer. It is certainly difficult to understand Dr. Berkeley's assurances.

There is, unfortunately, no way of knowing whether the material then given to the printer for publication is the same as the letters which subsequently made a first, partial appearance in 1767, forty-four years later. In that year, in an edition of Swift's letters printed for James Williams, Skinner's Row, Dublin, the following appears,

In the Appendix will be found some letters between the Dean and Mrs. Esther Vanhomrigh . . . . which did not come into the hands of the proprietors till the rest of the work was printed.

It adds,

The originals of these letters are in the hands of a gentleman of great eminence in the Law in Ireland,

A further note explains that the gentleman in question is:

Robert Marshall, Esq. late one of the Judges of His Majesty's Court of Common Pleas.

Robert Marshall had been forced to retire from the Bench, by ill-health, some years previously, and was, in 1767, living in Co. Dublin, presumably still in possession of the Swift-Vanessa correspondence, which had been so long suppressed. Dean Swift and Marshall's co-executor, Bishop Berkeley, both being dead for many years, the retired Judge must have felt that he could at last do tardy justice to his benefactress, but whether the selection of letters published in 1767 was the same as that approved by Dr. Berkeley as not casting *the least reflection on Cadenus*, there is no way of knowing. Since Dr. Berkeley undoubtedly knew sufficient French to understand *Soyez assurée que jamais personne du monde a été aimée, honorée, estimée, adorée par votre ami que vous*, one can only conclude that Dr. Berkeley saw nothing un-fitting in an elderly Dean assuring a young woman of his adoration, so long as he did so in a foreign language.

What had become of the originals of the letters was a mystery until May 1919, when the Morrison collection was offered for sale at Sotheby's. It included a volume, bound in a fine calf cover, which contained what is described on its first page in an eighteenth century script as:

> *Original Letters of Dr. Jonathan Swift, Dean of St. Patrick's, Dublin to Mrs. Van Homrigh, celebrated by him in his published works under the name Vanessa.*
>
> *With the foul copies of her Letters and Answers in her own Writing!*

This volume was bought for the British Museum.

Various suggested explanations — including blackmail — have been offered for the fact that Vanessa made and pre-served rough drafts of her letters to Swift. A simple reason for the *foul copies* could be that she was extremely conscious of the literary eminence of her correspondent and anxious to write as good a letter as she could. Since eighteenth century posts were very slow and erratic, a copy of her own last letter must have been almost essential in order to understand the deliberately enigmatic replies of Swift. The Dean himself both made and kept drafts of his letters to friends. This habit was probably widespread in an age when the art of letter-writing was both highly cultivated and much appreciated.

As to the charge of preserving Swift's letters, it is one which could be levelled against most lovers, since love became literate.

These letters, then, are all that now remains of the Correspondence between Cadenus, as Swift disguised himself, and Vanessa, and are worthy of some study.

Shortly after her death, one item amongst the papers did, somewhat mysteriously, find its way to the public: *Cadenus and Vanessa,* a long poem which Swift had written about ten years earlier. In this, he purports to give a history of their early relations. Its circulation, so soon after the flare of scandal following Vanessa's death, added a fierce fuel to the fire. Some idea of the atmosphere in Dublin can be given by a letter, written by Dr. Evans, Bishop of Meath, to the Archbishop of Canterbury, within a few weeks of Vanessa's death.

> *I think it not improper for me to acquaint your Grace with a passage lately happened here wherein Jonathan Swift is said to be pretty much concerned. A young woman, Mrs. Van Omrig (a pretended vain wit), and ye Dean had great friendship, many letters & papers passed betwixt them (the subject I know nothing of); they give out, there was a marriage promise between them, but this I can't affirm . . . In April, last, she discovered the D was married to Mrs. Johnson (a natural daughter of Sir W. Temple, a very good woman), upon which she expressed great indignation, making a new will and leaving all to Dr. Berkeley of this College . . . and to one Mr. Marshall, who was charged by her (on her deathbed) to print all the letters and papers*

which had passed between the D and herself . . . Ye Arch-
bishop of Dublin and ye whole Irish posse have (I fear)
prevailed with Mr. Marshall (ye lady's executor) not to
print the papers, etc., as she desired, lest one of their own
dear joyes should be trampled on by the Philistines.

The whole Irish posse may indeed have been working, as
the Bishop complains, to protect the reputation of *one of their
own dear joyes,* but the Dean himself had long fled the
battlefield. Obviously fearing some shattering scandal, on
the news of Vanessa's death, he immediately left Dublin,
without leaving any address, even to his Cathedral clergy.
Stella and her companion had already taken refuge in the
country, after Swift's mysterious break with Vanessa. None
of them returned to Dublin for many months.

It would be very interesting to know who spread the story
that there had been *a promise of marriage* between the dead
woman and the Dean, and what foundation existed for the
statement. It is at least possible that amongst the papers
Vanessa directed Mr. Marshall to publish was a copy of the
Van Homrigh *Family Petition.* As her mother's executrix,
she would certainly have had one.

The Bishop of Meath—enemy though he was to Swift—
would not have dared to write such a complaint to the Archbishop of Canterbury, unless he were quite certain that there
was a well-established fire to account for such volumes of
acrid smoke.

44

VII

TO revert to 1714: some four months after Vanessa's mother's death Swift left London for Berkshire, spending a few days in Oxford. When he writes to Vanessa on 8th June 1714, he is in lodgings as he explains, with the Rev. Mr. Geree, who held an Oxford College living at Letcombe Bassett, a couple of miles from Wantage in Berkshire.

He addresses the letter to—

Mrs. Esther Van-homrigh
at her lodgings over against the Surgeon's, in Great Rider
Street near St. James's Street,
London.

This address was almost certainly incorrect, as his three subsequent letters are addressed to,

Mrs. Van-Homrigh, at Mr.
Handcock's house in Little Ryder
Street, near St. James's Street
London.

It would seem that Vanessa and her sister had moved to new lodgings immediately after Swift's departure from London, and that he did not remember the correct address. This is important when considering the post-script of this letter which Vanessa has numbered I:

You see I am better than my word, and write to you be-
fore I have been a week settled in the house where I am.
I have not much news to tell you from hence, nor have I
one line from anybody since I left London, of which I am
very glad. But to say the truth, I believe I shall not stay
here so long as I intended. I am at a clergyman's house, an

old friend and acquaintance, whom I love very well; but he is such a melancholy thoughtful man, partly from nature and partly by a solitary life, that I shall soon catch the spleen from him . . . . His wife has been this month twenty miles off at her father's and will not return this ten days. I never saw her, and perhaps the house will be worse when she comes. I read all day, or walk, and do not speak as many words as I have now writ, in three days. So that in short, I have a mind to steal away to Ireland, unless I find myself take more to this way of living, so different in every circumstance from what I have left. This is the first syllable I have writ to anyone since you saw me. I shall be glad to hear from you, not as you are a Londoner, but a friend. For I care not threepence for news, nor have heard one syllable since I am here. The Pretender or the Duke of Cambridge may both be landed, and I never the wiser. But if this place were ten times worse, nothing shall make me return to Town while things are in the situation I left them . . . . I hope you are in good health and humour. My service to Moll. My cold is quite gone.

A vous etc.

I send my man two miles with this to the post town, so if there is a letter by chance from you, I shall not be able to tell you so now. I hope our maid carried your bandbox with the papers and deeds.

Unfortunately, Vanessa's reply is missing, as the next letter is numbered 3.

Several things in Swift's letter are worth noting. Apparently he suggests to Vanessa, for the first time, that he may possibly go over to Ireland, instead of remaining in Berkshire as he had intended. He also stresses the change in his manner of life, *so different in every circumstance from what I left.* And he ends with the surprising query whether *our maid carried your bandbox with the papers and deeds?* —

presumably as part of Vanessa's move to new lodgings, from some other where they had shared a maid.

The use of the word *friend* may be noted; but apart from Swift's constant caution and fear of letters being intercepted, he often used the word where a much more affectionate relationship is obvious. (In a later letter to Vanessa, who was a most devoted sister to Moll, Swift hopes *to see the sincerest friendship in the world long between you.*)

Some of the inexplicable happenings in the future might be explained by the assumption that Swift and this young woman who had never made any secret of her passionate love had been living together since his return to London in the Autumn of 1713. She considered herself his affianced wife; his most ardent defenders have never suggested that he was impervious to female charms. Swift had himself painted a glowing picture of sexual delights to an earlier love, *Varina*, (Miss Waring, daughter of the Archdeacon of Dromore, Co. Antrim.)

Surely, Varina, you have but a mean opinion of the joys that accompany a true, honourable unlimited love; yet either nature and our ancestors have hugely deceived us, or else all sublunary things are dross in comparison. Is it possible you cannot be yet unsensible to the prospect of a rapture and delight so innocent and so exalted? Trust me, Varina, Heaven has given us nothing else worth the loss of a thought. Ambition, high appearance, friends and fortune are all tasteless and insipid when they come in competition; yet millions of such glorious minutes we are perpetually losing, for ever losing, irrecoverably losing, to gratify empty forms and wrong notions. . . . To resist the violence of our inclinations in the beginning is a strain of self denial that may have some pretences to set up for a virtue; but when they are grounded at first upon reason, when they have taken firm root and grown to a height, it is folly—folly as well as injustice—to withstand their dictates; for this passion has a property peculiar to itself, to be more commendable in its extremes; and it is as possible to err in the excess of piety as of love.

To young, adoring Vanessa, the expression of such sentiments would be preaching to the converted. For several years, she had considered herself Swift's wife in all but name. She was alone in the world except for a delicate young sister and an unsatisfactory absent brother. She was her own mistress.

Some of Swift's most intimate friends were notorious, even by Eighteenth Century standards, for their lax morals—royal mistresses or ex-mistresses always ranked high in his esteem. He certainly was no prude. Under the conditions, he would have had to be superhuman to resist the loving young woman, whom he obviously found extremely attractive.

The letter to Varina quoted above, includes one sentence which might well serve as an epitaph to the story of Swift and Vanessa,

Love, with the gall of too much Discretion, is a thousand times worse than with none at all.

This *discretion* which Swift both practised himself and exacted from others, hangs like a fog over all their lives, only lifting occasionally to allow a tantalising glimpse of the truth. But the Dean must himself eventually have realised the havoc it could produce, for a poem was found, in his handwriting, amongst Vanessa's papers after her death. It ends—

. . . . curst Discretion, all the fault was thine;
Cupid and Hymen thou hast set at odds
And bred such feuds between those kindred gods
That Venus cannot reconcile her sons;

When one appears, away the other runs.
The former scales, wherein he used to poise
Love against love, and equal joys and joys
Are now filled up with avarice and pride,
Where titles, power and riches still subside.
Thou, gentle Venus, to thy father run
And tell him how thy children are undone;
Prepare his bolts to give one fatal blow
And send Discretion to the shades below!

In June 1714, Swift would have considered discretion more essential than ever, if Vanessa were about to have a child — that unexplained boy, who intrudes at least four times into Swift's later life.

Two letters are missing from the Correspondence, after his first letter from Letcombe. The next, a month later, numbered 3 by Vanessa, is almost entirely dealing with business arising from Mrs. Van Homrigh's death, and with his offers to be security, should Vanessa need to borrow money from his printers. The next letter, numbered 5, refers to two letters she had written, but which are also missing from the Correspondence. In this letter Swift tells her that he had actually made arrangements to go to Ireland, but had postponed his departure in order to visit Lord Oxford, who had finally been dismissed by the Queen, leaving Lord Bolingbroke to lead the Tory Ministry. Swift tells Vanessa that:

I expect to leave this in two or three days, one way or another . . . I am not of your opinion about Lord Boling-broke. Perhaps he may get the Staff, but I cannot rely on his love for me. He knew I had a mind to be Historiographer, though I value it not but for the public service; yet it is gone to a worthless rogue that nobody knows. I am writ to earnestly by somebody to come to Town and join these people in power, but I will not do it.

49

The worthless rogue that nobody knows was the eminent historian, Thomas Madox, author of *The History and Antiquities of the Exchequer of the Kings of England*, published some years previously. Swift was not always fair to his opponents.

The letter ends with instructions for the repair of some of his knives, which he has left in her keeping, giving her the address of *my toy-man in Exchange Alley*. And he adds,

> *Where's your discretion in desiring to travel with that body?*

that body being Swift's printer and close associate, Barber, who visited him in Letcombe, and with whom Vanessa had, possibly, suggested she might visit Swift there.

Although he was unaware of it, Queen Anne was already dead when Swift wrote this letter. On the first day of August 1714 the Stuart dynasty had lost their last tenuous grip on the throne and the Hanoverians had, curiously, become the British Royal Family. Vanessa's hopes that Lord Bolingbroke would re-establish Swift's fortunes had vanished with the Queen's last breath.

The realisation that he had actually considered leaving for Ireland without seeing her again was obviously too much for Vanessa. Swift's next letter to her, dated twelve days later, reproaches her—again—for her want of discretion.

> *I had your letter last post, and before you can send me another I shall set out for Ireland. I must go and take the oaths, and the sooner the better. I think, since I have known you, I have drawn an old house upon my head. You used to brag you were very discreet. Where is it gone? It is probable I may not stay in Ireland long, but be back by the beginning of winter. When I am there, I will write to you as soon as I can conveniently, but it shall always be under cover; and if you write to me, let some other direct*

it; and I beg you will write nothing that is particular, but
which may be seen; for I apprehend letters will be opened
and inconvenience happen. If you are in Ireland while I
am there, I shall see you very seldom. It is not a place for
any freedom; but is is probable we may meet in London in
winter, or if not, leave all to Fate, that seldom cares to
humour our inclinations. I say all this out of the perfect
esteem and friendship I have for you. These public mis-
fortunes have altered all my measures and broke my
spirits. God almighty bless you. I shall, I hope, be on
horseback in a day after this comes to your hand. I would
not answer your questions for a million, nor can I think
of them with any ease of mind. Adieu.

This letter, addressed to her *at Mr. Handcock's in Little
Rider Street*—Mr. Handcock being, presumably, *the Surgeon* of the address of the first letter Swift wrote after they
parted in London — refers to yet another indiscretion; the
visit she had paid him a very short time previously. It is not
clear, from his reproaches, whether the very idea of the visit
had alarmed him, or whether he merely objected to the fact
that Vanessa had travelled to Letcombe through so public a
place as the Post-town, Wantage. But in later times, *the
Berkshire Surprise* took its place in the litany of happy
memories of which he used to remind her. He explains to
her that he now *must* go to Dublin to take the oath of loyalty
to the new King, as Dean of S. Patrick's; and that he hopes
to be back again in England by the Winter. If he knew that
there was no question of her being able to travel to Ireland
for some months, then he may well have hoped that the
prospect of his speedy return would keep her safely in London. Since Vanessa's difficulties in getting control of her estate could be more easily solved in Mr. Partinton's Dublin
office than in London, she had every excuse to make a visit
to Ireland, and must have discussed such a visit with Swift.

So it is significant to read his warning that, if she *should* decide to come to Ireland, it would be practically impossible for them to meet there. His almost hysterical accounts of the dangers of being seen together in Dublin sound a note which was still echoing and re-echoing many years later, and raise the immediate queries: *what* was he so anxious to hide, and *what* were the questions this girl had asked him, which he would not answer *for a million*, the very thought of which robbed his mind of all its ease? Whatever the answers may be, Swift left his retreat in Berkshire, and travelled to Dublin in the middle of August 1714; and Vanessa, whose every instinct must have urged her to follow, remained behind in the Surgeon's house, Little Rider St., for almost three months.

VIII

A FEW weeks after Swift's return to Dublin, he wrote some verses which give a vivid picture of his state of mind.

In sickness.

'Tis true . . . then why should I repine
To see my life so fast decline?
But, why obscurely and alone,
Where I am neither loved nor known?
My state of health none care to learn;
My life is here no soul's concern:
And those with whom I now converse,
Without a tear will tend my hearse.
Some formal visits, looks and words,
What mere humanity affords
I meet perhaps from three or four,
From whom I once expected more;
Which those who tend the sick for pay
Can act as decently as they;
But no obliging tender friend
To help at my approaching end,
My life is now a burthen grown
To others, e'er it be my own.

Even allowing for his illness and subsequent depression, it seems quite clear that Stella was not at hand, in her old capacity of devoted confidant and attendant, and that she is numbered amongst those from whom he *once expected more*. Presumably, too many stories of the *obliging, tender friend* in London had reached her ears, in Dublin. Nevertheless, in spite of his desire for the warm devotion of Vanessa, he must have heard of her impending arrival with dismay. But, since the advantages of dealing with her complicated law-affairs on the spot were so indisputable, it was impossible to dissuade her. Apart from the joy of being near him again, Vanessa must have been extremely conscious of the urgent importance of freeing her fortune from Mr. Partinton's clutches. She was well aware that it was an essential condition for their marriage, just as a suitable English appointment for the Dean was another.

And so, somewhere during the early days of November, 1714, Vanessa set out on what she believed would be a short visit to Dublin. She was accompanied on the long, wearisome journey by her delicate young sister, Moll, and her servants. Possibly not by Ann Kindon, who had been servant to Mrs. Van Homrigh in London. Many years later, she and her daughter figured as beneficiaries in Vanessa's Will, after many years' faithful service. Ann Kindon may have been left behind in London in charge of an infant.

To Mrs. Van-homrigh
at her lodgings in Turn-Stile Alley,
near College Green, Dublin.

> *Philipstown,*
> *November 5th, 1714*

I met your servant when I was a mile from Trim and could send him no other answer than I did, for I was going abroad by appointment. Besides I would not have gone to Kildrohid [Celbridge] to see you for all the world: I ever told you that you wanted discretion. I am going to a friend upon a promise, and shall stay with him about a fortnight, and then come to Town; and I will call upon you as soon as I can, supposing you lodge in Turnstile Alley, as your servant told me, and that your neighbours can tell me your whereabouts. Your servant said you would be in Town on Monday; so I suppose this will be ready to welcome you there. I fear you had a journey

54

full of fatigues: pray take care of your health in this Irish air, to which you are a stranger. Does not Dublin look very dirty to you, and the country miserable? Is Kildrohid as beautiful as Windsor, and as agreeable to you as the Prebend's Lodgings there? Is there any walk about you as pleasant as Marlborough Lodge? I have rode a tedious journey to-day, and can say no more. Nor shall you know where I am till I come, and then I will see you. A fig for your letters and messages. Adieu.

This letter Vanessa has numbered I, as if she were opening a new series with her arrival in Ireland. Her letters to which Swift refers have not survived. All that is therefore certain is that Vanessa had recently arrived in Ireland, presumably with her delicate young sister, and had gone to the fine mansion, outside Celbridge, which her father had built.

This house is usually referred to as Marley Abbey, although it did not bear that name for years after Vanessa's death, when the Marley family bought the estate. It is ten miles from Dublin, and the river Liffey flows through its handsome pleasure grounds. Turnstile Alley, where the Van Homrighs had their town house, was a fashionable quarter in the Eighteenth Century, situated as it was off College Green, beside Chichester House where the Parliament met. It was a short distance from Dublin Castle and from Trinity College. It was also close to the Deanery of St. Patrick's. The house in Turnstile Alley had almost certainly been her father's house; as a Member of Parliament, he would have found it very convenient. It was also the house which Archbishop King advised Vanessa to sell, some years later, when her financial difficulties became acute. It is important to remember that Vanessa had a town and country house, and that she moved frequently between them.

Apparently, her first stay in Celbridge was short; Swift having made it perfectly clear that, under no circumstances would he visit her there. It is of interest to note that he never *did* visit her in Celbridge until August, 1720 — almost six years after her arrival in Ireland.

Swift's letter, stressing as it does the inferiority of the Irish scene to that she had just left behind her in London, was obviously intended to discourage her from any lengthy stay. It certainly sounded no note of welcome and must have given little comfort to Vanessa, after her *journey full of fatigues.*

The next letter, undated and endorsed *3rd,* is addressed to *Misshess Vanr* and is, presumably, a hand-delivered note.

I will see you to-morrow, if possible. You know it is not above five days since I saw you and that I would ten times more if it were at all convenient, whether your old dragon came or no, whom I believe my people cannot tell what to make of, but take him for some conjurer.

Adieu, Tuesday morning, ten

The old dragon who looked so strange to the Deanery staff, was probably a liveried man-servant whom she had brought with her from London. All that can be gathered, from Swift's somewhat enigmatic note is that Swift had been visiting her fairly frequently in her Dublin house and that he protests that he would have done so very much more often had it been *convenient* — which may be translated *discreet* — to do so.

The next letter, endorsed *4th,* is merely dated *Dublin,* 1714, and was also, almost certainly, delivered by hand. It is, like all the other correspondence, unsigned, and is to Swift from Vanessa. In this letter, she appears for the first time as the highly temperamental, emotional young woman, whom Swift later used to refer to as *Governor Huff* and beg not to quarrel with him. She was a victim of that

56

Eighteenth Century epidemic, *the Spleen,* and the correspondence is full of allusions to her feeling *so low.* In a
later letter the Dean complains, *I am confident you came
chiding into the world, and will continue so while you are
in it.* While admitting that Vanessa was a neurotic young
woman, it is also clear that this attractive, intelligent,
capable girl was extremely unfortunate in the situation in
which she found herself, and that under happier conditions
she would have been an unfrustrated, contented and
devoted wife.

*You cannot but be sensible, at least in some degree, of
the many uneasinesses I am slave to — a wretch of a
brother, cunning executors and importunate creditors of
my mother's — things I can in no way avoid being subject to at present, and weighty enough to sink greater
spirits than mine without some support. Once I had a
friend that would see me sometimes, and either commend
what I did or advise me what to do, which banished all
my uneasiness. But now, when my misfortunes are
increased by being in a disagreeable place, amongst
strange, prying, deceitful people, whose company is so
far from an amusement that it is a very great punish-
ment you fly from me and give me no reason but that we
are amongst fools and must submit. I am very well satisfied that we are amongst such but know no reason for
having my happiness sacrificed to their caprice. You once
had a maxim, which was to act what was right and not
mind what the world said. I wish you would keep it now.
Pray what can be wrong in seeing and advising an unhappy young woman? I can't imagine. You can't but
know that your frowns make my life unsupportable. You
have taught me to distinguish, and then you leave me
miserable. Now all I beg is that you will for once
counterfeit (since you can't otherwise) that indulgent*

57

friend you once were, till I get the better of these diffi-
culties, for my sister's sake; for were not she involved
(who, I know, is not so able to manage them as I am),
I have a nobler soul than to sit struggling with mis-
fortunes, when at the end I can't promise myself any real
happiness. Forgive me; and I beg you'd believe it is not
in my power to avoid complaining as I do.

The tone of the letter is very interesting; although she
asks, or rather demands his help, she does so as one who
has a perfect right to do so, clearly implying that his
discretion in dealing with her affairs is mere weakness and
subservience to public gossips — the *strange, prying,*
deceitful people to whom she refers. Turnstile Alley being
a short distance from Capel Street, where the Ladies then
lodged, it is easy to imagine the buzzing of rumour. Her
wretch of a brother, Bartholomew, owed a considerable
amount to his mother's estate, which was still unpaid in
May, 1715, when his Will was proved.

As usual when Vanessa really gets carried away, Swift
abjectly surrenders, whether from genuine love of the girl,
or from fear of what she might do, if driven too far. His
letter is undated, addressed to *Miss Hessy Van* and presumably delivered by hand.

I will see you in a day or two, and believe me, it goes to
my soul not to see you oftener. I will give you the best
advice countenance and assistance I can. I would have
been with you sooner if a thousand impediments had not
prevented me. I did not imagine you had been under
difficulties. I am sure my whole fortune should go to
remove them. I cannot see you, I fear, to-day, having
affairs of my place to do; but pray think it not want of
friendship or tenderness, which I will always continue
to the utmost. *Monday morning.*

Some short time later, Vanessa writes another letter, dated 1714. From it, it is obvious that the girl has had a very serious quarrel with Swift, in the course of which his terrible anger — so much feared by his closest associates — has had its way. As this is, it seems, the last existing letter for a considerable time, the fateful year 1714 ends with this explosion of Vanessa's misery.

Well, now I see plainly how great a regard you have for me. You bid me be easy, and you'd see me as often as you could. You had better said, as often as you could get the better of your inclinations so much, or as often as you remembered there was such a one in the world. If you continue to treat me as you do you will not be made uneasy by me long. 'Tis impossible to describe what I have suffered since I saw you last; those killing, killing words of yours. Sometimes I have resolved to die without seeing you more; but those resolves, to your misfortune, did not last long. For there is something in human nature that prompts one so to find relief in this world, I must give way to it, and beg you'd see me and speak kindly to me; for I am sure you'd not condemn anyone to suffer what I have done, could you but know it. The reason I write to you is because I cannot tell it to you, should I see you; for when I begin to complain, you are angry, and there is something in your look so awful, that it strikes me dumb. Oh! that you may but have so much regard for me left, that this complaint may touch your soul with pity. I say as little as ever I can: did you but know what I thought, I am sure it would move you. Forgive me, and believe I cannot help telling you this, and live.

After that letter, there is silence, until a note from Swift, which may well be dated 1715 because of the allusion to Dr. Pratt, Provost of Trinity College, who was an

59

executor of the will of Vanessa's brother, Bartholomew. At his recent death, May 1715, he left his estate for life, to his sisters, so it seems natural that Vanessa should be in touch with Dr. Pratt.

(In Bartholomew Van Homrigh's will, which was put into probate by Dr. Pratt and Peter Partington on the 15th May, 1715, he left directions for the immediate repayment of the money he owed to his mother's estate for the expenses of his very considerable travel, as well as for his board and lodging while living in her London household. This will was drawn up in London, within a few weeks of his mother's death. He left a legacy to *Mr. Thomas Bacon of the Middle Temple, London* — presumably the same Thomas Bacon who had recently witnessed his mother's will. He also left a legacy to the Rev. Mr. Periam, *heretofore my Tutor in Christchurch, Oxford.* and to Erasmus Lewis.

Although Bartholomew states that he is *in good health of body*, his will seems oddly pessimistic for a young man of twenty-two. He shows an almost frantic desire for the perpetuation of the name, Van Homrigh, either through his father's godson, Bartholomew Partington, should he consent to assume that name, or, failing such consent, by the erection of a Van Homrigh building in Trinity College, Dublin. At twenty-two, he apparently believed himself incapable of fathering a child.)

The note was obviously written by Swift in Vanessa's house in Turnstile Alley.

I dined with the Provost and told him I was coming here, because I must be at prayers at six. He said you had been with him, and would not be at home this day, and went to Celbridge tomorrow. I said I would however go try. I fancy you told him so that he might not come tonight. If he comes you must piece it up as you can, else he will think it was on purpose to meet me, and I hate anything that looks like a secret. I cannot possibly call after prayers, and therefore came here in the afternoon, while people were at Church, hoping certainly to find you. I am truly afflicted for poor Moll, who is a girl of infinite value; I am sure you will take all possible care of her; and I hope to live to see the sincerest friendship in the world long between you. I pray God of Heaven protect you both, and am entierement—

Four o'clock.

After that note there is nothing, until a very long letter, written by Swift, in French, dated 12th May, 1719. It is addressed to *Madame Hester Vanhumri*, and begins by explaining that it is not true that he has left Dublin for three months; that he has merely gone to visit some friends in the country to improve his health. He continues,

Croyez moy, s'il y a chose croyable au monde, que-je pense tout ce que vous pouvez souhaiter de moy, et que tous vos desirs seront toujours obèi comme des commandements qu'il sera impossible de violer.

After warm good wishes for her health and hopes that she will spend part of the summer in her Celbridge home, he continues,

Il faut vous connoitre long temps de connoitre toutes vos perfections; toujours en vous voyant et entendant il en paroissent des nouvelles, qui estoient auparavent cachées . . . vous, qui estes incapable d'aucune sottise, si ce n'est l'estime qu'il vous plaist d'avoir pour moy. Car il n'y a point de merite, ni aucun preuve de mon bon goût de trouver en vous tout ce que la Nature a donne a un mortel. Je veux dire l'honneur, la vertue, le bon sens l'esprit, la doueur, l'agrement et la fermité d'ame. Mais en vous cachant commes vous faites, le monde ne vous connoit pas, et vous perdez l'eloge des millions de gens.

61

Depuis que j'ai l'honneur de vous connoitre, j'ay toujours remarqué que ni en conversation particuliere ni generale aucun mot a echappe de votre bouche, qui pouvoit etre mieux exprimé; et je vous jure qu'en faisant souvent la plus severe critique, je ne pouvois jamais trouver aucun defaut, ni en vos actions ni en vos parolles. La coquetrie, l'affectation, la pruderie sont des imperfections que vous n'avez jamais connu. Et avec tout cela, croyez vous qu'il est possible de ne vous estimer au dessus du reste du genre humain? Quelle bestes en juppes sont les plus excellentes de celles que je vois semées dans le monde au prix de vous. En les voyant, en les entendant, je dis cent fois le jour, Ne parle, ne regarde, ne pense, ne fait rien comme ces miserables. Sont ce du meme sexe, du meme espece de creatures? Quel cruantè de faire mepriser autant de gens, qui sans songer de vous seront assès supportable. Mais il est tems de vous delasser, et dire adieu avec tous le respecte, la sincerete et l'estime du monde. Je suis et sera toujours — — — — —.

If, as Lord Orrery charged, Vanessa was *in her own opinion superior to all her sex,* she had Swift's authority for it. *What beasts in petticoats are the most excellent of those I see everywhere in comparison with you . . . What cruelty to make so many people appear despicable, who would seem tolerable if I didn't remember you.* And Swift ends this letter with five dashes, to be filled in by the loving heart of the girl to whom he had written this truly remarkable letter.

Obviously, the lovers had reached some *modus vivendi,* although, with Swift's temperament, it was not very stable.

There is a curious, undated letter, written to Vanessa, and obviously delivered to her Dublin house.

I received your letter when some company was with me on Saturday night; and it put me in such confusion, that I could not tell what to do. I here send you the paper you left me. This morning, a woman who does business for me, told me she heard I was in love with one—naming you, and twenty particulars, that little master and I visited you, and that the A-B did so; and that you had an abundance of wit, etc. I ever feared the tattle of this nasty town, and told you so; and that was the reason why I said to you, long ago, that I would see you seldom in Ireland. And I must beg you to be easy if for some time I visit you seldomer, and not in so particular a manner. I will see you at the latter end of the week if possible. These are accidents in life that are necessary and must be submitted to; and tattle by the help of discretion, will wear off. Monday morning, ten o'clock.

Discretion *had* indeed been lacking, if the conversation Swift reports were true. But, remembering that proud, violent-tempered man, whom even his best friends took very good care not to annoy; remembering Orrery's description of him *when the sternness of his visage was increased by rage, it is scarce possible to imagine looks, or features, that carried on them more terror;* remembering Vanessa's complaint that anger produced in him *looks so awful* as to strike her dumb, *is* it possible to believe the story? No woman, or man, from his Archbishop down, would have dared, or been permitted, to repeat such tittle-tattle to the Dean of St. Patrick's. To imagine that formidable man listening patiently, while some female caller repeated local gossip, *with twenty particulars*, is impossible. It is an incredible story.

Some other explanation must be found. It may well be that, finding his relationship had got out of control, Swift used the gossip of a fictitious woman to explain or excuse a general tightening up. But the accusations he repeats are extremely interesting. Apart from the charge of being in love with Vanessa—with *twenty particulars*—there is also the assertion *that little master and I visited you.* The question naturally arises, who was *little master*, whose visits to Vanessa were giving food for scandalous gossip?

If Vanessa had had a son, about October 1714—the child, whose imminent birth prevented her from following Swift to Ireland in the August of that year — he would now be about five or six years old. Once Vanessa had realised that there was little chance of Swift's speedy return to England, and that her own disastrous legal affairs would drag on indefinitely, she would have arranged to have their child in her neighbourhood. Visits of the boy to her house, arranged so as to coincide with Swift's, might well have seemed to Vanessa a way of strengthening their bond. To the Dean, such an arrangement would have appeared appallingly dangerous, but his position was so full of pitfalls that he could only act with extreme caution. Rather than refuse, openly, to continue such meetings—so running the risk of driving Vanessa to unknown lengths — he may have invented the story of the tattling woman, using it as a perfectly reasonable excuse for greater discretion. Vanessa herself would have had to acknowledge the danger to the Dean of such a discovery, and the disastrous results it would have on his career, both in and outside Ireland.

The fact that his letter ends with the promise of visiting her within a few days would seem to discount any genuine alarm on his part, about the *tattle of this nasty town.*

The next long letter from Vanessa is undated, but is assigned to about 1720. Although she complains, yet there is gaiety and confidence in her tone, and, apparently, her complaint is that he doesn't visit her every day.

Is it possible that again you will do the very same thing I warned you of so lately? I believe you thought I only rallied when I told you, the other night, I would pester

64

you with letters. Did not I know you very well, I should think you knew but little of the world, to imagine that a woman would not keep her word whenever she promised anything that was malicious. Had not you better a thousand times throw away one hour, at some time or other of the day, than to be interrupted in your business at this rate? For I know 'tis as impossible for you to burn my letters without reading them, as 'tis for me to avoid reproving you when you behave yourself so wrong. Once more I advise you, if you have any regard for your quiet, to alter your behaviour quickly; for I do assure you I have too much spirit to sit contented with this treatment. Now, because I love frankness extremely, I here tell you that I have determined to try all manner of human arts to reclaim you, and if all those fail, I am resolved to have recourse to the black one, which it is said, never does. Now see what inconveniences you will bring both me and yourself into. Pray think calmly of it. Is it not much better to come of yourself than to be brought by force, and that, perhaps, at a time when you have the most agreeable engagement in the world? For when I undertake anything, I don't love to do it by halves. But there is one thing that falls out very luckily for you, which is that, of all the passions, revenge hurries me least, so that you have it yet in your power to turn all this fury into good humour, and, depend upon it, and more I assure you. Come at what time you please, you can never fail of being very well received.

To which Swift replied, with equally light-hearted banter,

If you write as you do, I shall come the seldomer, on purpose to be pleased with your letters, which I never look into without wondering how a Brat, who cannot read, can possibly write so well. You are mistaken; send me a letter without your hand on the outside, and I hold you a crown I shall not read it. But, raillery apart, I think it inconvenient for a hundred reasons that I should make your house a sort of constant dwellingplace. I will certainly come as often as I conveniently can, but my health and the perpetual run of ill weather hinders me from going out in the morning; and my afternoons are taken up, I know not how, that I am in rebellion with a dozen people beside yourself, for not seeing them. For the rest, you need make use of no other black art besides your ink. 'Tis a pity your eyes are not black, or I would have said the same of them; but you are a white witch and can do no mischief. If you have employed any of your art on the black scarf, I defy it, for one reason: guess. Adieu.

Eight years before, in London, she had made him another black scarf, which may provide the clue to Swift's invitation to *guess*.

In July, 1720, Swift wrote to her, to her house in Celbridge:

I am now writing on Wednesday night, when you are hardly settled at home; and it is the first hour of leisure I have had, and it may be Saturday before you have it, and then there will be Governor Huff; and to make you more so, I here enclose a letter to poor Malkin, which I will command her not to show you, because it is a love-letter. I reckon by this time the groves and fields and purling streams have made Vanessa romantic, provided poor Malkin be well. Your friend sent me the verses he promised, which I here transcribe:

Nymph, would you learn the only art
To keep a worthy lover's heart,
First, to adorn your person well
In utmost cleanliness excell;
And though you must the fashions take,
Observe them but for fashion's sake.

66

The strongest reason will submit
To virtue, honour, sense and wit.
To such a nymph, the wise and good
Cannot be faithless, if they would:
For vices all have different ends
But virtue still to virtue tends:
And when your lover is not true,
'Tis virtue fails, in him or you;
And either he deserves disdain,
Or you without a cause complain.
But here Vanessa cannot err,
Nor are these rules applied to her:
For who would such a nymph forsake
Except a blockhead or a rake?
Or how could she her heart bestow
Except where wit and virtue grow?

In my opinion these lines are too grave, and therefore may not fit you, who I fear are in the spleen; but that is not fit either for yourself or the person you tend, to whom you ought to read diverting things. Here is an epigram that concerns you not:

Dorinda dreams of dress a-bed,
'Tis all her thought and art;
Her lace hath got within her head
Her stays stick in her heart.

If you do not like these things, what must I say? This town yields no better. The questions which you were used to ask me, you may suppose to be all answered, just as they used to be after half an hour debate — entendez-vous cela? You are to have a number of parsons in your neighbourhood, but not one that you love, for your age of loving parsons is not yet arrived. What this letter wants in length it will have in difficulty, for I believe you cannot read it. I will write plainer to Malkin, because she is not much used to my hand. I hold a wager there are some lines in this letter you will not understand, though you can read them. So drink your coffee and remember you are a desperate chip, and that the lady who calls you bastard will be ready to answer all your questions. 'Tis now Sunday night before I could finish this.

Swift wrote this letter over five days, taking up the thread of easy thought as time offered, in affectionately jocose style. The mysterious *lady who calls you bastard* and who was ready to supply all answers is probably Venus. In the poem *Cadenus and Vanessa,* she assures her fellow-goddess that the infant Vanessa so closely resembles Cupid that she appears to be a child of Apollo. The answering of *questions,* which appears so often in the later letters, first poses its enigma here, and, because he is not certain that *she* will understand the phrase, he adds *Entendez-vous cela?*

In her reply from Celbridge, 28th July, 1720, she makes it clear that she does understand.

I thought I should have heard from you in a week, according to your promise, but that week consisted of fourteen days, which were to me, after the first seven, very long, long ones. I own I never expected to have another letter from you, for two reasons: first, because I thought you had quite forgot me, and because I was so very ill that I thought I should have died. But, ever since I received your letter, which was last Friday, I have been pretty well. I have done all that lay in my power to follow your example, for fear of teasing you, but I find I cannot defer writing to you any longer. When I opened your letter, I thought you had wrote me two, as you said perhaps you might; but instead of that to find 'twas a letter to another, and that a love-letter — how do you think I could support it? But upon my word, when I see you I have a vast deal to say to you about that letter. I have asked you all the questions I used, ten thousand times, and don't find them answered at all to my satisfaction.

The letters *poor Malkin* got from Swift have not survived, but the kindness which prompted his notes to the dying girl is one of his pleasanter traits. Mary Van Homrigh had apparently been in bad health since he had first known her. In July, 1720, she had only a few months to live. Almost certainly, in nursing her, Vanessa had herself become infected with tuberculosis; and the psychological stresses which that disease produces are added, from now on, to the other tensions which drove Vanessa to her early grave.

Swift to Vanessa:

If you knew how many little difficulties there are in sending letters to you, it would remove five parts or six of your quarrell; but since you lay hold of my promises, and are so exact to the day, I shall promise you no more, and rather choose to be better than my word, than worse. I am confident that you came chiding into the world, and will continue so while you are in it. I was in great apprehension that poor Malkin was worse, and till I could be satisfied on that particular, I would not write again. But I little expected to have heard of your own ill health, and those who saw you since made no mention to me of it. I wonder what Malkin meant by shewing you my letter: I will write to her no more, since she can keep secrets no better. It was the first love-letter I have writ these dozen years, and since I have so ill success I will write no more — never was a belle passion so defeated. But the Governor, I hear, is jealous and upon your word you have a vast deal to say to me about it. Mind your nurse-keeping, do your duty and leave off your huffing. One would think you were in love, by dating your letter August 29th, by which means I received it just a month before it was written. You do not find that I answer your questions to your satisfaction. Prove to me first that it was ever possible to answer anything to your satisfaction, so as that you would not grumble in half an hour. I am glad my writing puzzles you, for then your time will be employed in finding it out; and I am sure it costs me a great many thoughts to make my letters difficult. Sure Glass Heel is come over, and gave me a message from John Barber about the money on the jewels, which I shall answer. Malkin will be so glad to see Glass Heel — ay, Malkin. Yesterday I was half-way towards you, where I dined, and returned weary enough. I asked where that road to the left led, and they named the place. I wish your letters were as difficult as mine, for then they would be of no consequence, if they were dropped by careless messengers. A stroke thus — — — — signifies everything that may be said to Cad, at beginning or conclusion. It is I who ought to be in a huff that anything written by Cad should be difficult to Skinage. I must now leave off abruptly, for I intend to send this letter to-day. August 4th — — — — —

Glass Heel was the nickname the Van Homrighs used for their good friend, Charles Ford, with whom Swift had been very intimate in London. Ford had a handsome property near Dublin and is one of the few people who knew both Vanessa and Stella. The jewels referred to are almost certainly the diamond and pearl necklaces and earrings, which Mrs. Van Homrigh, in her will, bequeathed to her daughters, and which Vanessa had pledged to John Barber.

Swift's fear of his letters being opened leads to his invention of expressing his love by strokes. Vanessa's next letter, undated, but obviously a reply to the last, begins in an ecstasy:

Celbridge, 1720

—. —, —, —, —, Cad —, you are good beyond expression, and I will never quarrel again if I can help it; but, with submission, 'tis you that are so hard to be pleased, though you complain of me. I thought the last letter I wrote to you was obscure and constrained enough: I took pains to write it after that manner. It would have been much easier for me to have wrote otherwise. I am not so unreasonable as to expect you should keep your word to a day, but six or seven days are great odds. Why should your apprehensions for Malkin hinder you from writing to me? I think you ought to have wrote the sooner to have comforted me. Malkin is better, but in a very weak way. Though those that saw me told you nothing of my illness, I do assure you I was for twenty-four hours as ill as 'twas possible to be, and live. You wrong me when you say I did not find that you answered my questions to my satisfaction. What I said was, I had asked those questions but could not find them answered to my satisfaction. How could they be answered in absence, since Somnus is not my friend? We have had a vast deal of thunder and lightning. Where do you think I wished to be then? And do you think that was the only time I wished so since I saw you? I am sorry my jealousy should hinder you from writing more love-letters, for I must chide sometimes, and I wish I could gain by it at this instant, as I have done and hope to do. Is my dating my letter wrong the only sign of my being in love? Pray tell me, did not you wish to come where that road to the left would have led you? I'm mightily pleased to hear you talk of being in a huff. 'Tis the first time you ever told me so. I wish I could see you in one. I am now as happy as I can be without seeing —, —, —, Cad. I beg you'll continue happiness to your own Skinage.

In spite of her attempts at obscurity, it is clear that, in Swift's absence, *questions* can only be satisfactorily answered in dreams; and Vanessa doesn't sleep. Thunder-storms remind her of Cad's protecting arms and of her constant desire to find herself there. She must chide, sometimes, for the joy of making up the quarrel, as she has done before and hopes to do again. She is as happy as she can ever be in the absence of —, —, —, *Cad*. She gladly admits his charge of being in love. It is the happy letter of a loving woman to a man who, she knows, loves her, too.

A few days later, Swift replies:

"*August 12th, 1720.*
I apprehended, on the return of the porter I sent with my last letter, that it would miscarry, because I saw the rogue was drunk; but yours made me easy. I must neither write to Malkin nor not write to her. You are like Lord Pembroke, who would neither go nor stay. Glass Heel talks of going to see you, and taking me with him, as he goes to his country house. I find you have company with you these two or three days: I hope they are diverting, at least to poor Malkin. Why should Cad's letters be difficult? I assure you — —'s are not at all.
I'm vexed that the weather hinders you from any pleasure in the country, because walking, I believe, would be of good use to you and Malkin. I reckon you will return a prodigious scholar, a most admirable nursekeeper, a perfect huswife and a great drinker of coffee. I have asked, and am assured there is not one beech in all your groves to carve a name on, nor a purling stream, for love or money, except a great river, which sometimes roars, but never murmurs — just like Governor Huff. We live here in a very dull Town, every valuable creature absent, and Cad — says he is weary of it, and would rather drink his coffee on the barrenest, highest mountain in Wales, than be King here.

A fig for partridges and quails;
Ye dainties, I know nothing of ye,
But on the highest mount in Wales
Would choose in peace to drink my coffee.

What would you give to have the history of Cad and
——, exactly written, through all its steps, from the
beginning to this time? I believe it would do well in verse,
and be as long as the other. I hope it will be done. It
ought to be an exact chronicle of twelve years, from the
time of spilling the coffee to drinking coffee, from Dun-
stable to Dublin, with every single passage since. There
would be the chapter of the blister; the chapter of Madam
going to Kensington; the chapter of the Colonel's going
to France; the chapter of the wedding, with the
adventure of the lost key; of the strain; of the joyful
return; two hundred chapters of madness; the chapter
of long walks; the Berkshire surprise; fifty chapters of
little times; the chapter of Chelsea; the chapter of
swallow and cluster; a hundred whole books of myself
and "so low"; the chapter of hide and whisper; the chapter
of Who made it so? My sister's money. Cad bids me tell
you, that if you complain of his puzzling you with
difficult writing, he will give you enough of it.

See how much I have written without saying one word
of Malkin, and you will be whipped before you deliver
her a message with honour. I shall write to J. Barber next
post, and desire him to be at no pains about his money;
and I will take not one word of notice of his riches, on
purpose to vex him. If Heaven had looked upon riches
to be a valuable thing, it would not have given them to
such a scoundrel. I delivered your enclosed letter to our
friend, who happened to be with me when I received it.
I find you are very much in his good graces; for he said
a million of fine things upon it, though he would let
nobody read a word of it but himself, though I was so

*kind to shew him yours to me, as well as this, which he
has laid a crown with me you will not understand —
which is pretty odd for one that sets up for so high an
opinion of your good sense.*
I am ever, with the greatest truth, yours etc.
                                                    August 13.

Swift's attempts at *obscurity and constraint* were sufficient,
no doubt, to mislead an untrustworthy messenger, but his
letter can have offered little difficulty to the delighted eyes
of Vanessa.

He was actually coming to Celbridge! . . . the visit she
had dreamed about for six long years . . . he would see her
home . . . she could show him her beautiful house, the fine
pleasure-grounds sloping down to the lovely stretch of Liffey
. . . Cad was coming, —, —, —, Cad. And, as if that news
were not enough happiness for one letter to hold, he shows
her that he has forgotten nothing of the past . . . reminds
her of the times they have shared . . . tantalises her with
the hope that he might even continue their own private history, *Cadenus and Vanessa.* He suggests chapter headings
. . . Does she remember? Could she possibly forget?

To her shining eyes, each detail was as clear as noonday;
but the dust of Time has blurred everything which it has not
totally obliterated. Today the real significance lies in the
fact that Swift, sharing Vanessa's memories, should have
chosen to recall them to her. That so often remembered
coffee, spilt years before in a Dunstable inn . . . *the Colonel,*
her wild, young scamp of a brother . . . Swift had packed
him off to France, with an introduction to his good friend,
Prior, to get him away from mischief in London . . . and
then the frantic apeals to his mother from a debtor's prison
in Paris . . . poor, foolish Bartholomew, in his too early
grave . . . These have left faint traces. But *the blister?* A
clue lies, perhaps, in the circumstances surrounding Swift's

fearful attack of shingles in London? *The wedding . . .* whose?

This memorable wedding, more fully described in a later letter as *the London Wedding,* was very probably that of Lady Mary Butler, younger daughter of the Duke of Ormond, who married Lord Ashburnham on the 20th October 1710. This young girl was a constant visitor at the Van Homrigh home and a close friend of Vanessa. In a letter from Swift to her cousin, Anne Long, he says of Vanessa (December 1711),

> *Her greatest favourites at present are Lady Ashburnham, her dog and myself.*

Both Swift and the Van Homrighs would certainly have been guests at this fashionable wedding. Swift describes Lord Ashburnham in the *Journal* as *the best match in England.* When she died a couple of years later, Swift wrote:

> *She was my greatest favourite, and I am in excessive concern for her loss.*

The strain . . . ? In a later letter, Swift expands this to *the strain by the box of books in London,* reminding her that, each time he changed lodgings, he invariably had a wooden-case of newly acquired books to be shifted and stored. *Chelsea . . .* ? That happy, happy time, when he came to see them twice a day, changing into his fine new wig and gown before going amongst the great . . . laughter in the Sluttery . . . fragrance of roasting oranges . . . the tang of strong, black coffee . . . O happy, happy Chelsea! . . . *The Berkshire Surprise?* He had been angry at first . . . . . . angry and embarrassed, when he looked up and saw her at the Vicarage gate . . . *Who* had seen her in the coach at Wantage? . . . *Whom* had she told she was coming? . . . *What* would the Reverend Mr. Geree suspect? . . . A stern sermon on his favourite subject, Discretion, and then, half-way through, she was in his arms . . . The happiness of being together again, even for a few short hours . . . And he ventures *a Crown* that she will not understand!

Swift, too, must have been in one of his rare completely happy moods when he wrote that letter. It bubbles with gaiety. Even his good, faithful friend, John Barber, becomes *a scoundrel*, and he invents yet another personality for himself, *our friend*, to whom he delivers Vanessa's letter, *I find you are very much in his good graces, for he said a million of fine things upon it. . . . So low*, his pet name for her when she moped. . . .

People of Vanessa's temperament tend to swing between the heights of joy and the depths of despair. On the 13th August 1720, as she read that letter, she must have spent some hours on a sunbathed peak. Her ardent joy fills her immediate reply:

> *Celbridge,* 1720.
> -, -, -, *Cad, is it possible you will come and see me? I beg for God sake you will. I would give all world to see you here, and Malkin would be extremely happy. Do you think the time long since I saw you? I did design seeing you this week, but will not stir, in hopes of your coming here. I beg you'll write two or three words by the bearer, to let me know if you think you'll come this week: I shall have the note tonight. You make me happy beyond expression by your goodness. It would be too much once to hope for such a history. If you had laid a thousand pounds that I should not understand your letter, you had lost it. Tell me sincerely, did those circumstances crowd on you, or did you recollect them to make me happy?*

Her messenger was to wait for his answer. There is no record of that visit to Celbridge. The only thing of note in the letter is that it shows that she was in the habit of visiting Dublin, from time to time, and seeing him there. Presumably the country air of Celbridge was considered better for her dying sister, and so they had to stay there.

The next surviving letter is from Swift, and there is a gap of two months between it and the last:

October 15th 1720.

I sit down with the first opportunity I have to write to you; and the Lord knows when I can find conveniency to send this letter; for all the morning I am plagued with impertinent visits, or impertinent business, below any man of sense or honour to endure, if it were in any way avoidable. Dinners and afternoons and evenings are spent abroad and in walking, to help and avoid spleen, so far as I can; so that when I am not so good a correspondent as I could wish, you are not to quarrel and be Governor, but to impute it to my situation, and to conclude infallibly that I have the same respect, esteem and kindness for you I ever professed to have and shall ever preserve, because you will always merit the utmost that can be given you—especially if you go on to read, and still further improve your mind and the talents nature has given you. I had a letter from your friend, John Barber, in London, in answer to what I told you Glass-heel said about the money. J. B.'s answer is that you are a person of honour, that you need give yourself no trouble about it, that you will pay when you are able, and he shall be content until then. Those are his very words; and you see he talks in the style of a rich man, though terribly pulled down by the fall of stocks. I am glad you did not sell your annuities, unless somebody were to manage and transfer them while stocks were high. I am in much concern for poor Malkin and the more because I am sure you are too. You ought to be as cheerful as you can, for both your sakes, and read pleasant things that will make you laugh, and not sit moping with your elbows on your knees on a little stool at the fire. It is most

77

infallible that riding would do Malkin much more good than any other thing, provided fair days and warm clothes be provided; and so it would to you; and if you lose any skin, you know Job says: Skin for skin will a man give for his life. It is either Job or Satan says so, for aught you know.

October 17th—I had not a moment to finish this since I sat down to it. A person was with me just now, and interrupted me as I was going on with telling me of great people here losing their places; and now some more are coming about business, so adieu till by and by or to-morrow.

October 18th—I am getting an ill head in this cursed town, for want of exercise. I wish I were to walk with you fifty times about your garden, and then—drink your coffee. I was sitting last night with half a score of both sexes for an hour, and grew as weary as a dog. Glass Heel takes up abundance of my time, in spite of my teeth; everybody grows silly and disagreeable, or I grow monkish and spleenatic, which is the same thing. Conversation is full of nothing but South Sea, and the ruin of the Kingdom, and scarcity of money. I had a thousand times rather hear the Governor chide two hours without reason.

October 20th—The Governor was with me at six o'clock this morning, but did not stay two minutes, and deserves a chiding, which you must give when you drink your coffee next. I hope to send this letter to-morrow. I am a good deal out of order in my head after a little journey I made, and ate too much, I suppose, or travelling in a coach after it. I am now sitting alone, and will go write Malkin. So adieu — — — — —.

In this letter, he warmly advocates his cure-all for ill-health—exercise; horse-riding will help even poor Malkin, apparently in the last stages of tuberculosis. All through

Swift's life, he exercised himself mercilessly, from the early days when he used to run up a hill at Moor Park, to those darker days towards the end, when in wet weather, he used to rush up and down the Deanery stairs, until he calculated that he had covered ten miles. In 1720, his ill health was increasing, his attacks of Meniere's disease were more frequent and its giddy spells left him ever more shaken and depressed. Ill and weary, he wishes he could leave *this cursed town* and take refuge with her in the quiet Celbridge garden, walking around it fifty times, *and then—drink your coffee.* Many people have speculated as to what the words mean. What Vanessa understood by the phrase is one of the many secrets in this strange adventure in love.

Dublin can talk of nothing but the bursting of the South Sea Bubble; rather than listen to the wearisome talk, he would willingly be chided by Vanessa for two hours on end, even though he didn't deserve to be scolded. And then, next day, he adds a postscript to tell her that he has been dreaming about her, in the early hours; that the dream was too brief and that there would be reproaches *when next she drank her coffee.* He ends this touching letter with no less than seven strokes, each one a warrant for the most loving words she cares to substitute.

When Swift wrote this letter, he was almost fifty-three and Vanessa was thirty one. They had known one another for some fourteen years, through good times and bad, and they had arrived at a relationship which this letter makes clear.

The next, dated merely 1720, is from Vanessa:

Celbridge.
You had heard from me before, but that my messenger was not to be had till today; and now I have only time to thank you for yours, because he is going about his business this moment, which is very happy for you, or you would

79

have had a long letter full of spleen. Never was human creature more distressed than I have been since I came. Poor Malkin has had two or three relapses, and is in so bad a way that I fear she will never recover. Judge now what a way I am in, absent from you and loaded with melancholy on her score. I have been very ill with a stitch in my side, which is not very well yet.

Her next letter, also is dated:

Celbridge 1720.
Believe me 'tis with the utmost regret that I now complain to you, because I know your good nature, such that you cannot see any human being miserable without being sensibly touched. Yet what can I do? I must either unload my heart and tell you all my griefs, or sink under the unexpressible distress I now suffer by your prodigious neglect of me. 'Tis now ten long weeks since I saw you, and in all that time I have never received but one letter from you and a little note, with an excuse. Oh —, —, —, how have you forgot me! You endeavour by severities to force me from you; nor can I blame you, for with the utmost distress and confusion, I behold myself the cause of uneasy reflections to you. Yet I cannot comfort you, but here declare that 'tis not in the power of art, time or accident to lessen the unexpressible passion, which I have for -, -, -. Put my passion under the utmost restraint, send me as distant from you as the earth will allow, yet you cannot banish those charming ideas, which will ever stick by me, whilst I have the use of memory. Nor is the love I bear you only seated in my soul, for there is not a single atom of my frame that is not blended with it. Therefore, don't flatter yourself that separation will ever change my sentiments, for I find myself unquiet in the midst of silence, and my heart is at once pierced by sorrow and love. For Heaven's sake, tell me what caused this prodigious change

*in you, which I have found of late. If you have the least
remains of pity for me left, tell me tenderly. No, don't
tell it, so that it may cause my present death; and don't
suffer me to live a life like a languishing death, which is
the only life I can lead, if you have lost any of your tenderness for me.*

Ill herself, and worn out with the care of her dying sister,
Vanessa is driven, by some unexplained break, to a depth of
misery and despair, out of which rises her poignant cry *I find
myself unquiet in the midst of silence, and my heart is at
once pierced by sorrow and love.* Both as an artist and as a
lover, Swift must have envied her that phrase.

Her next letter, which also bears the date 1720, is written
in the same despairing mood:

Celbridge 1720.
*Tell me sincerely if you have once wished with earnestness
to see me since I wrote to you. No, so far from that, you
have not once pitied me, though I told you how I was distressed. Solitude is insupportable to a mind which is not
easy. I have worn out my days in sighing, and my nights
with watching and thinking of -, -, -, -, -, -, who thinks
not of me. How many letters must I send before I shall
receive an answer? Can you deny me, in my misery, the
only comfort which I can expect at present? Oh! that I
could hope to see you here, or that I could go to you. I
was born with violent passions, which terminate all in one
—that unexpressible passion I have for you. Consider the
killing emotions which I feel from your neglect of me, or
I shall lose my senses. Sure, you cannot possibly be so much
taken up but you might command a moment to write to
me, and force your inclinations to do so great a charity.
I firmly believe, could I know your thoughts (which no
human creature is capable of guessing at, because never
anyone living thought like you), I should find that you*

have often, in a rage, wished me religious, hoping then I should have paid my devotions to Heaven. But that would not spare you, for was I an enthusiast, still you'd be the deity I should worship. What marks are there of a deity but what you are known by? You are present everywhere; your dear image is always before my eyes; sometimes you strike me with that prodigious awe I tremble with fear; at other times, a charming compassion shines through your countenance, which revives my soul. Is it not more reasonable to adore a radiant form seen, than one only described?

Vanessa is spending her nights watching beside her sister's sickbed, her days in the cold, bleak, winter climate of Celbridge, listening to the river storming through her gardens, the wind howling in the trees. She is herself sick, in body and in mind, deserted by her God. There is no explanation of Swift's apparent neglect of her. But, somewhere during this period, he was writing his masterpiece, *Gulliver*, and the genius that drove him into immortality may have dealt ruthlessly with mere human needs. His next letter to Vanessa is a short one, almost surely delivered by hand at her Dublin home:

To Mrs. Esthr. Va.

I am surprised and grieved beyond what I can express. I read your letter twice before I knew what it meant, nor can I yet well believe my eyes. Is that poor good creature dead? I observed she looked a little ghastly on Saturday, but it is against the usual way for one in her case to die so sudden. In God's sake get your friends about you, to advise and to order everything in the forms. It is all you have to do. I want comfort myself in this case, and can give little. Time alone must give it to you. Nothing now is your part but decency. I was wholly unprepared against so sudden an event, and pity you most of all creatures at present. — *Monday.*

It would seem that, when her case was hopeless, Mary Van Homrigh may have been moved back to Dublin, where medical help would have been more easily available. This note was written on the day she died, and Swift had apparently visited her two days before. She was buried, near her father, on 3rd March 1720-21, in St. Andrew's Church. Swift's letter is a curious mixture of genuine sorrow for the girl's death and an obvious fear lest, in her emotional crisis, Vanessa should in any way publicly involve *him*. He implores her to rely entirely for advice and assistance on her *friends*, making it quite clear that he (who was, at the least, her best and oldest friend) was not available. It would be revealing to know whether his discretion kept him away from St. Andrew's Church, when Vanessa, the last of the Van Homrighs, stood beside poor Malkin's grave, or whether fear of the watchful eyes in *this cursed town* held him within the Deanery walls.

With her sister's death, Vanessa became a completely free agent. Presumably, she now spent most of her time in Dublin, saw Swift frequently and had no need of letters. One short note, from Swift, is addressed to

Mrs. Esth. Vanhomrigh. June 1st.
-, -, -, -, -, -, -, I cannot contrive to get this catalogue copied out, and therefore have delivered it to Mr. Worrall for you, and told him it was some papers directed to me for you from England. Pray God protect you. Adieu.

Once again, there are seven dashes to be filled in with whatever words of love she pleases. Mr. Worrall was his Vicar at St. Patrick's who did much confidential business for the Dean. The reference to the catalogue may be explained by an allusion in one of Doctor Berkeley's letters to Prior, some years later, in which he states that, after Vanessa's death, he had seen a *catalogue of her debts clearly stated, drawn up by her order.*

The next letter is written by Swift:

July 5th 1721 Gaulstown, near Kinnegad.
It was not convenient, hardly possible, to write to you be-
fore now, though I had a more than ordinary desire to do
it, considering the disposition I found you in last; though
I hope I left you in a better. I must here beg you to take
more care of your health, by company and exercise; or else
the spleen will get the better of you, than which there is
not a more foolish or troublesome disease; and what you
have no pretences in the world to, if all the advantages of
life can be any defence against it. Cad - assures me he
continues to esteem and love and value you above all
things, and so will do to the end of his life, but at the same
time entreats that you will not make yourself or him un-
happy by imaginations. The wisest men of all ages have
thought it the best course to seize the minutes as they fly,
and to make every innocent action an amusement. If you
knew how I struggle for a little health, what uneasiness I
am at in riding and walking, and refraining from every-
thing agreeable to my taste, you would think it but a small
thing to take a coach now and then, and to converse with
fools or impertinents, to avoid spleen and sickness.
Without health, you will lose all desire of drinking your
coffee, and so low as to have no spirits.
I answer all your questions that you were used to ask Cad
-, and he protests he answers them, in the affirmative.
How go your affairs? You were once a good lawyer, but
Cad - hath spoiled you. I had a weary journey in an
Irish stage-coach, but am pretty well since. Pray write to
me cheerfully, without complaints or expostulations, or
else Cad - shall know it and punish you.
What is this world, without being as easy in it as prudence
and fortune can make it? I find it every day more silly
and insignificant, and I conform myself to it for my own

ease. I am here as deep employed in other folks' planta-
tions and ditchings as if they were my own concern, and
think of my absent friends with delight, and hopes of
seeing them happy and of being happy with them. Shall
you, who have so much honour and good sense, act other-
wise, to make Cad - and yourself miserable? Settle your
affairs, and quit this scoundrel island, and things will be
as you desire.

I can say no more, being called away, mais soyez assurée
que jamais personne du monde a été aimée, honorée, es-
timée, adorée par votre ami que vous. I drank no coffee
since I left you, nor intend to till I see you again. There
is none worth drinking but yours, if myself may be the
judge.

Rest assured that you are the only person on earth who has
ever been loved, honoured, esteemed, adored by your friend.
Swift could scarcely have made a clearer declaration of his
love, and it must either be accepted as a genuine expression
of his emotions (after an acquaintance of fourteen years), or
else as a despicable lie from an elderly hypocrite.

This is the only surviving letter which was undoubtedly
written during the year 1721; it came from the fine Meath
estate of Swift's friend, Chief Baron Rochford. His visit
there was, it seems, planned to last a couple of months, and
the impending separation probably accounts for the mood in
which he had found Vanessa, and which he hoped he had improved before he left her. Once again, he urges her to take
exercise and go into company. He himself, as he writes to
the Archbishop a few days later, is *rowing after health like a*
waterman and riding after it like a postboy. He is also deeply
interested *in other folks' plantations and ditching, as if they*
were my own affair. Swift could never resist such activities;
of the garden he made in Dublin there is scarcely a trace, and
at Laracor, only his willows survive, straggling along his
well-loved *Canal* and the River Walk.

It would be interesting to know what company he urges her to keep, for the names of few of her friends survive, and they mostly in her will. Near Celbridge, there were Mr. and Mrs. George Finey, to whose son, poor Malkin's godson, she left £25. To Mrs. Finey and her sister, she left money for mourning, so that they may have been connections. She only mentions one relative, *the Reverend Mr. John Antrobus my cousin*, to whom she left money for a ring. There is no way of knowing who were the *fools or impertinents*, whom she was to take a coach and visit.

Poor Vanessa's legal affairs were still in such an inextricable tangle, in spite of all her efforts, that she must often have been reduced to despair, her brother's and sister's estates being now added to the muddle. Nevertheless, Swift assures her that she enjoys *all the advantages of life.* Swift's injunction to settle her affairs and leave this *scoundrel island* must have produced, at best, a wry smile.Only Vanessa could have told the meaning of his next words, *and things will be as you desire.* About this time, it is probable that Swift had begun to consider the possibility of re-establishing himself in the English scene. Seven years of absence is a long time, and even the most virulent political feuds die away. Besides, Swift must have been well aware that, with the publication of *Gulliver,* he had a brilliant chance of real literary fame; and it seems that MSS. copies were being discreetly circulated. A little later, Lord Bolingbroke wrote to him, *I long to see your Travels;* and Swift wrote to his good friend, Pope, pointing out that there was now no reason why he should not be treated, with *at least tolerable quarter,* by the ruling Whigs. Vanessa would have been well aware of such plans, and needed only Swift's reminder that he hoped very soon to be back in England, for most of his time, with her and his old friends. How gladly she would have left *this scoundrel island,* where no seclusion could protect her from rumours of *the Ladies,* around whom so much of the Deanery social life revolved. The shadow of Esther Johnson, even as an old friend of Swift's youth, must often have fallen, dark, across Vanessa's moods; even had Swift quoted to her his recent lines on Stella, *But her graceful black locks were all mingled with grey.*

In almost a year, there is no existing letter, and then Swift writes from,

Clogher, June 1st 1722.
This is the first time I have set pen to paper since I left Dublin, having not been in any settled place till ten days ago, and I missed one post by ignorance, and that stopped me five days. Before that time, I was much out of order, by usual consequences of wet weather and change of drink; neither am I yet established, though much better than I was. The weather has been so constantly bad that I wanted all the healthy advantages of the country, and seems likely to continue so. It would have been infinitely better once a week to have met Kendall and so forth, where one might pass three or four hours in drinking coffee in the morning, or dining tête-à-tête, and drinking coffee again till seven. I answer all the questions you can ask me in the affirmative. I remember your detesting and despising the conversations of the world. I have been so mortified with a man and his lady here two days, that it has made me as peevish as—I want a comparison. I hope you have gone or are going to your country seat, though I think you have a term upon your hands. I shall be here long enough to receive your answer, and perhaps to write to you again; but then I shall go further off (if my health continues) and shall let you know my stages. I have been for some days as spleenatic as ever you were in your life, which is a bold word. Remember I still enjoin you reading and exercise for the improvement of your mind and health of your body, and grow less romantic and talk and act like

*a man of this world. It is the saying of the world, and I
believe you often say, I love myself; but I am so low, I
cannot say it, though your new acquaintance were with you,
which I heartily wish, for the sake of you and myself.
God send you through your law and your reference; and
remember that riches are nine parts in ten of all that is
good in life, and health is the tenth. Drinking coffee comes
long after, and yet it is the eleventh; but without the two
former you cannot drink it right; and remember the china
in the old house, and Ryder Street, and the Colonel's journey to France, and the London Wedding, and the sick
lady at Windsor, and the strain by the box of books at
London. Last year, I writ you civilities, and you were
angry; this year, I will write you none, and you will be
angry, yet my thoughts were still the same, and I give you
leave to be the carver, and will be answerable for them. I
hope you will let me have some of your money when I see
you, which I will pay you honestly again. Repondez-moy
si vous entendez bien tout cela, et croyez que je seray toujours tout ce que vous desirez.   Adieu.*

In this highly enigmatic letter, Swift once again reminds
her of the high points of their past; but gives no clue which
might identify the anniversary he refers to, *this* year, without
last year's civilities.

The most significant reminder, however, begins, *It would
have been infinitely better once a week to have met Kendall,
and so forth, where one might pass three or four hours in
drinking coffee in the morning, or dining* tête-à-tête *and
drinking coffee again till seven.* Almost exactly two months
later, he expands this: *The same scene has passed forty
times . . . yet each has* ses agréments particuliers.

According to the City Records, a Thomas Kendall became
a Freeman of Dublin, in 1749. In his will, he is described
as a bookbinder. He lived in St. Andrew's Parish, as did

Vanessa; he married a woman named Anne M'Loghlin. It is quite clear that *someone* named Kendall provided a place where they could meet, weekly and regularly; this bookbinder may well have been the man. The many commentators who have brushed aside the relationship of Swift and Vanessa—a relationship now in its seventeenth and last year —as one in which an importunate woman harassed an indifferent man, have chosen to ignore Swift's own statement that they met regularly, once a week, over a long period. These meetings took place as the other letter specifies *at ten in the morning*, when they passed *three or four hours*, and sometimes *from two till seven*, each having *its particular pleasures*. (Once again the difficulty arises as to the real significance of coffee-drinking and of the ritual asking and answering of Vanessa's *questions*. Whatever be the solution, it is quite obvious that the words do not mean precisely what they appear to say.) And, although Swift assures her that *riches are nine parts in ten of all that is good in life, drinking coffee comes long after, and yet is the eleventh; but without riches and health, you cannot drink it right*, it is clear that Swift, who had thrown discretion to the winds of Dublin by meeting Vanessa weekly and regularly, must still have been very deeply in love with her: It would seem that such meetings, often involving a *tête-à-tête* dinner, must have required an extremely discreet and trustworthy host; and it is perhaps another minute piece missing from the puzzle, that the host should be closely connected with a family named M'Loghlin. Of this, more later.

The phrase, *my thoughts are still the same and I give you leave to be the carver and will be answerable for them* has puzzled editors, but Swift—as so often—provides his own answer in a poem . . .

To a Lady, who desired the author to write some Verses for her.

You must learn, if you would gain us
With good sense to entertain us.
Scholars, when good sense describing
Call it tasting and imbibing;
Metaphoric meat and drink
Is to understand and think;
We may *carve* for others thus
And let others carve for us;
To discourse and to attend
Is to *help* yourself and friend.
Conversation is but *carving*,
Carve for all, yourself is starving;
Give no more to ev'ry guest
Then he's able to digest;
Give him always of the prime,
And but little at a time.
Carve to all, but just enough;
Let them neither starve nor stuff;
And, that you may have your due
Let your neighbours *carve* for you.

The italics are Swift's.

His final request for the loan of her money when next he saw her—she was always in financial straits and he was a relatively wealthy man— must obviously be classed amongst the group of things which do not mean what is, apparently, said. To stress that, he adds his query in French, ending with the assurance that he will always be everything she can wish.

Vanessa's next letter, undated, but almost certainly an answer to the last, is written from her Dublin house:

-, -, -, Cad, I thought you had quite forgot both me and your promise of writing to me. Was it not very unkind to be five weeks absent, without sending me one line to let me know you were well and remembered me? Besides,

you have had such bad weather that you could have no diversion abroad. What then could you do but write and read? I know you do not love cards, neither is this a time of year for that amusement. Since I saw you, I have gone more into this world that I did for some time past, because you commanded me; and I do here protest that I am more and more sick of it every day than other. One day this week, I was to visit a great lady that has been a-travelling for some time past, where I found a very great assembly of ladies and beaux, dressed (as I suppose) to a nicety. I hope you'll pardon me now, if I tell you that I heartily wished you a spectator; for I very much question if in your life you ever saw the like scene or one more extraordinary. The lady's behaviour was blended with so many different characters, I cannot possibly describe it, without tiring your patience. But the audience seemed to me a creation of her own, they were so very obsequious. Their forms and gestures were very like those of baboons or monkeys. They all grinned and chattered at the same time, and that of things I did not understand. The room being hung with arras, in which were trees, very well described, just as I was considering their beauty, and wishing myself in the country with -, -, -, one of these animals snatched my fan and was so pleased with me, that it seized me with such a panic, that I apprehended nothing less than being carried up to the top of the house, and served as a friend of yours was; but in this, one of their own species came in upon which they all began to make their grimaces; which opportunity I took, and made my escape.

I have not made one single step, either in law or reference since I saw you. I meet with nothing but disappointments, yet I am obliged to stay in Town attending on Mr. Partinton, etc. which is very hard. I do declare I have so little joy in life, that I don't care how soon mine ends. For God's sake, write to me soon and kindly, for in your

absence your letters are all the joy I have on earth; and
sure you are too good-natured to grudge one hour in a
week to make any human creature happy. -, -, -, -, Cad,
think of me and pity me.

Clearly, what with the weather, her failing health, her
social life, her executor, Mr. Partinton and her absence from
Swift, poor Vanessa was *so low.* It would be interesting to
know the identity of the much-travelled *great lady.* The
most significant item in this letter is her allusion to an incident
in *Gulliver's Voyage to Brobdingnag,* in which he is carried
off by a monkey. This reference shows that she had either
been shown the MSS, or had discussed the work with Swift.
It was not published for more than four years afterwards.
There is also internal evidence that Vanessa was shown the
MSS of *Gulliver's Voyages to Lilliput* and that some words
in the Lilliputian *language* contain private jokes between
herself and Swift. Otherwise, it is difficult to account for the
very first words Gulliver hears fram a Lilliputian, who
lifting up his hands and eyes by way of admiration cried out,
Hekinah degul! Swift had a habit of conferring pet-names,
and amongst those which he gave to Vanessa—itself a name
which he invented for her—was Heskinage. It is impossible
to believe that when he wrote those two words, which include
every letter of that very curious name except one, he did so
by accident. As is well known, Swift had always had a passion
for playing with words; cyphers, puns and anagrams constantly appear in his work. It would indeed be very remarkable if he had resisted the temptation when inventing
new *languages.* The word *hurgo,* which he assures us, is
Lilliputian for *a great Lord,* looks suspiciously like an anagram for *rogue;* and the shameful antics of the courtiers are
described as *a summerset,* a name Swift could not possibly
have written without remembering his bitter enemy, the
Duchess. Perhaps someone will decipher the *languages* in

Gulliver's travels. So far as Vanessa is concerned, they are only important in so far as they appear to show how intimately she was associated with Swift's masterpiece.

Swift was still on his country tour when he wrote the next letter.

To Mrs. Vanhomrigh,

Lough-Gall, County of Armagh. July 13th 1722

I received yours, and have changed places so often since that I could not assign a place where I might expect an answer from—; and if you be now in the country, and this letter does not reach you in due time after the date, I shall not expect to hear from you, because I leave this place the beginning of August. I am well pleased with the account of your visit and the behaviour of the ladies. I see every day as silly things among both sexes, and yet endure them for the sake of amusements. The worst thing in you and me is that we are too hard to please, and whether we have not made ourselves so, is the question. At least, I believe we have the same reason. One thing I differ from you in, that I do not quarrel with my best friends. I believe you have ten angry passages in your letter, and every one of them enough to spoil two days apiece of riding and walking. We differ prodigiously in one point: I fly from the spleen to the world's end, you run out of your way to meet it. I doubt the bad weather has hindered you much from the diversions of your country house, and put you upon thinking in your chamber. The use I have made of it was to read I know not how many diverting books of history and travels.

I wish you would get yourself a horse, and have always two servants to attend you, and visit your neighbours, the worse the better. There is a pleasure in being reverenced, and that is always in your powers, by your superiority of sense and an easy fortune. The best maxim I know in this

93

life, is to drink your coffee when you can, and when you cannot, to be easy without it. While you continue to be spleenatic, count upon it I will always preach. Thus much I sympathise with you, that I am not cheerful enough to write, for I believe coffee once a week is necessary to that. I can sincerely answer all your questions as I used to do; but then I give all possible way to amusements, because they preserve my temper as exercise does my health; and without health and good humour I had rather be a dog. I have shifted scenes oftener that I ever did in my life, and I believe have lain in thirty beds since I left town, and always drew up the clothes with my left hand, which is a superstition I have learned these ten years.

These country posts are always so capricious that we are forced to send our letters at a call, on a sudden; and mine is now demanded, though it goes not out till to-morrow. Be cheerful, and read and ride and laugh, as Cad - used to advise you long ago. I hope your affairs are on some better settlement. I long to see you in figure and equipage; pray do not lose that taste. Farewell.

Here once again are the mysterious allusions to the drinking of coffee and the answering of questions; but this time he tells her (reminding her of *Kendall*), that, in order to be cheerful it is necessary to drink coffee once a week. Presumably, the fact that he had learned a superstition about strange beds in 1712 also revived some mutual memory.

The next letter is the last which has survived from Vanessa to Swift. It is a reply to his letter of the 13th July, and is probably written during that month.

-, -, -, Cad, I am and cannot avoid being in the spleen to the last degree. Everything combines to make me so. Is it not very hard to have so good a fortune as I have and yet no more command of that fortune than if I had no title to it? One of the Doctors is—I don't know what

to call him. He behaved so abominably to me the other day that, had I been a man he should have heard more of it. In short, he does nothing but trifle and make excuses. I really believe he heartily repents that he ever undertook it, since he heard counsel first plead, finding his friend more in the wrong than he imagined. Here am I, obliged to stay in this odious town, attending and losing my health and humour. Yet this and all other disappointments in life I can bear with ease, but that of being neglected by -, -, -, Cad. He has often told me that the best maxim in life, and always held by the wisest of all ages, is to seize the moments as they fly; but those happy moments always fly out of the reach of the unfortunate. Pray tell -, -, -, Cad I don't remember any angry passages in my letter, and am very sorry if they appeared so to him. Spleen, I cannot help, so you must excuse it. I do all I can to get the better of it and it is too strong for me.

I have read more since I saw Cad than I did in a great while past, and chose those books that required most attention, on purpose to engage my thoughts; but, I find the more I think the more unhappy I am. I had once a mind not to have wrote to you, for fear of making you uneasy to find me so dull, but I could not keep to that resolution. For the pleasure of writing to you, the satisfaction I have in your remembering me, and the delight I have in expecting one from -, -, -, Cad, makes me rather choose to give you some uneasiness than to add to my own.

She is still hopelessly embroiled with law and lawyers, forced to remain in *this odious town,* ill, depressed and, above all her other miseries, absent from Swift. In that state of mind, Vanessa vanishes into a void. In ten months, she is dead, aged thirty-four.

The correspondence ends with a last letter from Swift, *To Mrs. Vanhomry, August 7th,* 1722.

I am this hour leaving my present residence, and if I fix anywhere, shall let you know it; for I fain would wait till I get a little good weather for riding and walking, there never having been such a season as this remembered; though I doubt you know nothing of it but what you learn by sometimes looking out at your back windows to call your people. I had your last, with a spleenatic account of your law affairs. You were once a better solicitor, when you could contrive to make others desire your consent to an Act of Parliament against their own interest, to advance yours. Yet at present, you want neither power, nor skill, but disdain to exercise either. When you are melancholy, read diverting or amusing books: it is my receipt, and seldom fails. Health, good humour and fortune are all that is valuable in this life, and the last contributes to the two former.

I have not rode in all above four hundred miles since I saw you, nor do I believe I shall ride above two hundred more till I see you again. But I desire you will not venture to shake me by the hand; for I am in mortal fear of the itch, and have no hope left, but that some ugly vermin called ticks have got into my skin, of which I have pulled out some and must scratch out the rest. Is not this enough to give one the spleen? For I doubt no Christian family will receive me. And this is all a man gets by a northern journey. It would be unhappy for me to be as nice in my conversation and company as you are, which is the only thing wherein you agree with Glass-heel, who declares there is not a conversable creature in Ireland except Cad -. What would you do in these parts, where politeness is as much a stranger as cleanliness?

I am stopped, and this letter is intended to travel with me, so Adieu till the next stage.

August 8th. Yesterday, I rode twentyeight miles without being weary, and I wish little Heskinage could do as much.

Here I leave this letter to travel one way, while I go another, but where I do not know, nor what cabins or bogs are in my way.

I see you, this moment, as you are visible at ten o'clock in the morning; and now you are asking your questions round, and I am answering them, with a great deal of affected delays; and the same scene has passed forty times as well as the other from two till seven, longer than the first by two hours, yet each has ses agremens particuliers. *A long vacation, law lies asleep, and bad weather: how do you wear away your time? Is it among the fields and groves of your country seat, or among your cousins in Town, or thinking in a strain that will be sure to vex you, and then reasoning and forming teasing conclusions from mistaken thoughts? The best companion for you is a philosopher, whom you would regard as much as a sermon. I have read more trash since I left you than would fill all your shelves, and am abundantly the better for it, though I scarce remember a syllable.*

Go over the scenes of Windsor, Cleveland Row, Ryder Street, St. James's, Kensington, the Sluttery, the Colonel in France etc. Cad thinks often of these, especially on horseback, as I am assured. What a foolish thing is Time, and how foolish is man, who would be as angry if Time stopped as if it passed. But I will not proceed at this rate, for I am fast writing myself into the spleen, which is the only thing I would not compliment you by imitating. So adieu till the next place I fix in, if I fix at all till I return, and that I leave to fortune and the weather.

His reference here to the circumstances leading up to the Act of Parliament has already been commented on; no one can doubt that Swift had full knowledge of them.

In spite of bad weather, he is still dogged by the necessity of exercising to improve his health. Fully conscious that his lengthy absence is greatly aggravating her increasing melancholia, he tries to lighten it by reminding her of their weekly meetings, with the questions and answers—*the same scene has passed forty times, as well as the other,* each with its *special pleasures.* For the third time, he recalls the incidents of their past; and in this last surviving letter, he returns, appropriately, to their beginnings, to *the Sluttery, which I have so often found to be the most agreeable chamber in the world.*

IX

THERE follow months of unbroken silence. On the 8th August, 1722, Swift wrote his last letter, reminding Vanessa fondly of their weekly *rendez-vous* and holding out hope of seeing her soon; on the 1st May, 1723, she made her last will, leaving the bulk of her considerable property to strangers and pointedly omitting the name of Jonathan Swift. There is no reliable account of what happened between these two dates, but there is a general agreement that *something* did—something so terrible that it hastened Vanessa's death and also caused a complete break between Stella and Swift. The Reverend Dr. Delany, intimate friend of both, says,

> *I have good reason to believe that they both were greatly shocked and distressed (tho' it may be differently) upon the occasion.*

Various explanations have been suggested by other contemporary writers. Lord Orrery states that Vanessa wrote to Swift, proposing marriage and that Swift rejected her. Deane Swift says that her unrequited passion was the remote cause of her death, as *Dr. Swift never once made her the most distant overtures of marriage.* He adds, that she only heard that Swift was married to Stella a couple of months before her death. Dr. Delany suggests that the situation was complicated by the fact that, as he delicately put it, *she certainly gave herself up (as Ariadne did) to Bacchus, from the day she was deserted.* The most widespread version is that Vanessa wrote a letter, either to Stella or Swift, asking whether they were married; that Swift rode immediately to Celbridge, threw down her letter in a black fury, and rode away, for ever.

Only conjectures fill the gap, between the 8th August, 1722, and the end of April, 1723, and no very satisfactory conjecture has yet been produced. The suggestion that this three-fold rupture was caused by an enquiry as to whether Swift and Stella were married is not a reasonable one.

These two women had, for some nine years, been living in the small circle of Dublin society. The miraculous thing is that they seem to have managed never to meet; they had at least three friends in common, Archbishop King, Dr. Pratt, Provost of Trinity, and Charles Ford...*Glass Heel* to the Van Homrighs, *Don Carlos* to the Ladies. For nine years, Stella's friends had been constantly speculating about a possible marriage between her and the Dean. (This speculation continues to this day.) If Vanessa did, finally, demand an answer to this over-due question, it is conceivable that, having since 1711 regarded herself as Swift's affianced wife, she might well have felt outraged had she been told that he and Stella *were* married. Such a shocking betrayal would very reasonably account for Vanessa's subsequent anger; for the new will, the instructions for publication of her papers and her death within a few weeks.

But this explanation does not account for the extraordinary behaviour of Stella and the Dean. To quote their mutual good friend, Dr. Delany, again:

> *I have good reason to believe that they both were greatly shocked and distressed (tho' it may be differently) upon this occasion. The Dean made a tour to the South of Ireland for about two months, at this time, to dissipate his thoughts and give place to obloquy. And Stella retired (upon the earnest invitation of the owner) to the house of a cheerful, generous, good-natured friend of the Dean's whom she also much loved and honoured. There my informant often saw her and, I have reason to believe, used his utmost endeavour to relieve, support and amuse her in this sad situation.*

Dr. Delany, being himself *my informant*, had every opportunity of observing Stella's shocked and distressed condition, during the six months she spent at Charles Ford's sheltering house, where he did his utmost to relieve her *sad situation.*

Surely the condition he pictures is a very exaggeratedly tragic one for a woman who had merely been asked whether she were married? And what *obloquy* was the Dean escaping from? Had Vanessa written to ask Stella whether she were the Dean's wife, she might very well have been annoyed, particularly if she could not answer in the affirmative. Had Vanessa written her query to Swift, he *might* have flown into one of his furies — unreasonably, since over the years he must often have discussed his relationship with Stella, recognising that Vanessa had a perfect right to know where he stood between the two women. But his angers were transient, and such an incident could not account for his subsequent behaviour.

Immediately after Swift's dramatic break with Vanessa, Stella and her companion, Mrs. Dingley, fled from Dublin —rumour says without seeing the Dean—taking refuge at Wood Park, where they remained for over six months, without ever setting foot in Dublin, some ten miles distant. There, they were *relieved and supported* in their *sad situation* by their circle of friends, headed by Dr. Sheridan and Dr. Delany. Swift, who apparently did *not* visit them, remained in Dublin during the few weeks while Vanessa was dying, probably in her house in Turnstile Alley. *What* he feared would happen at her death is not known; that he *did* fear something is obvious, and the town was probably buzzing with speculations about the dying woman. The proof of his apprehensions of a shattering scandal is the letter he wrote, at midnight, to his friend Knightley Chetwode, on the day Vanessa died,

2nd June, 1723 — *past twelve at night . . . I am forced to leave this town sooner than I expected . . .*

On 4th June, Vanessa was buried, near her father and her sister, in St. Andrew's Church. Swift was not at the funeral; he had left Dublin the previous day, according to Dr. Sheridan, leaving no address, so that not even the clergy of his own Cathedral could contact him. Weeks passed, and they were extremely worried, until in August he wrote to Dr. Sheridan, saying that he proposed returning some weeks later. In that letter he asked, *Are the Ladies in town, or in the country? If I knew I would write to them. Are they in health?*

So the break between the unhappy Ladies and the fugitive Dean had been complete.

Since none of the proffered explanations can be held to account reasonably for these happenings, there is at least room for another conjecture which might better explain the disaster which overtook these three unhappy people. The known facts give support to the following theory.

By the Spring of 1723, Vanessa must have been far advanced in tuberculosis, and forced to realise by the tragically early deaths of her brothers and sister that she, too, was doomed. All her life, she had been an easy prey to depression — *the spleen.* By 1723, there were many circumstances which may well have reduced her to despair. All hope of ever marrying Swift—himself in bad health—must have vanished. Not Marriage but Death was now *in prospect.*

The years of frantic efforts to rescue her estate from the lawyers' clutches, *to get it into her own hands,* as Swift had written so long ago, had proved utterly fruitless. She no longer had the health or the hope necessary to struggle on. Indeed, Vanessa can scarcely be blamed if, as Dr. Delany alleges, she had tried to drown her misery by turning to Bacchus for comfort. It may be that with everything in tragic disorder, one thing remained which now urgently demanded settlement—a boy, aged about eight, who was boarded with a Dublin family named M'Loghlin. Before her death some provision must be made for his future—for Swift's son.

Although the two women had never met, it is reasonable to believe that, in the course of sixteen years, through conversations with Swift, a very clear picture of Stella must have been gradually formed in Vanessa's mind—this good, kindly, intelligent woman, the faithful friend of Swift's youth, who had a sister's devotion to him. Quite certainly, no other description of Stella can ever have been offered to Vanessa by Swift. He would have told her, as he told posterity, that *no scandal, censure or detraction ever came out of her mouth*, and also that *the follies of her own sex, she was inclined to extenuate, or to pity.*

Little wonder, then, if in her final despair, Vanessa's thoughts should turn to this benevolent, middle-aged friend of the Dean's, who, in her charity would *extenuate and pity* Vanessa's misfortunes, and, because of her sisterly devotion to Swift, be willing to give Swift's son that security which his mother had never been able to provide. There lay Vanessa's only hope, since, for a multitude of reasons, it was clearly impossible that Swift should take open responsibility for the boy.

And so, one day late in April, 1723, Vanessa — who would be dead in five weeks—wrote a letter to Stella. Remembering the passionate fervour which burns in so many of her letters, it is not difficult to imagine the eloquence with which she made her plea and the picture she drew of her intimate relations over sixteen years with Swift; her marriage-engagement; her life with him in London; her hopes and fears; the birth of the child; her relations with Swift since her return to Ireland. Secure in her absolute certainty of Stella's sisterly relationship with Swift, Vanessa would have anticipated nothing worse than a preliminary shock and surprise at Swift's weakness, followed immediately by Stella's loving *extenuation and pity.* When she had written her letter, Vanessa, worn out with emotion, must have felt certain that her appeal could not fail to touch Stella's warm heart and secure the child's future.

There is abundant testimony from her friends that Stella was, in every respect, a most admirable person. Even Dr. Evans, Bishop of Meath and Swift's bitter enemy, describes her as *a very good woman,* and Lord Orrery, who wastes little praise, is lyrical about her prefections. Swift, on the night of her death, described her as *the truest, most virtuous and valuable friend that I, or perhaps any other person, was ever blessed with.* He also stated that *when she was once convinced, by open facts, of any breach of Truth or Honour, in any person of high station, especially in the Church, she could not conceal her indignation.* He adds, *Honour, Truth, Liberality, Good-nature and Modesty were the virtues she chiefly possessed, and most valued in her acquaintance.*

Stella had been in love with Swift from her girlhood and had certainly suffered considerably because of his failure to marry her. Nevertheless, she had accepted his will and, but for periods of jealous misery, had contented herself with a highly privileged friendship.

She was, however, capable of jealousy and, about this time, wrote these lines:

On Jealousy

Oh! shield me from his rage, Celestial Powers!
This Tyrant that embitters all my hours.
Oh! Love, you've poorly played the Monarch's part,
You conquered, but you can't defend my heart;
So blessed was I throughout thy happy Reign,
I thought this Monster banish'd from thy Train;
But you would raise him to support thy Throne,

And now he claims your Empire as his own;
Or tell me, Tyrants, have you both agreed
That where One reigns, the Other shall succeed?

One version of the letter episode relates that, when Stella had read Vanessa's letter, she sent it to the Dean and, without giving time for an answer, fled from Dublin to hide herself in the country. Vanessa's letter, written in her absolute confidence that Stella had never been anything more than Swift's sisterly friend, would have carried a terrible conviction to the stricken woman. For Swift, no appeal was possible.

Most stories agree that he rode to Celbridge, threw Vanessa's letter before her and, after a terrible interview, stormed away, leaving Vanessa half-conscious. She had brought upon Swift the most dreaded of all eventualities: Stella, lover of Truth and Honour, had seen him in his naked shame.

It is easy to imagine the torrent of foul invectives that tore away the last shreds of Vanessa's endurance — Swift's appalling weapon, which he himself once described, in an apology to Stella,

And when indecently I rave,
When all my brutish passions break
With gall in every word I speak—

After the storm of rage and obscenity had passed over her, there was nothing—nothing but the terrible echoes of those *killing, killing words.* Later would come the feeble struggle to cleanse herself of the filth in which he had drowned her . . to rescue the long years he had distorted and defiled . . . to defend herself (above all, perhaps in Stella's eyes) from the horrible charges . . . She had not been his harlot . . . foisting her bastard . . . she was his affianced wife . . . She was . . . she *had* been . . . *the one person on earth he had loved, honoured, esteemed and adored* . . .

There was so little time . . . A day or two later, she made a new will. By then, the pain was numbed; her mind was clear again. She left the bulk of her considerable property to two strangers: to the Reverend George Berkeley, Fellow of Trinity College, whom she knew to be a good and upright man, on whose honesty and good faith she could rely to defend her good name, and to Robert Marshall a law student, whom she could summon to her bedside for her instructions about the publication of her papers. Between these two grateful men, she could be sure that the truth would be made clear. To the Archbishop of Dublin, her father's friend and her own, she left £25 for a mourning ring and the same bequest to the Archbishop of Clonfert. Swift had been on good terms with neither. They would be on *her* side. The first person named in her will, *Erasmus Lewis of London, Esq.* had known the truth from the beginning, when he used to forward her letters, under his cover, to Swift. She left a legacy to Dr. Bryan Robinson, one of Dublin's leading physicians, who had probably attended both Vanessa and her sister. A bequest to her faithful servant, Anne Kindon[1], who had come with her from London, where she had been Mrs. Van Homrigh's servant. Anne Kindon knew the truth too. Half a dozen other small bequests. *In witness thereof I, the said Esther Van Homrigh, have hereunto set my hand and seal, this first day of May, in the year of Our Lord* 1723.

The lawyer folded his papers and went away, tiptoeing, perhaps, as people tend to do in a sickroom. Outside, Turnstile Alley was very quiet.

She had made no provision in her will for the child. She could not, without naming—and branding—him. She could

---

[1]Anne Kindon witnessed an I.O.U. which Vanessa gave to one of her mother's creditors, in February 1713-14 (Monck Berkeley, *Literary Relics*).

only hope and trust in the ultimate goodness of the woman who had, unwittingly, brought this final catastrophe upon her. She had no other living soul to turn to . . . She was too tired to struggle any more.

A few weeks later, Vanessa was dead.

The Archbishop of Dublin must have been extremely perturbed to hear from the Reverend Dr. Sheridan that Mrs. Van Homrigh, recently dead, had left her executors instructions to publish letters which had passed between herself and the Dean of St. Patrick's. The Archbishop was no friend of the Dean, but he was concerned, very naturally, about the good name of the Church; and when the very agitated Dr. Sheridan told him that the papers were actually in the printers' hands, things must have looked most alarming. To increase the awkwardness of the situation, it seemed that the Dean had vanished from Dublin the day of Esther Van Homrigh's death, and Dr. Sheridan assured the Archbishop that neither his clergy nor his friends had the least idea where he had gone, and were, therefore, unable to make any contact. Meanwhile, Mr. Marshall had taken his dying benefactress' wishes very seriously indeed, and all appeals from the Dean's clerical friends had failed to induce him to stop publication. Hence, Dr. Sheridan's despairing visit to the Archbishop — the last person to whom Swift's friends would have wished to admit the Dean's dilemma. By his flight, Swift had left them powerless. His behaviour in this emergency was exactly described in his own words:

Nothing more unqualifies a man to act with prudence than a misfortune that is attended with shame and guilt.

With complete lack of all prudence, he ran away. It is to be hoped that *shame and guilt* were aggravated by sorrow— sorrow for the dead woman whom he had loved for so many years, and for the living woman whom he had also grossly betrayed.

To the Archbishop, the danger of scandal would have been paramount—scandal which he may well have feared would prove only too well-grounded. As friend of both Esther Van Homrigh and of her father, he was well placed to advise young Robert Marshall as to his proper course. There were other powerful pressures which could be brought to bear on a law student, not yet called to the Bar, with his career to consider. A word here, a word there could make him realise the strength of the power he was challenging. Young Mr. Marshall was eventually induced to have second thoughts.

As Dr. Evans, Bishop of Meath reported, a few weeks later to the Archbishop of Canterbury,

The Archbishop of Dublin and the whole Irish posse have (I fear) prevailed with Mr. Marshall not to print the papers etc. as she desired, lest one of their own dear joyes should be trampled over by the Philistines.

So, young Mr. Marshall was *prevailed* upon to remove the letters and papers from the printer's press; but he resolutely resisted suggestions that they should be destroyed. Some copies of the poem *Cadenus and Vanessa* rather mysteriously got into circulation, giving gossip plenty of food and adding to Stella's misery. But that was the only item of Vanessa's papers which reached the public for forty-four years. In 1767 the elderly Judge Robert Marshall, late of His Majesty's Court of Common Pleas, gave a small selection of the *Vanessa-Swift Correspondence* for publication. In 1921, all the surviving papers were published, for the first time, almost two centuries after Vanessa's death.

It is quite obvious from Vanessa's own numbering of the letters that many have been removed from the file. And not a single one has survived that was written during the last nine months of her life. Who did the censoring will never be known. Dr. Berkeley was far too occupied with his Bermuda scheme to have spared much time for such trifles. If, as seems likely, Mr. Marshall decided which letters should survive, he probably removed those which too obviously proved the existence of a child.

X

IN October 1723, five months after Vanessa's death, a reconciliation had taken place between Stella and Dean
Swift, and the Ladies were back in their lodgings, *Near
Liffey's stinking tide in Dublin,* to quote the verses with
which he celebrated their return. Possibly, he may still have
dreaded the ordeal that the ailing Stella would have to face in
Dublin—and the impetus her return might give to the
scandalmongers—because, about this time, he gave a money-
order for £100 to Rebecca Dingley. Perhaps he hoped that,
with the money, the Ladies might be persuaded to pay the
expenses of a visit to their native land, possibly to one of the
Spas to which they were so addicted. Swift was not the man
to part lightly with so large a sum of money. But Mrs.
Dingley never made any use of the £100, nor did she return
it to Swift, but disposed of it, in her will, many years later—
one of the very minor mysteries of the story.

But Stella did return to Dublin. Scandal died away, and
the *obloquy* from which Swift had fled had spent the force
of its first venom. A very solid phalanx had formed to protect the Dean's reputation, both from the truth, and also
from the lies of popular report. His friends had assiduously
spread the story that the innocent, luckless Dean had been
the victim of an hysterical young woman's unruly passion;
that only his kindness of heart had prevented him from dealing with her as ruthlessly as she deserved; that he was a
blameless, much maligned man, meriting nothing but sympathy. Those who had heard more or less detailed reports
about the letters—which, after all, had been seen by printers
and very likely discussed by young Mr. Marshall, before he
was *prevailed* upon to forget them—were assured, on no less
high an authority than that of the Reverend Doctor Delany,

that *his letters contain nothing but curt compliments, excuses, apologies and thanks for little presents ... but not the least hint of criminal commerce between them, in the letters of either.*

The conspiracy of silence was complete amongst those who knew the *whole* truth; Stella, Swift and probably the Reverend Dr. Sheridan, loving friend of both and later an executor of Stella's will. To their number must be added whoever censored the Correspondence. The Archbishop and his clergy were silent because they had to protect the Church from scandal. Swift's enemies, amongst whom the Bishop of Meath and Dean Smedley ranked prominently, threw what stones local rumours made available to their hands, with unseemly enthusiasm. But the staunch friends of Stella and of the Dean stood firm and protected his reputation against all attacks.

There was nobody to protect Vanessa's good name, her executors having been *prevailed upon* to retire, and the most sympathetic picture of her is that of a young woman *who loved the reluctant Dean greatly but extremely unwisely.* Nevertheless, in *one* hope the luckless Vanessa may not have failed, trusting as she did in the basic goodness of Stella.

There have always been rumours that a boy existed, who was a son of Swift and Stella. Such stories were told during their lifetimes.

When Monck Berkeley, grandson of Vanessa's heir, came to Dublin about 1788, he found Richard Brennan, then an elderly man, a member of the staff of St. Patrick's Cathedral. He had been Dean Swift's last servant, and had protected the old man on the occasion of his alarming experience with the Reverend Dr. Wilson. This is the account of Brennan, published in Monck Berkeley's *Literary Relics*:

My informant was Richard Brennan, at present a bell-ringer in St. Patrick's, and in a state of penury. (Such should not be the case—the servant in whose arms Swift breathed his last, and who attended him during the six years immediately preceding his death.) My informer, who is still living in Dublin, told me that, when he was a boy at school, there was a boy boarded with the Master, who was commonly reputed to be the Dean's son by Mrs. Johnson. He added that the boy strongly resembled the Dean in his complexion; that he dined constantly at the Deanery on Sunday, and that, when the other boys were driven out of the Deanery yard, he was suffered to remain there and divert himself. This boy survived Mrs. Johnson by a year or two at the most.

If Robert Brennan had been about the same age as this schoolmate, he would have been about seventy-four when Monck Berkeley interviewed him in Dublin in 1788; about twenty-five when he went to the Deanery as Swift's last man-servant, and about nine in 1723 when Vanessa died. There is no reason to discount the accuracy of Brennan's school memories, nor to doubt that rumours of this mysterious child —*little master?*—were in circulation in Dublin soon after Vanessa's death. Monck Berkeley was sufficiently impressed with Brennan's bona fides to give him a pension.

The reference to the boys playing in the Deanery yard would seem to point to the school of St. Patrick's Cathedral as being the one at which the child was a boarder. There is no explanation of how this reputed son of Stella and Swift got there unless, indeed, Vanessa's last desperate appeal bore fruit when Stella returned to Dublin, after recovering from her shock and heartbreak. From everything that is known of that remarkable woman, with her love of truth and justice, it is extremely likely that on her return to Dublin she would have lost little time in finding the child—this boy who so *resembled the Dean*. With or without Swift's immediate consent, she would have insisted on this child's right to proper schooling and care. The moral courage of this woman—whose physical courage had been sufficient for her to shoot dead a man who was breaking into her lodgings —would not have been daunted by the fear of provoking further scandal, where the child's future was at stake. But, during the few years she had still to live, when ill-natured rumours buzzed, Stella must often have been bitterly hurt and sorely tempted to defend her innocence with the truth. About this time, Swift wrote some lines, *On Censure*, which may very well have been written to encourage her, ending, as they do, with the suggestion that she ignore gossip, since *ten hundred thousand lyes* cannot make her *less virtuous, learn'd or wise.*

> *Bare innocence is no support*
> *When you are tried in scandal's court . . .*
> *The world, a willing stander-by,*
> *Inclines to aid the specious lye;*
> *Alas, they would not do you wrong,*
> *But all appearances are strong.*
> *Yet whence proceeds this weight we lay*
> *On what detracting people say?*
> *For let mankind discharge their tongues*
> *In venom, till they burst their lungs,*
> *Their utmost malice cannot make*
> *Your head, or tooth, or finger ake:*
> *Nor spoil your shape, distort your face*
> *Or put one feature out of place.*
> *Nor will you find your fortune sink*
> *By what they speak, or what they think;*
> *Nor can ten hundred thousand lyes*
> *Make you less virtuous, learn'd or wise.*
> *The most effectual way to baulk*
> *Their malice is . . . to let them talk*

From the Dean's point of view, any amount of *talk* was better than a declaration that the child's real mother was

Vanessa. Such an avowal might have saved Stella's reputation, but would certainly have given new life to the old scandals about his relationship with the dead woman. That, he could or would not face.

Nevertheless, Stella's consciousness of her false position may well explain the curious story of a half-overheard conversation between herself and the Dean, during her last illness. He is reported to have said,

Well, my dear, if you wish it, it shall be owned.

To which Stella answered, with a sigh,

It is too late.

This is usually explained as Swift's last-moment offer to admit a secret marriage; but it is more likely that the Dean, tormented by sorrow at the sight of her sufferings, was at last offering to clear her reputation from the stigma of being the mother of the child who was then living with her, *on charity*.

Unfortunately for this child, Stella had only a few years left in which to supervise his life and, during her last years, she was often at death's door. Hence, perhaps, his period at a boarding school.

In 1727, she made a will, a few weeks before her death. Being the prudent, orderly woman she was, and remembering her constant illnesses over years, it is difficult to believe that she had never made a previous will, so that the one she made in December 1727 may have a special significance. For the last months of her life, she had been living near the Phoenix Park, in the hope, perhaps, that the good country air might ease the tortures of asthma. She described herself as *being in tolerable health in body and perfectly sound mind* and she bequeathed the bulk of her small fortune to her mother and sister for their lives, and afterwards to Steevens Hospital, Dublin, for the support of a Chaplain.

She also gave instructions that, should the Church of Ireland ever be dis-established, her money should immediately revert to her nearest living relative. The Church of Ireland was dis-established in 1871, and her sister, Mrs. Filby, had no less than nineteen children.

Stella left several other legacies, amongst them one which seems to have remained unnoticed:

> *I bequeath to Bryan M'Loghlin (a child who now lives with me and whom I keep on charity) twenty-five pounds, to bind him out apprentice, as my executors and the survivors of them shall think fit.*

In 1727, £25 was a fairly considerable sum of money; in that year, the fee paid to apprentice a boy, by the parish school of St. Nicholas Without, Dublin, was *£3 and a suit of clothes*. Over and above this legacy, Swift has recorded that, in her strong-box, which she bequeathed to him, there was about £150 in gold. Perhaps this money, too, was intended to provide indirectly for the child, as the relatively wealthy Dean had no particular need for it. During the three years that Stella had given a home to Bryan M'Loghlin, the childless woman may well have become very attached to the boy and much concerned about his future. That Bryan was an affectionately established member of Stella's household is curiously corroborated by Dean Swift himself.

Rebecca Dingley had all her life been a dog-worshipper, and when her adored Tiger died, Swift wrote a cruelly jocose verse on her loss The introduction runs as follows:

> *Elegy upon Tiger*
> *Her dear Lady's joy and comfort*
> *Who departed this Life*
> *The last day of March 1727,*
> *To the great joy of Bryan*
> *That his antagonist is gone.*

Tiger, surprisingly, was a female, as Swift adds this note:

N. B. *She died in Puppy and left two helpless infants behind. And that Mrs. Sally and Jane and Robin cryed three days for.*

The pampered lap-dog may well have been less popular with the twelve year old Bryan! Presumably Mrs. Sally, Jane and Robin were the *two maids and one man* to whom Swift alludes later in his description of Stella's household. In March 1727, that household was nearing its end, since Stella spent the last months of her life with friends, where she died nine months later.

Amongst Stella's executors, who were to decide Bryan's future was one of her oldest and most devoted friends, whom she could trust to obey her wishes, the Rev. Dr. Sheridan. He constantly attended her during her last illness, and would have done his utmost to carry out any instructions she gave. He and Swift had a serious quarrel immediately after Stella's death, and it was a long time, according to his son, before they made friends again. It is reasonable to believe that Stella's death produced yet another crisis about the child's future, and that Swift and Sheridan disagreed violently.

There is another signficant feature of this will, made by a dying woman a few weeks before her death—the detailed description of the boy's status. It is as if in her last public declaration, Stella were determined to silence the malicious rumours, which had so embittered her final years. Bryan M'Loghlin had no other claim upon her than her *charity*.

And the name, M'Loghlin? Kendall, who provided facilities for the weekly meetings of Vanessa and the Dean must, undoubtedly, have been a person whom they both knew to be utterly trustworthy. Kendall married a woman named M'Loghlin, and it is a reasonable surmise that

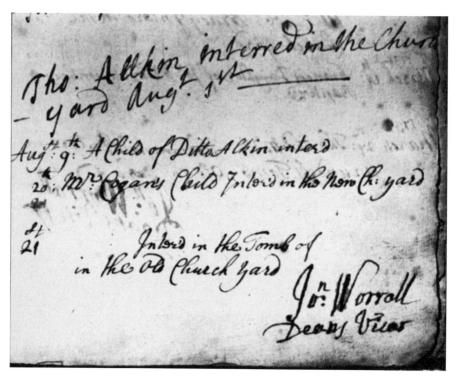

PLATE II

The anonymous burial entry in the Register of Saint Patrick's Cathedral, Dublin.

Vanessa boarded her son with this family and that they lent this nameless child their own name.

According to Richard Brennan, the boy *survived Mrs. Johnson a year or two at most.* Stella died at the beginning of 1728. Some two and a half years later, there appears a very curious entry of a burial in the Register of St. Patrick's Cathedral,

21st August, 1731.
          inter'd in the tomb of
in the old Churchyard.

Immediately beneath this entry is the signature of the Rev. John Worrall, who was Swift's Dean's Vicar and his trusted man of business. Apparently Mr. Worrall was content to sign this extraordinary registration, although no similar one exists in the Records of St. Patrick's Cathedral: an unidentified corpse, interred in some unidentified owner's unidentified tomb. It is also significant that this should have taken place in the only cemetery where such a burial could be arranged, without any awkward questioning, and that the date was within *a year or two* of Stella's death, as Brennan had reported.

The mystery surrounding this extraordinary interment is very unlikely to be cleared away, but a possible solution would point to this nameless tomb as the last resting place of *little Master,* of the anonymous schoolboy who so resembled the Dean, of little Bryan M'Loghlin, who lived with Stella and was jealous of the lap-dog—of the ill-fated son of Esther Van Homrigh and Jonathan Swift, Dean of St. Patrick's Dublin.

*

Swift survived, for many years, both the women who loved him. During that time, he wrote a collection of verses on women and *Love*, so grossly appalling that, to quote Carl Van Doren, *they made even the Eighteenth Century squirm.* That was not a squeamish period, yet Letitia Pilkington records in her Memoirs that her mother vomited when first she read *The Lady's Dressing-room.* It is as if some demon drove a lapsed lover to desecrate, with obscene scrawlings, the shrine at which he had once worshipped.

A persistent legend relates that, when his terrible years ended at last in the Winter of 1745, amongst his papers was found an envelope, on which he had written: *Only a woman's hair.* Inside was a brown tress. Stella's hair, as Swift has recorded, was *black as a crow.*

APPENDICES & BIBLIOGRAPHY

Appendix I: The Paternity of Thomas, Jane and Jonathan Swift

In the Burial Register of the Church of St. Andrew, Northborough, Northamptonshire, the following entry is to be found for the date, 3rd December, 1737.

Thos. Swift, Bro. to Dr. Jon. Swift, Dean of St. Patrick's, Dublin.

This very remarkable entry is, according to the present Rector, the Reverend A. Lister, *in writing similar to several previous entries.* There is no doubt that Thomas Swift was buried in the churchyard of St. Andrew, on 3rd December 1737 as brother of Dean Swift.

Mr. P. I. King, M. A. Archivist at the Northamptonshire Record Office has kindly supplied the information that the clergyman then in charge of St. Andrew's was the Reverend William Richardson, Rector of the nearby Parish of Elton from 1717 to 1741. He took his B.A. at St. John's College, Cambridge in 1696 when he was twenty-two; so that, at the time of Thomas Swift's burial, Mr. Richardson would have been about sixty-four and have been in charge of the parish for over twenty years. The entry and identification could not have been made without his knowledge and, presumably, approval. But the contemporary transcripts of the St. Andrew Register, which are deposited in the Northamptonshire Archives, do *not* contain this entry.

As Mr. King explains, . . . *every year, at the Archdeacon's Visitation of the Parishes, the Rector hands him a copy of the entries in his Register, for the previous year.* Mr. King confirms that this entry has been omitted from the copy of the 1737 Register, given to the Archdeacon. This omission is, in itself, very curious. It would seem that it was one thing to acknowledge Thomas Swift's identity in a small community, where his background was probably well known, but quite another to announce, to the wider world outside, that the dead man was brother of the famous, still living, Dean of St. Patrick's.

Regarding the wording of the burial entry, Mr. King says, *it is* not *usual to give details of relationships in* 18*th century burial registers, except that children have their parents' names given. I should think it very rare to mention that somebody was a brother.*

Mr. King also gives the information that there *were Swifts residing in the Northborough and neighbouring parishes.* There were also Temples living at Sulby, some thirty miles from Northborough. Any wills or documents relating to local Swifts would seem to show that they were humble folk, shepherds and such like; lowly connections, possibly, of the Swifts of Dublin, amongst whom it would be convenient to find suitable foster-parents for a boy of that name, whose birth followed a marriage too soon for comfort.

This marriage, for which the Archbishop of Armagh issued a Special Licence, in June 1664, was that of Jonathan Swift and *Abigail Erick, of the City of Dublin, Spinster.* The advantage of this expensive form of marriage licence is that the ceremony is performed in private and therefore no date need be registered.

The bride, an Englishwoman from Leicestershire, was some ten years older than her bridegroom, and was given an annuity of £20, in English Funds, ostensibly by her husband, who possessed no apparent means.

Denis Johnston, in his book, *In search of Swift,* has put up a well-reasoned argument that Sir John Temple, Master of the Rolls in Dublin, was the father of Jonathan Swift, the last child of this marriage. It would seem that his contention would be enormously strengthened by arguing that

Sir John was the father of *all* Abigail Erick's children, and that Thomas, born probably about the Winter of 1664, was the eldest.

In that case, the procedure after birth, with both sons would have been the same; Thomas was removed to England because he was born *too soon* after the marriage by which Swift gave Abigail Erick the protection of his name, while Jonathan was removed to England because he was born *too late* after the death of his putative father.

Between these two sons, there was born a daughter, Jane, baptised in St. Michan's Church, Dublin, in May 1666, almost two years after the marriage. She spent the greater part of her youth in Dublin, and will be considered later.

Soon after Jonathan Swift's birth, he was removed from Dublin. The story is that he was kidnapped by an over-affectionate nurse, who had to go to England, and could not bear to leave the infant behind her. This episode Swift himself characterises as *very unusuell*, which it certainly was; but not more so than the subsequent events. The infant remained in this woman's keeping by the direction of the mother, who feared a sea-journey for the child, but had no fear of leaving him in charge of the woman who had criminally removed him from his mother's Dublin home. Odder still, Mrs. Swift returned to her native Leicestershire, after some years, making her permanent home there and living frugally on her £20 annuity. As Denis Johnson points out, it would seem natural that she would then have taken immediate steps to be reunited with the child she had not seen for some years. But it would appear that this was not so; the infant Jonathan was, according to Hawkesworth, *again carried to Ireland by his nurse and replaced under the protection of his Uncle Godwin.*

Had poverty been the reason that Mrs. Swift relinquished her child to her brother-in-law, it is obvious that a very small part of the money which was henceforth spent on the young boy would have supported him comfortably in his mother's care. Why, then, was *this* child brought back to Dublin?

Swift himself tells that he was an infant prodigy; by the time the erring nurse brought him back to Ireland he could spell and read any chapter of the Bible. Although neither Swift himself nor other authorities agree as to his exact age at this time—the highest estimate is five—there is no doubt that the small boy already showed very great promise round about the year 1671.

By one of those odd coincidences which sometimes make truth far stranger than fiction, in that same year, Sir Philip Skippon of Wrentham, Suffolk, wrote to his friend, Mr. John Ray, on 18th September, 1671,

> *I shall somewhat surprise you with what I have seen in a little boy, William Wooton, five years old last month, son of Mr. Wooton, Minister of this Parish, who hath instructed his child, within the last three quarters of a year, in the reading of the Latin, Greek and Hebrew languages, which he can read almost as well as English, and that tongue he could read at four years and four months old, almost as well as lads thrice his age.*

This William Wooton, infant prodigy, so nearly Swift's exact contemporary, became in due course a close friend of Bentley and, with him, disputed with Sir William Temple in the controversy about Ancient and Modern Learning. Later Wooton was a severe critic of Swift's *Tale of a Tub*, and was a victim of Swift's wit.

It was the age of the Infant Prodigy in England. John Evelyn's son had died, some years before, already famous at five. At two and a half, his father records that he could read perfectly *any of the English, Latin, French or Gothic letters, pronouncing the three first languages exactly.* His accomplishments at the time of his death, aged five, were too long to list here.

Evelyn's child had obviously had every possible assistance and encouragement in acquiring his terrifying load of learning, while the baby Jonathan, presumably, had only whatever poor facilities were available in his foster-mother's humble circle.

Sir John Temple, Master of the Rolls in Dublin, was himself a man of learning. His father had been Provost of Trinity College, Dublin. Sir John had been a Scholar of that College, became a B.A. when he was under eighteen and an M.A. in 1620. In the same year, he was admitted to Lincoln's Inn. If it had been reported to him that this nurse-child in England were showing promise of very remarkable intelligence he might well have decided to make an entirely new arrangement for his future, which would give this infant prodigy opportunities for an education worthy of his talents. The boy's return to Dublin provided this fully and the presence of the Swift brothers made arrangements very easy for Sir John. They were reasonably prosperous lawyers more than willing to oblige the powerful Master of the Rolls. Henceforth, a great deal of money was spent on Jonathan Swift's education, for which he never showed the slightest gratitude, which is all the more remarkable since very few of the Swifts' own sons had any comparable opportunities. There has never been any satisfactory explanation offered as to why this destitute child should have been singled out for a far more expensive education than should have been his normal lot.

Sir John Temple lived on in Dublin, until his death in 1677, and must have taken a keen interest in the progress of this unusual child; his will was never published, and as it is now destroyed, it is impossible to know what, if any, arrangements he made for his family; but his son John

Temple continued in Dublin and was in a position to see that his father's wishes were carried out.

There is no open avowal of any Temple interest whatever in Mrs. Abigail Swift's children, until 1689, when Deane Swift, reporting an imaginary recommendation which she gave to Jonathan, whom she was sending to Sir William Temple for a start in life, makes her say,

> . . . *his father, Sir John Temple, had a regard and friendship for your father and your uncles until his last hour.*

Swift, in his Autobiography, referring to Sir William Temple, states,

> . . . *his father had been a great friend to the family.*

How that great friendship manifested itself is not explained by either Deane Swift or the Dean of St. Patrick's.

However, from 1689 onwards, the Temple family became open patrons of Jane and Jonathan Swift, and remained in this role for very many years. He spent a considerable time as a member of Sir William's household; his sister paid lengthy visits there.

Jane Swift, (born about April 1666, some two years after the marriage of Abigail Erick), is described by Deane Swift as *rather beyond what is called agreeable,* meaning, presumably, that she was rather a pleasant girl. According to F. Elrington Ball, she was married from the house of William Swift, and it would appear that, during her early life, she was probably a member of his household. Little is known about William Swift, except dates, but there is evidence that he was a kindly man. He was very helpful to Abigail Swift after her husband's death, aiding her to clear up the muddle in which he had left his legal accounts; he was on good terms with Jonathan, who seems to have felt kindly towards him. When Swift's mother finally left Dublin for her native Leicestershire, she must presumably have been content with an arrangement by which her baby daughter was left behind in someone's keeping. It may well have been in William Swift's family.

He came to Dublin, from England, in 1661, bringing a new wife. In Dublin, he was admitted an attorney. He married four times, he fathered and lost a number of children. At the outbreak of the Williamite Wars, his family shared the flight to England of the frightened Anglo-Irish community. Presumably, young Jane went with them, and later returned with her guardian's family, to Dublin, where life soon became normal again.

Jane Swift certainly spent long periods at Moor Park and at the London home of the Temple family. In a letter to William Swift, her brother Jonathan wrote:

Moor Park, November 29, 1692.

Sir,

My sister told me you was pleased (when she was here) to wonder I did so seldom write to you ... I knew your aversion to impertinence; and God knows so very private a life as mine can furnish a letter with little else; for I often am two or three months without seeing anybody besides the family; and now that my sister is gone, I am likely to be more solitary than before.

This letter also contains about the only tribute ever paid by Swift to his relations,

I am sorry my fortune should fling me far from the best of my relations, but I hope I shall have the happiness to see you some time or other.

There is a letter to Jane, in a collection of Swift's letters, edited by Deane Swift and published in Dublin by Faulkner in 1768. Deane Swift heads the letter, *Dr. Swift to Mrs. Jane Swift* and adds a note, *The Doctor's sister.* It is dated 1696 and is obviously written from Moor Park to a member of the Temple household then in residence in Sir

William's house in London. As Lady Temple (who had made her home there for many years before her death) had died in London not very long previously, her sister-in-law Lady Giffard (who all that time had been head of Sir William's establishment in Moor Park) may well have been making a prolonged stay in the Pall Mall house.

For some reason this letter has been *re-addressed* to Stella or to her mother, Mrs. Bridget Johnson, by some subsequent editors, the reason perhaps, being that they could not imagine Swift writing a humorously affectionate letter to anyone else. Here is the letter to Jane Swift.

1696.

I received your kind letter from Robert, by word of mouth, and think it a vast condescention in you to think of us in your greatness; now shall we hear nothing from you for five months but We courtiers. *Loory is well, and presents his humble duty to my Lady, and love to his fellow servant: but he is the miserablest creature in the world; eternally in his melancholy note, whatever I can do; and if his finger do but ake, I am in such a fright you would wonder at it. I pray return my service to Mrs. Filby in payment of hers by Robert.*

Nothing grows better by your absence but my Lady's chamber-floor, and Tumble-down Dick. Here are three letters for you, and Molly will not send one of them; she says you ordered her to the contrary. Mr. Mose and I desire you will remember our love to the King, and let us know how he looks.

Robert says the Czar is there, and is fallen in love with you, and designs to carry you to Muscovy, pray provide yourself with muffs and sable tippets etc.

Aeolus has made a strange revolution in the rook's nests; but I say no more, for it is dangerous to meddle with things above us.

I desire your absence heartily; for now I live in great state, and the cook comes in to know what I please to have for dinner; I ask, very gravely, what is in the house, and accordingly give orders for a dish of pigeons, or etc. You shall have no more ale here; unless you send us a letter. Here is a great bundle, and a letter for you; both came together from London. We all keep home like so many cats.

Regarding the date, the allusion to Peter the Great's visit to England would seem to show that 1696 should read 1698, since that was the year in which the Czar used to amuse himself by being pushed in a wheel-barrow through John Evelyn's magnificent beech hedges, as the owner indignantly records. On the other hand, the entire letter is written in a jocose humour, and rumours of the Czar's impending visit may have long anticipated the event. The account of the health and behaviour of Lady Giffard's adored *Loory* might have helped to place the letter, had her brother, Sir William, dated the poem he wrote for her, on the death of that much lamented bird—

. . . and now, alas, embalmed with her tears . . .
. . . Company, Love, Playfellow and Friend . . .

The importance of this letter is that it shows that Jane is again spending many months as a member of the Temple household. It also shows, by its atmosphere of easy affection, that the *disagreement that subsisted between* the brother and sister, according to Deane Swift, had not yet arisen.

But the days of the Temple household at Moor Park were rapidly drawing to a close. In May, 1699, Sir William Temple died, and that hospitable home was broken up.

It may have been no coincidence that six months later Jane married Joseph Fenton. The marriage was bitterly opposed by her brother, who, according to Deane Swift, offered her £500 if she would break it off. While it seems extremely unlikely that Swift had so large a sum to dispose of, the story at least proves the strength of his objections. Nevertheless, Jane married Fenton and, from some unexplained source, was provided with a comfortable dowry of £300.

The marriage was unhappy, and some ten or eleven years later she left her husband, a perilous step for an ostensibly penniless gentlewoman, with at least two children, who had no other home to go to in Dublin, her kind guardian, William Swift, having died six years earlier.

In May, 1710, Jonathan Swift made this entry,

On Wednesday, between seven and eight in the evening, I received a letter in my chamber at Laracor from Mrs. Fenton, dated 9th May, with one enclosed sent from Mrs. Worrall at Leicester to Mrs. Fenton, giving an account that my mother, Mrs. Abigail Swift, died that morning, Monday, April 24th, 1710, about ten o'clock after a long illness; being ill all winter and lame and extremely ill a month or six weeks before her death. I have now lost my barrier between myself and death. God grant I may live to be as well prepared for it as I confidently believe her to have been. If the way to Heaven be through piety, justice and charity, she is there.

In January, 1710-11, Swift explains in his *Journal to Stella* that,

Mrs. Fenton has written me another letter about some money of hers, in Lady Giffard's hands, that is entrusted to me by my mother, not to come to her husband.

Mrs. Fenton was still, apparently, in Dublin, and Lady Giffard was handling some money belonging to Jane, which she was anxious her husband should know nothing about. Within a matter of months, Mrs. Fenton had joined Lady

Giffard's establishment in England, where, in company with Stella's mother, she remained until old Lady Giffard's death in 1722, broke up yet another Temple shelter.

But, to return to 1711, there is a curious entry in the Journal, dated 17th July,

It is damned news you tell me about Mrs. F., it makes me love England less a great deal. I know nothing of the trunk being left or taken; so 'tis odd enough if the things in it were mine; and I think I was told there were some things for me, that my mother left particularly for me.

Unfortunately, the trunk and its contents are not again referred to, so it is not possible to know what *papers* may have reached Swift from his dead mother or what family secrets he may then have learned. But it may well be of significance that, according to Deane Swift, the Doctor was *upon no Terms of Friendship* with any of the Swift family, nor they with him, after his return to Ireland from this London visit. Whatever tenuous ties held him to his relatives in Dublin were now broken, for very many years.

What his sister had said or done to make him *love England less a great deal* is not known, but the cause of his anger was not, apparently, her leaving her husband, as a few weeks later he writes,

I pity poor Jenny, but her husband is a dunce, and with respect to him she loses little by her deafness.

In the same month, the Journal records that

Mrs. Fenton was to see me about a week ago; and desired I would get her son into the Charter House.

The relevance of these extracts appears only when they are contrasted with a letter, written by Dean Swift to Benjamin Motte, his English man of business, dated 25th October, 1735.

Dublin.

. . . Here lives one Mr. Hatch, who is a manager for the Temple family. He came lately to the Deanery, and talked with great melancholy of Mrs. Fenton not having received any money from me, for a long time; whereupon I paid him ten guineas and took his receipt; for, to say the truth, having not heard from you in a long time, nor caring one straw whether the woman had received one penny or what became of her, who, during her whole life, disobliged me in most circumstances by her conduct, I did not employ one thought upon her except to her disadvantage, and I heartily wish you had demanded your money of me, as you paid it, because then it would not have been such a load upon me as now it will . . . . I desire, therefore that you will pay her no more, but only send me how her account lies, including the ten guineas I sent by Mr. Hatch, who was to send her a bill . . . . I would much rather assist my poor cousin Lancelot, if it was in my power, for she was always kind and obliging to me. I did not know Mrs. Fenton had a son, nor will ever believe such a breed had either worth or honour — — ?

Some explanation of this letter is necessary. Mr. Hatch (who gave his name to a Dublin street) was, as Swift explains, the Irish agent of the Temple estates. It seems extremely unlikely that Mr. Hatch would have had the temerity—or the impertinence—to call upon Dean Swift to reproach him for not having paid Mrs. Fenton's allowance, if the payment of that allowance were not part of his business as the Temple family's agent. Swift's anger at the interview (at which he actually paid ten guineas to Mr. Hatch, on behalf of Mrs. Fenton) is quite apparent in this letter; had the annuity to his sister been a matter of his own private charity, there is little doubt of the reception Temple's agent would have got from the infuriated Dean. As it was, since Swift had had no account for a year from Motte, he had no option but to pay the money to the Temple's agent, on behalf of his sister. It would seem very clear that the money Mrs. Fenton received was Temple money, of which Swift was merely the channel; the fact that Mrs. Fenton (then living again near Moor Park in Surrey) should have applied to the Temple agent when her annuity was in arrears, is proof that she *knew* the money was Temple money.

A further proof that the payment to Mrs. Fenton was not a voluntary offering from the Dean is given by his allusion to his cousin, Mrs. Lancelot, whom he would much rather assist *if it were in my power, for she was always kind and obliging to me.* (This lady, formerly Mrs. Patty Rolt, had always been a favourite of Swift's; he sympathised with her poverty, in London, where she lived in the absence of her first husband. For some reason, various editors have surmised that he was a good-for-nothing, runaway spouse, although it seems obvious from an entry in the *Journal* (10th April, 1713) that he was a soldier in the English forces, stationed in Minorca. The Eighteenth Century Army provided no allowance for wives, and poor Mrs. Rolt had to live on £18 a year.) From the Dean's furious outburst against his sister, it seems extremely unlikely that he would have continued to support her, had he any option whatsoever. He goes so far, in his diatribe, as to deny any knowledge of Mrs. Fenton's son, whom he had been trying to get into the Charter House, some years before. It is satisfactory to see, in a letter from Mr. Motte to the Dean, that he considers *Mr. Fenton a man of worth and honour.*

When Lady Giffard died, in 1722, she left Mrs. Fenton some of her clothes, the furnishings of her bedroom, a small silver cup, and thirty guineas. After Lady Giffard's establishment was broken up, Jane Fenton went straight back to

Guilford in Surrey, to the neighbourhood of the Temples in Moor Park. The *silver cup* which Jane Fenton inherited from Lady Giffard is presumably the *silver cann*, which Mrs. Fenton left to *Anne, wife of Richard Fenton, son of my late husband, Joseph Fenton, by his first wife.*

Her will, dated February, 1733-4, and put into Probate in March, 1735-6, has also been overlooked. It is of interest for several reasons; it proves that Mrs. Fenton did *not* die in 1738, as stated by the Rev. Dr. Lyon and quoted by W. Monck Mason and others; it also proves that Joseph Fenton, at the time of his marriage to Jane Swift, was a widower with at least two children. By her marriage with Fenton, she also had at least two children: a son, to whom reference has already been made, and a daughter, who married Jonathan Jackson, who had a daughter, Jane.

Although the amount of her property is unspecified, it is obvious from her will that Mrs. Fenton was in comfortable circumstances and in no way dependent on the money which the Temples' agent, Mr. Hatch, was demanding from the Dean, a few months before her death. She leaves £10 to the poor, £2 to the clergyman who preached at her funeral, a few small bequests including one to Stella's mother, who had become Mrs. Mose by her second marriage, who is described as *now or late of Farnham.*

Incidentally, the will shows that Mrs. Fenton and Mrs. Mose were *not* living together in Farnham, as is usually stated. The legacy to Mrs. Swift is another tiny link with the Temples, whose Chaplain her husband had been.

But the real interest of the will is that it shows that Jane Fenton, whose husband had been a bankrupt, had sufficient property to set up a trust for the support and education of her granddaughter, Jane Jackson. Since Mrs. Fenton's only visible sources of income were a salary of £12 a year, during her service with Lady Giffard, and £20 from her brother, Dean Swift, it is difficult to see where the property came from which she disposed of in her will, unless it were the same mysterious source, which had provided her dowry, some thirty years earlier.

Jane Fenton died in Guilford on the 26th February, 1735-6, in the neighbourhood of Moor Park. She died, as she had lived, in the protecting shadow of the Temples.

With regard to Swift's possible knowledge of the paternity of his family, there are a few small clues remaining, which may help to strengthen conjectures. In a letter to Lord Bolingbroke, the Dean wrote,

Dublin, 31st October, 1729.

. . . . . My birth, although from a family not undistinguished in its time, is many degrees inferior to yours. All my pretensions upon person and parts, infinitely so. I am a younger son of younger sons. You are born to a great fortune . . . .

It must be remembered that Swift claimed his *mother's* family was one of great importance and antiquity. The phrase *I am a younger son* is, at least, unexpected from an *only* son.

Again, in No. VI of the *Drapier Letters*, he writes a name, which raises a query:

A gentleman, now in Dublin, affirms that, passing some months ago through Northampton . . . . . that large town . . . . directly on our way to London . . . .

Did the Dean of St. Patrick's learn — perhaps from his mother's delayed trunk — of the existence of Thomas Swift . . . . and did they ever meet?

In the MS. of the Rev. Dr. Lyon, Minor Canon of St. Patrick's during Swift's lifetime, he records that, in 1738, *the Dean put on mourning for his sister.* As is now known, Mrs. Fenton had then been dead for several years. But in December 1737, *Thos. Swift, Bro. to Dr. Jon Swift, Dean of St. Patrick's, Dublin,* was buried in the Churchyard of St. Andrew's, Northborough, Northampton.

Appendix II: The Family Petition to the House of Lords (1711-12)

To the Right Hon.*ble* the Lords Spiritual & Temporal in Parliam*t*. Assembled.

The humble Petition of Hester Vanhomrigh widow and relict of Bartholomew Vanhomrigh late of the City of Dublin Esq*r* and Hester Vanhomrigh their daughter and Bartholomew and Mary Vanhomrigh Infants by their said Mother their guardian.   Sheweth

That your Petitioners Husband and Father Bartholmew Vanhomrigh deced Did by his last Will & Testament bearing date the 2nd day of June 1701 Give and Devise That all his Lands Tenements Chattles Real and Personal Goods of all kind of Worldly Substance that he had or should have or be Intituled unto at the time of his death should within two Months after his decease be Inventoried valued and appraised (and after his debts and ffuneral charges satisfied) should be divided into so many equal parts as he should have children living att the time of his death and one part more to be put out to Interest, which Interest he did thereby direct to be paid to your Pet*r*. Hester his wife dureing her Life, with other Devises over and made his said Wife Hester, John Pearson and Peter Partington Executors and Overseers as in and by the said Will may more fully appear.

Your Pet*rs*. further shew that the said Devisor dyed sometime after making his said Will leaving the said Hester his widow the said Hester and Mary his two daughters and Ginkell and Bartholomew his two sons all under the age of 21

PLATE III

The burial entry of Thomas Swift in the Register of Saint Andrew's Church Northborough, England.

years and that the Will was afterwards Established by Decree in the High Court of Chancery in Ireland as by the said Decree relation being thereunto had may appear

That the said Ginkell is since dead under the age of 21 years and Hester the daughter is now come to age, and in prospect of marriage but cannot receive her portion by reason the said Bartholomew her Brother being only of the Age of 19 years cannot sell any part of the Devised premises without the aid of an Act of Parliament.

That the said Peter Partington hath ever since the death of the said Devisor taken upon himself the Mannagement of the said Estate which being dispersed in severall Counties in Ireland and all the Petitioners living in this Kingdom are desireous to sell and dispose of the said Estate so left to them, and bring the produce thereof into this Kingdom which will tend very much to the advantage of your Petitioners.

Therefore your Petitioners humbly pray your Lordships to permit them to bring in a Bill to vest the lands tenements and hereditaments of which the said Devisor died seized in Trustees and their heirs to be sold and that the purchase money to be gott for the same may be divided into five equal parts, one part whereof to be enjoyed by the said Hester the Widow dureing her life with power to dispose of ffive hundred pounds thereof as by the said Will directed, and the other four parts together with what shall remain of the said fifth part after the decease of the said Hester the Widow to be equally divided between the other Petitioners the Children of the said Bartholomew Vanhomrigh.

And your Petrs. shall ever pray etc.

E. Van Homrigh
E. Van Homrigh
B. Van Homrigh
Mary Van Homrigh

137

Appendix III: The opinion of the Judges on the Family Petition

(1711-12)

To the Right Hono: ^{ble} the Lords Spiritual and Temporal in Parliament Assembled

May it please Your Lordships

In pursuance of Yr Lordship's Order, bearing date the 22nd of January last past hereunto annext We have considered of the Bill therein mencioned and hereunto annext and considered of the matters refer'd do find the state of the Case to be as followeth Viz:

That Bartholomew Vanhomrigh late of the City of Dublin in the Kingdom of Ireland Esqr deceased by his last Will and Testament in Writeing bearing date the second day of June in the Year of Our Lord 1701 did Will and Devise that all his Lands and Tenements Chattles Real and Personal Debts due to him Money Plate Jewells Household goods and furniture living Cattle Corn and all and every kind of Worldly Substance whatsoever which he had or were Intituled to at the time of his death should be Inventoried Valued and appraised (and after his Debts and funeral charges satisfied) the remainder thereof according to such Valluation should be divided into so many equal parts as he should have Children living at the time of his Decease and one part more that is if he had 4 Children living at his Death his said Estate to be divided into five parts and if had five Children at the time of his Death the same to be divided into six parts and so more or less according to the Number of his Children so as there be always One part more than he should have Children at the time of his Death and that the Vallue in money of one part or Division of the said Estate Real and personal so vallued and divided should be put out at Interest which Interest he did thereby direct to be paid half Yearly to his Wife Hester during her life for her support and maintenance with a power to dispose of £500 out of the same at the time of her Decease and made his said Wife Hester during her Widowhood John Pierson and Peter Partinton Executors and Overseers of his said Will.

That the said Bartholomew Vanhomrigh some time after the making of his Will dyed leaving the said Hester his Widow Hester and Mary his two daughters and Bartholomew and Ginkell his two sons all under the age of one and twenty years. That the said Ginkell is since dead under the age of one and twenty years intestate and not married that Hester the Daughter has attained the age of one and twenty years But the said Bartholomew the brother being but of the age of nineteen years and the said Mary the sister of fifteen years, no part of the Lands and Tenements and Hereditaments which their said father dyed seized of can be sold without the aid of an Act of Parliament.

That the Premises lye disposed in several Counties in the Kingdom of Ireland and all Parties concerned in Interest in the same are now residing and intend to make their residence in England and are desireous that the said Premises be sold and the produce thereof brought into this Kingdome which will be more beneficial for all the Parties concerned therein than where the same now lies dispersed and remote from them

That the said Will was proved in Ireland (but by reason of the danger of the Seas) the parties concerned could not safely produce the Originall Will but only a probate thereof under the Seale of the Prerogative Court there whereas the Original Will ought to be produced and proved.

And we further certifie that the said Hester the Mother Bartholomew Hester and Mary the Son and Daughters acknowledged their hands to the Peticion and gave their Consents to the Bill hereunto annext and the said Hester the Mother and guardian of the said Son and Daughter Bartholomew and Mary consented also for them and the said John Pierson and Peter Partinton the Trustees and Executors in the said Will being in Ireland and not able to appear before Us proof was made of their consents to the said Bill under their hands and Seals by two Witnesses sworn at Your Lordships Bar. And there appears to be no other Parties concerned in the Consequences of the said Bill and that the Sale of the said Esate in Ireland will redound very much to the advantage of the Petitioners.

Wherefore We are humbly of Opinion It will be for the advantage of all parties concerned in the premisses if the Bill annext do pass into an Act which Bill we have perused and signed

All which We humbly submit to Your Lordships Consideration

Signed

ROBERT PRICE
ROBERT DORMER

Appendix IV: The Will of Mrs. Van Homrigh (1713-14)

In the Name of God Amen

I Hester Vanhomrigh of the Parish of St. James's Westminister in the County of Middlesex Widow Relict of Bartholomew Vanhomrigh late of Dublin in the Kingdom of Ireland Esq being sick and weak in body but praise be God for it of sound and disposing mind and memory do make and ordain this my last Will and Testament in manner and form following That is ffirst and principally I recommend my Soul into the hands of Almighty God that gave it And my body do remitt to the Earth to be buried in a decent but very private manner at the discretion of my Executrix thereinafter named And as for such wordly Estate as it hath pleased God to bless me with and which I have disposal of I do give desire and bequeath the same as is hereinafter mencioned Viz: ffirst I will and desire that all my proper and just debts which I shall owe at the time of my decease be paid and satisfied as soon as conveniently may be And I do give and bequeath unto my loving Son Bartholomew Vanhomrigh my silver dressing plate gold seal and large silver medal And unto my loving daughter Hester Vanhomrigh my diamond ear-rings and necklace and one pair of my silver candlesticks with my silver Snuffers and Snuff pan and my wedding Ring and Ruby ring with diamonds between and my furr-Tippett And unto my loving daughter Mary Vanhomrigh my pearl necklace and Ear-rings and the other pair of my silver candlesticks and my cornelian Ring with one diamond Also my Will is that my two small enamelled pictures and all my lockets shall be divided into two parts of equal value as near as may be and I do give one of the parts thereof unto my said daughter Hester Vanhomrigh and the other part thereof unto my said daughter Mary Vanhomrigh And my intencion and desire is that the same being so equally divided as aforesaid my said daughter Hester shall have the liberty of choosing which of the said two parts she shall think fitt Also I do give and bequeath unto my good friends Mr. John Pierson and Mr. Peter Partinton both of the said City of Dublin the sume of Ten Pounds apiece to buy them mourning Also I do give and bequeath unto Mary Whitlock my servant (if she shall be living with me at the time of my decease) all my wearing cloaths of silk linnen and woollen which shall have been worn by me And whereas my said husband Bartholomew Vanhomrigh in and by his last Will and Testament in writing bearing date the second day of June one thousand seven hundred and one did (amongst other things) will and bequeath that I might at my death by my Will attested by three or more credible witnesses dispose of the sum of five hundred pounds sterling to any ffriend of ffriends use or uses out of such part or share of his Estate as is therein for that purpose mencioned as by the said Will of my said late husband may more at large appear Now I do by this my last Will and Testament (executed in the presents of and attested by three or more credible Witnesses) give devise and dispose of the said sume of ffive hundred pounds and all and every sume and sums of money and all benefitt and advantage of or belonging unto me or at my disposal by vertue of the said Will of my said late Husband or of a late Act of Parliament for vesting the Estate of my said late Husband in Trustees or otherwise out of his Estate And also all the Rest and residue of my ready Money Securities for money Plate Jewells Goods Chattles and personal Estate whatsoever and wheresoever (my said debts Legacies and ffuneral charges being paid) unto my said son Bartholomew Vanhomrigh and my said daughters Hester Vanhomrigh and Mary Vanhomrigh their heirs Executors and Administrators respectively equally to be divided between them share and share alike. And I do hereby make constitute and appoint my said daughter Hester Vanhomrigh full and sole Executrix of this my last Will and Testament And I do hereby revoke and make void all former and other Wills and Testaments by me at any time heretofore made either in Word or Writing and do declare this to be my last Will and Testament   In witness thereof I the said Hester Vanhomrigh have hereunto set my hand and seal this sixteenth day of January 1713 and in the Twelfth year of the

Reign of our Soveraign Lady Queen Anne over Great Britain E. Van Homrigh (signed and sealed)
Published and declared by the said Testatrix Hester Vanhomrigh for and as her last Will and Testament in the presence of us (who attest the same by subscribing our names in the presence of her the said Testatrix)

John White   Henry White   Thos. Bacon

Mrs. Van Homrigh's will was put into probate on the 11th February 1713-14.

Appendix V: Will of Bartholomew Van Homrigh Jnr. (1715)

In the name of God Amen.
I Bartholomew Van Homrigh of St. James's Westminister in the County of Middlesex Gent (only surviving son of Bartholomew Van Homrigh late of the City of Dublin in the Kingdom of Ireland Esq. deceased) being in good health of body and of sound and disposing mind and memory praise be God for it and considering the certainty of Death and the uncertainty of the time when it may happen to me make and ordaine this my Last Will and Testament in manner and forme following that is to say ffirst and principally I recommend my Soul into the hands of God that gave it and my body I commit to the earth to be decently buried att the discretion of my Executors hereinafter named and my Will and desire is that in case I shall happen to dye in Ireland that then my body be interred in the Parish Church of St. Andrews in the City of Dublin as near the body of my said Late ffather as conveniently may be and if I shall happen to dye

in Great Britain that then my body be interred in the parish Church of St. James's Westminster aforesaid as near as conveniently may be to the body's of my late deceased Mother and Brother and as for such Worldly Estate as it hath pleased God to bless me withall I do give devise and bequeath the same as hereinafter is mentioned. Whereas by the Last Will and Testament in writing of my said Late ffather bearing date the second day of June one thousand seven hundred and one all his Estate both reall and personall which he had or was intituled unto at the time of his Death was willed and devised to be valued and appraised and after payment of his Debts ffuneral and other charges the Remainder thereof was to be divided amongst and had and received by my said Late Mother and Brother (both since deceased) and my sisters and myself in the several parts shares and proportions and in the manner therein mentioned and whereas by an Act of Parliament made in or about the Eleventh year of her present Majestie's Reigne for vesting of my said late ffather's Estate in Ireland in Trustees to be sold all and singular the Lands and Tenements and hereditaments which my said late ffather or any other person or persons in Trust for him or to his use was seized or possessed of at the time of his Death were and are invested in John Peirson and Peter Partington therein named their Heirs Executors and Administrators respectively in Trust to sell and dispose of the same and to divide the moneys arising thereby and the profitts thereof according to the said Last Will and Testament of my said late ffather and the said Act of Parliament may now at large appear. Now my Will and Desire is that the said Estates of my said Late ffather and Premises or all my Parts Shares and proportions Right Title and Interest in or unto the same or any part thereof be sold and disposed of by the said John Peirson and Peter Partington their Heirs or Administrators respectively to the best Purchaser or Purchasers that can be gotten for the same and be converted into

144

ready money as soon as may be after my decease and that all such summes of money as my late Mother did advance pay or disburse unto or for me or for my share of House-keeping Dyett Lodging and Travelling Charges in Equal proportion with her and with my said Brother and Sisters as have dwelt with her from time to time and all other just debts as I shall owe at the time of my decease be thereout and out of the Proffits untill such Sale or Sales paid and satisfyed in the ffirst place and I do give and bequeath unto the Reverend Doctor Benjamin Pratt Provost of Dublin Coledge in the said Kingdom of Ireland and Peter Partington of the said City of Dublin Gent the Summe of ffifty pounds a peice of Lawful Money of Great Britain also I doe give and bequeath unto Bartholomew Partington son of the said Peter Partington and unto John Hookes of Gaunts in the County of Dorsett and unto Erasmus Lewis Esq. the summe of ffifty pounds apeice of like money to buy them Mourning And unto the Reverend Mr. Periam Rector of Wimerton in the County of Wilts (heretofore my Tutor att Christchurch Colledge in Oxford) the Summe of thirty pounds of like Money to buy him Mourning And unto Mr. Thomas Bacon of the Middle Temple London the summe of Twenty pounds of like money to buy him Mourning And all the Rest and Residue of the moneys which shall be raised by such Sale or Sales as aforesaid and of the Rents and profitt until the makeing the same and whatsoever doth or shall belong unto me by virtue of the said Last Will and Testament of my said late ffather or the said Act of Parliament or either of them and of all other my Goods Chattells and personal Estate whatsoever and wheresoever not hereby otherwise disposed of after payment of my Debts ffuneral and other charges I doe give devise and bequeath unto the said Doctor Pratt and Peter Partington their Executors and Administrators upon Trust and Confidence Nevertheless and to and for the Intents and purposes hereinafter mentioned that is to say upon Trust and my Will is that they the said Doctor Pratt and Peter Partington their Executors Administrators doe and shall from time to time as any considerable part thereof shall come to their hands place the same out at Interest upon such Security as he or they shall be advised and conceive to be good and sufficient or otherwise secure and dispose of the same so as the greatest Interest proffits or Advantage may be made thereof that conveniently may be and doe and shall pay the Interest Produce or proffits thereof from time to time as the same shall arise or become due can be gotten in or received by them unto my loving sisters Esther Van Homrigh and Mary Van Homrigh equally to be divided Share and Share alike dureing the terme of their natural Lives and from and after the Death of either of my said Sisters then to the Survivor of them during the terme of her natural life And from and after the Death of the Survivor of my said Sisters my desire is that the said Bartholomew Partington son of the said Peter Partington and Godson of my said ffather if he shall be then living or otherwise the Heir male of his body Lawfully begotten do and shall take upon him and be constantly written and called by the Surname of Van Homrigh and in case he the said Bartholomew Partington if living or otherwise the Heir male of his body then living shall think fitting soe to doe then my Will and Mind is and I doe direct that as soon as may be after the Death of the survivor of my two said Sisters the said Doctor Benjamin Pratt and Peter Partington or the Survivor of them or the Executors or Administrators of such Survivor doe and shall (with the approbation of the said Bartholomew or in case of his Death of the Heir male of his body) by and with the said Rest and Residue of the Moneys to be raised by such Sale or Sales aforesaid and of my Goods and Chattells and personal Estate (after payment of my Debts Legacys and ffuneral and other Charges) Purchase a

Messuage or Messuages Lands Tenements and Hereditaments of Inheritance of as great yearly Value as may be had
and purchased with the same and that the said Lands Tenements and Hereditaments so to be purchased therewith be
settled and conveyed in the manner hereinafter mentioned
(that is to say) to the use of the said Bartholomew for the
terme of ninety-nine years if he shall so long live without
impeachment of Wast and to Trustees and their Heirs during
the Life of the said Bartholomew for preserving of the con-
tingent Estates thereof from being barred and from
and after his Death to the use of ffirst second third
ffourth and all and every other son and sons of the Body of
the said Bartholomew Lawfully Issuing severally and successively in Taile male The elder of such Son and Sons and
the Heires Male of his body Issuing provided that the said
Bartholomew and all and every person and persons who shall
be intituled to the Estate to be purchased as aforesaid doe,
always take upon thcm or beare and be constantly written
and called by the Sirname of Van Homrigh my Intention
and Desire being that the Estate soe to be purchased shall
be enjoyed forever by a person of that Name But in case the
said Bartholomew Partington at his Death shall leave no
Issue Male of his body Lawfully begotten or if the said
Bartholomew or his Heir Male or any other person who by
virtue or in pursuance of this my Will shall become intituled
to the Estate so to be purchased as aforesaid shall refuse to
take or be written or called by the Sirname of Van Homrigh
then my Will is that from and after the Death of the Survivor of my said Sisters and of the said Bartholomew without Issue Male of his body surviving or from and after such
refusal of taking the said Name of Van Homrigh as aforesaid which shall first happen respectively then the said Doctor Benjamin Pratt and Peter Partington or the Survivor of
them or the Executors or Administrators of such survivor
doe and shall pay all the rest and residue of the moneys to

be raised by such Sale or Sales as aforesaid and of my said personal Estate or Assigne and convey the Securities for the same if not laid out in the Such Purchase as aforesaid, or if such Purchase be made that the Estate so purchased shall be sold and the Money raised thereby with the Proffits till Sale shall be paid to Dublin Colledge in the said Kingdom of Ireland and shall be appropriated applyed and disposed of on and for the Erecting and finishing of some convenient Building, of use in or adjoining to and for the benefitt of the said last mentioned Colledge and not otherwise and that the Building soe to be erected therewith shall forever beare or be called by the name of Van Homrigh and I doe hereby make constitute and appoint the said Doctor Benjamin Pratt and Peter Partington Executors of this my Last Will and Testament and Earnestly Intreat them to see the same duly performed to the utmost of their power and for their care and paines therein I doe give and bequeath unto each of them (besides what I have hereinbefore given to them) the Summe of ffifty pounds apeice to be had and received by them, as soon as may be after they respectively shall prove this my Will and take upon them the Trusts hereby reposed in them Provided always nevertheless and for the Encouragement of my said Executors and Trustees to act in the Executorshipp and Trusts my Will and meaning is that it shall and may be Lawfull to and for the said Doctor Pratt and Peter Partington their Executors and Administrators from time to time in the first place to deduct detaine and satisfye unto themselves out of what shall come to their hands by virtue hereof all such reasonable Charges Costs and Expences as they respectively shall expend or sustaine or be put unto in the performance or execution of this my Will or the Trusts hereby reposed in them or in anywise touching or concerning the same and that they shall not be answerable for or chargeable with more of my said Estate than shall actually

come to their hands respectively nor for any Involuntary
Losses or Losses which shall or may happen without his or
their owne willfull Default respectively nor one of them for
the Receipts Payments Acts or Doeings of the other of them
But each of them respectively for his owne Receipts Payments Acts and Doeings only anything herein before contained to the contrary thereof not withstanding.

In witness I the said Bartholomew Van Homrigh have
put unto this my Last Will and Testament Comprized or
Written in six sheets of paper and part of the seventh sheet
att the Topp thereof sett my Seale this third day of March
Anno Domini 1713 and the twelfth year of the Reigne of
Our Soveraigne Lady Anne by the Grace of God of Great
Britain France and Ireland Queen Defender of the ffaith
(B. Van Homrigh) Signed sealed published and declared
by the said Testator Bartholomew Van Homrigh for and as
his Last Will and Testament in the presence of us (who
attest the same by subscribing our names in the presence of
him the said Testator

Ri Tanner   William Lingard   John Turner
Put into Probate 17th May 1715.·

Appendix VI: The Will of Mrs. Jane Fenton (1735–6)

In the name of God Amen I Jane Fenton of Guldesford in
the County of Surrey Widow do make my Last Will and
Testament in manner and form following First I Commend
my soul to God hoping to be saved by the death of Jesus
Christ and I order my body to be decently buryed and as

concerning my Worldly Estate I give and dispose thereof as followeth to wit I give and bequeath unto Alice Fenton daughter of my late husband Joseph Fenton deceased by his first wife my gold watch also I give and bequeath to Richard Fenton son of my said late husband by his first wife my silver hand candlestick and snuffers and to Anne his wife my silver Cann Also I give and release to my son-in-law Jonathan Jackson all money that shall be due and owing from him to me at the time of my decease Also I give and bequeath to my granddaughter Jane Jackson all my linnen of all sorts and all my wearing apparell to be delivered to her at her age of one and twenty years or day of Marriage which shall first happen and in case of her death before such time then give the same to the said Richard Fenton Also I give and bequeath unto Mrs. Mose now or late of Farnham Mrs. Swift of Puttenham and Mrs. Hewatson of Dublin if she be living if not to her husband one guinea apiece to buy them rings Also I give and bequeath the sum of ten pounds to be applied to such charitable uses as my Executors hereinafter named shall think fit Also I give and bequeath to the Reverend Mr. Bannister of Guldeford or whom else shall preach a funeral sermon for me two guineas. Also I give and bequeath to William Herswell of Guldeford aforesaid Mealman the sum of ten pounds in case he shall accept of the trust hereinafter by me reposed in him Also I give and bequeath unto the said Richard Fenton and William Herswell all the rest and residue of my Goods Chattells rights Credits ready money and personal estate whatsoever (after my debts and funeral expenses paid and discharged) in trust to pay and apply the yearly income interests and profits that can be made thereof towardes the maintenance education and bringing up of my said granddaughter Jane Jackson until her age of one and twenty years or day of Marriage which shall first happen and then to pay her thereout the sum of one hundred pounds of lawful money of Great Britain And from thenceforth I will that the said Richard Fenton shall have the yearly income interest and profits that can be made of the residue thereof during his natural life for his own use and property and at his decease I will the said residue thereof to be paid to my said Granddaughter Jane Jackson her executors or administrators But in case she shall happen to dye before she shall attain the age of one and twenty years or be marryed then and from thenceforth I will and bequeath all the said rest and residue of my said goods Chattells rights credits ready money and Personal Estate to the said Richard Fenton his executors and administrators for his and their own property But in such case I will he or they shall pay ten pounds thereout to his sister Alice Fenton her executors or administrators and I nominate and appoint the said Richard Fenton and William Herswell to be joynt executors of this my last Will and Testament And my further will and meaning is that neither of my said Trustees and Executors shall be charged or chargeable with or for any part of my estate further or otherwise than only for such and so much thereof as shall come to each of their respective hands and disposals And in case any moneys shall happen to be lost by being put out on bad security or otherwise that my said trustees and executors or either of them shall not be charged or chargeable with or answerable for the same And I revoke all Wills by me made In testimony whereof I have hereto set my hand and seal the eight and twentyth day of February in the seventh year of the Reign of King George the Second of Great Britain and so forth and in the year of Our Lord one thousand seven hundred thirty and three Jane Fenton Signed sealed published and declared by the said Jane Fenton to be her last Will and Testament in the presence of us. Humphrey Harrison. John Shotter.

Put into Probate 8th March 1735-6.

Appendix VII: Vanessa's Will

In the name of God, Amen. I Esther Vanhomrigh, one of the daughters of Bartholomew Vanhomrigh, late of the City of Dublin, Esq., deceased, being of sound and disposing mind and memory, do make and ordain this my last will and testament, in manner and form following, that is to say: —First, I recommend my soul into the hands of Almighty God, and my body I commit to the earth, to be buried at the discretion of my executors hereinafter named. In the next place, I give and devise all my worldly substance, whether in lands, tenements, hereditaments or trusts, and all my real and personal estate, of what nature or kind soever, unto the Reverend Doctor George Berkly, one of the fellows of Trinity College, Dublin, and Robert Marshall of Clonmell, Esq., their heirs, executors and administrators, chargeable nevertheless with, and subject and liable to the payment of all such debts of my own contracting, as I shall owe at the time of my death, as also unto the payment of the several legacies hereinafter bequeathed, or which shall hereafter be bequeathed by an codicil to be attached to this my last will and testament: *Item*, I give and bequeath to Erasmus Lewis of London, Esq., the sum of twenty-five pounds sterling, to buy a ring: *Item*, I give and bequeath to Francis Annesley of the city of London, Esq., twenty-five pounds sterling, to buy a ring: *Item*, I give and bequeath to John Hooks, Esq., of Gaunts in Dorsetshire, twenty-five pounds sterling, to buy a ring: *Item*, I give unto the Right Reverend Father in God, William King, Lord Archbishop of Dublin, twenty-five pounds sterling, to buy a ring: *Item*, I give and bequeath unto the Right Reverend Father in God, Theop. Bolton, Lord Archbishop of Clonfert, twenty-five pounds sterling, to buy a ring: *Item*, I give and bequeath unto Robert Lindsey, of the city of Dublin, Esq., twenty-five pounds sterling, to buy a ring: *Item*, I give and bequeath unto Edmund Shuldam of the City of Dublin, Esq., twenty-five pounds sterling, to buy a ring; *Item*, I give and bequeath unto William Lingin of the Castle of Dublin, Esq., twenty-five pounds sterling, to buy a ring; *Item*, I give and bequeath unto the Rev. Mr. John Antrobus, my cousin, the like sum of money, to buy a ring: *Item*, I give and bequeath unto Bryan Robinson, doctor of physic in the City of Dublin, fifteen pounds sterling, to buy a ring: *Item*, I give and bequeath unto Mr. Edward Cloker of the City of Dublin, fifteen pounds sterling, to buy a ring: *Item*, I give and bequeath to Mr. William Marshall of the city of Dublin, fifteen pounds sterling, to buy a ring: *Item*, I give and bequeath to John Finey, son of George Finey of Kildrought in the county of Kildare, and godson to my sister, the sum of twenty-five pounds sterling, to be paid him when he shall attain the age of twenty-one years: Also I give and bequeath to his mother, Mrs. Mary Finey, the sum of ten pounds sterling, to buy mourning; and to Mrs. Ann Wakefield, her sister, of the parish of St. Andrews in the city of Dublin, the like sum, to buy mourning: *Item*, I give and bequeath unto Ann Kindon, who is now my servant, the sum of twenty-five pounds sterling, to buy mourning; and to her daughter, Ann Clinkskells, the like sum of money, to buy mourning: *Item*, I give and bequeath unto every servant that shall live with me at the time of my death half a year's wages; and to the poor of the parish, where I shall happen to die, five pounds sterling: And I do hereby make, constitute and appoint the said Dr. George Berkly, and Robert Marshall, Esq., of Clonmel, sole executors of this my last will and testament: And I do hereby revoke and make void all former and other wills and testaments by me in any wise heretofore made, either in word or writing, and declare this to be my last will and testament. In witness whereof I, the said Esther Vanhomrigh, have hereunto set my hand and

153

seal, this first day of May, in the year of Our Lord 1723.

E. Van Homrigh.   (Seal)

Signed, published and declared by the said Esther Van-homrigh, for and as her last will and testament, in presence of us, who attest the same by subscribing our names in the presence of her the said testatrix.

Jas. Doyle.   Ed. Thrush.   Darby Gafny.

The last will and testament of Esther Vanhomrigh, late deceased (having, and so forth), was proved in common form of law, and probate granted by the most Reverend Father in God Thomas, and so forth, to the Reverend George Berkely and Robert Marshall, the executors, they being first sworn personally.

Dated the 6th day of June, 1723.

A true copy, which I attest.

John Hawkins, Dep. Reg.

Appendix VIII: Swift's membership of Freemasonry

The important fact that Dean Swift was a Freemason has not been taken into consideration by editors of his work, some of which requires an understanding of Freemasonic cere-monies and symbolism.

There is no existing record of Swift's having been a member of any Irish Lodge, but, according to information kindly supplied by the Grand Lodge, London, in a letter dated 8-XII-59, he was a member of a Lodge

which was granted Warrant No. 16, on 3rd April 1723, to meet at the Red Lion, Tottenham Court Road, London. In 1729, the Lodge moved to The Goat, at the foot of the Haymarket. It was erased from the List of Lodges on 21st November 1745. *The Grand Lodge minute book, under heading* List of the Names of the Members of all the regular Lodges, as they were returned in the year 1730, *records the name of Jonathan Swift as a member of the Lodge meeting at The Goat, at the foot of the Haymarket: The date of initiation is not shown, but the Dean is known to have been in London in* 1726 *and* 1727 *as the guest of Pope, and it is probable that he became a Mason during that time.*

Not only Alexander Pope, but also Swift's other close friend, Dr. Arbuthnot, was a member of that Lodge.

Although there is not any existing record that Swift belonged to an Irish Lodge, many of his friends did, and in the Dean's opposition to *Mr. Wood's Halfpence,* he was given invaluable support by Irish Freemasonry.

It is not known what Degree was reached by Dean Swift, so it cannot be asserted that he was a Member of The Royal Arch. According to F. de P. Castell's *Antiquity of the Holy Royal Arch,* this Degree of Masonry existed prior to 1723. But, during Swift's last, terrible phase of mental decay, his household reported that the old man used to repeat, *I am what I am . . . . . I am what I am . . . .*

A very slight alteration in those words would suggest that, in his last fearful ordeal, a Member of the Royal Arch Degree was calling for help.

Appendix IX: Swift and Vanessa

Chapter III; paragraph 5.
Since the available evidence would seem to show that this poem was written for Esther Van Homrigh *before* Swift became a dean, the use of the anagram *Cadenus* for *Decanus* has caused a great deal of speculation. A possible explanation

may be that this name—specially invented by Swift for intimate use between himself and the girl for whom he also invented the name Vanessa—had a totally different derivation. The Oxford Dictionary gives a XVII Century meaning of the word *Cad*, as *a familiar spirit*, and quotes two extracts from writers of that period, in which the word is so used. Swift's handwriting was not always very legible, and his *V* might have been easily misread as U by a stranger. If this mistake had been made, their secret name may, in reality, have been an anagram of *Cad Es Vn* i.e. *The familiar spirit of Esther Van* (*Homrigh*). Several times in their letters allusions are made to witchcraft; Swift constantly used diminutives of *Esther*, and in his *Journal to Stella* he habitually referred to her family as the *Vans*.

After Vanessa's death, the poem was found among her papers, and copies were surreptiously distributed in Dublin. The name would, very reasonably, have been taken to be an anagram of *Decanus*, Swift being then long a dean. Some years later, Swift would have accepted the happy alteration, when he himself edited the poem.

Vanessa's use of the name *Cad*, in her letters to Swift, would be very much more significant if the XVII Century meaning of the word were accepted instead of its being a somewhat clumsy abbreviation.

Bibliography

The following is a list of the chief sources which have been consulted.

The Works of the Rev. Jonathan Swift D.D. edited by John Hawkesworth. London 1755.

The Words of the Rev. Jonathan Swift, D.D. arranged by

Thomas Sheridan, A.M., revised by John Nichols, F.S.A., London 1808.

Remarks on the Life and Writings of Dr. Jonathan Swift, by John, Earl of Orrery. Dublin 1752.

Observations upon Lord Orrerys Remarks, by Dr. Delaney 1754.

Essay upon the Life, Writings and Character of Dr. Swift, by Deane Swift. 1755.

The Life of the Revd. Jonathan Swift, Hawkesworth, 1755.

Letters written by the late Dr. Jonathan Swift, Dean of St. Patrick's, Dublin. Published from the originals collected and revised by Deane Swift. Dublin 1768.

The Drapier Letters. Faulkner, Dublin. 1762.

The Life of the Rev. Dr. Jonathan Swift. T. Sheridan 1784.

Enquiry into the Life of Dean Swift. George Monck Berkeley 1789.

Literary Relics. George Monck Berkeley 1789.

The Diary of John Evelyn, edited by Austin Dobson. Macmillan 1908.

Memoirs of Mrs. Letitia Pilkington - 1748. George Routledge & Sons, London 1928.

History and Antiquities of the Collegiate Church of St. Patrick, W. Monck Mason 1820.

The Correspondence of Jonathan Swift D.D., edited by F. Elrington Ball, G. Bell & Sons, London, 1910.

The Poems of Jonathan Swift, edited by Harold Williams, Clarendon Press, Oxford, 1937.

Journal to Stella, edited by Harold Williams, Clarendon Press, Oxford, 1948.

Gulliver's Travels, edited by Harold Williams, London.

Vanessa and her Correspondence with Jonathan Swift, edited by A. Martin Freeman, London 1921.

Jonathan Swift, a critical essay, W. D. Taylor 1933.

The Closing Years of Dean Swift's Life. Sir W. Wilde 1849

The Life of Jonathan Swift. Sir Henry Craik. 1882.
The Life of Jonathan Swift. John Foster 1875
Jonathan Swift, a biographical and critical study, John Churton Collins 1893.
Swift. Sir Leslie Stephens. 1889
Swift or the Egoist. Rossi and Hone 1934
Swift. Carl Van Doren 1931
In Search of Swift. Denis Johnston, Dublin 1959
The Conjured Spirit. Evelyn Hardy. 1949.
Martha, Lady Giffard, Life and letters, Julia Longe 1911
Stella, a Gentlewoman of the Eighteenth Century, Herbert Davis 1942.
Swift's Marriage to Stella. Maxwell Gold. 1935
The Life and friendships of Dean Swift. Stephen Gwynn 1933
Dean Swift and his writings. G. P. Moriarty 1893
Jonathan Swift. J. Middleton Murry 1954
Betham's Geneological Abstracts, Records Office, Dublin.
Registers of St. Patrick's Cathedral, Dublin.
Calender of Ancient Records of Dublin, edited by J. T. Gilbert.
Dictionary of National Biography.
Publications of the Parish Register Society of Dublin.
Gentleman's Magazine, November, 1757
Foundation of the Hospital of King Charles II in Dublin. F. R. Falkiner.
Records of the House of Lords, London.
Parish Register of St. Andrew's Church, Northborough, England.
Parish Register of St. James's Church, London.
Principal Probate Registry, Somerset House, London.
Transcript of Northborough Parish Register, 1738
Antiquity of the Holy Royal Arch, F. deP. Castells, London 1927

Index

APPENDICES

SYBIL LE BROCQUY

Swift's Most Valuable Friend

THE DOLMEN PRESS

IN MEMORY OF ÉMIL PONS

INTRODUCTION

Esther Johnson died, after a long illness, on the 28th January, 1727-8. Some hours after receiving the news of her death, Dean Swift began to make notes about the dead lady, and continued them during the actual time when her funeral was taking place a short distance from his house.

In these writings — afterwards published under the title *On the Death of Mrs. Johnson* — Swift revealed, wittingly or unwittingly, much information about the shadowy figure of the woman who as *Stella* played so important a part in the tragicomedy of his life.

Here I have tried to fill in some of the gaps in Swift's own account of Esther Johnson, who has been variously described as his secret wife, his long-suffering mistress and, in his own words,

The truest, most virtuous and valuable friend that I, or perhaps any other person, was ever blessed with.

Sybil Le Brocquy
Dublin
June, 1967.

7

SOME RELEVANT DATES

1667 Jonathan Swift born in Dublin.
1682 entered Trinity College, Dublin.
1689 entered the service of Sir William Temple, in Moor Park, Surrey, England.
1690 left Sir William's home, Moor Park, and went to Ireland.
1691 returned to Moor Park.
1694 left Moor Park and returned to Ireland.
1695 ordained a Church of Ireland clergyman in Dublin.
1696 returned to Moor Park.
1699 death of Sir William Temple. Swift returned to Dublin as Chaplain to the Earl of Berkeley.
1700 appointed to a living in Co. Meath.
1701 returned to England as Chaplain to the Earl of Berkeley.
1701 Stella and Rebecca Dingley arrived to live in Dublin, on Swift's invitation.
1701 Swift returned to Dublin.
1702 Swift returned to London, where he spent much of his time for five years.
1707 Swift met Esther Van Homrigh (Vanessa) in England.
1710-13 Swift spent in England. During this time he wrote the letters afterwards published as "The Journal to Stella".
1713 Swift spent a few weeks in Dublin, where he was installed as Dean of St. Patrick's Cathedral. He returned to England.
1714 Queen Anne died. Swift left England on the disruption of the Tory Government. Some months later, Vanessa followed him to live on her Irish estates.
1723 Vanessa died.
1728 Stella died.
1742 Commission decided that Swift was "of unsound mind and memory, and not capable of taking care of his person or fortune".
1745 Swift died, in the Deanery of St. Patrick's Cathedral, Dublin.

CHAPTER I

This day, being Sunday, January 28, 1727-8, about eight o'clock at night, a servant brought me a note, with an account of the death of the truest, most virtuous and valuable friend that I, or perhaps any other person, was ever blessed with. She expired about six in the evening of this day; and as soon as I am left alone, which is about eleven at night, I resolve, for my own satisfaction to say something of her life and character.

(On the Death of Mrs. Johnson)

In the damp gloom of a Dublin winter's night, Dean Swift wrote these words, in the Deanery of St. Patrick's Cathedral. The little group of faithful Sunday visitors had paid him their usual respects, and had gone silently away, presumably after the arrival of the message that Esther Johnson's long, painful struggle for life had ended. There would have been awkward attempts at condolence; Swift had never been a man to welcome sympathy. And there was the further complication of embarrassment caused by the ever-present doubt as to the real relationship between the dead woman and the Dean; a doubt which had kept gossip simmering for over twenty-five years. Was the old man mourning his secret wife, his mistress, or his dearest friend? No one had ever had the temerity to question the Dean, and the unsolved mystery still teases, after more than two hundred and fifty years.

Esther Johnson (whom, as *Stella,* Swift has thrust into a melancholy fame), had died, it is said, at the house of her friend, Lady Eustace, after a final illness which had lasted many months. The house, near the Phoenix Park, was no great distance from the Deanery; a coach would have carried him there in half an hour. The Cathedral Close was outside the city walls, but no great difficulty would have prevented the Dean from hurrying to the deathbed of his beloved friend, where, at the least, he could have comforted her devoted companion, Rebecca Dingley and her sorrowing friends.

But, curiously enough, the Dean did not hurry to the house at Harbour Hill, any more than he had hurried back from England, the previous year, when close friends had written that her death was then imminent. On that occasion, Swift's reaction was to write a very remarkable letter to Dr. John Worral, his Vicar at St. Patrick's Cathedral, ordering him to see that his housekeeper at the Deanery carried out the strict instructions previously given her : under no conditions should Stella be allowed to die in the Deanery. So far as Swift was concerned, *the truest, most virtuous and valuable friend that I, or perhaps any other person was ever blessed with,* could under no circumstances be permitted to die under his roof, lest further food be given to gossip about himself and the dying lady.

In most of his human relationships, Swift's behaviour wove a tangled web of inconsistency, which has since hampered most efforts at reasonable conjecture. It is obviously impossible to reconcile the man, who so genuinely loved and valued a woman over many years, with the Dean, whose chief concern was lest her death cause him embarrassment by taking place in his Deanery. This extremely divided personality is, perhaps, more evident in Swift's dealings with Esther Johnson than in any of his other relationships, and the curiously revealing account of her life, which Swift began on the night she died, provides a convenient framework within which to place the enigmatic story of Swift and Stella.

CHAPTER II

She was born at Richmond in Surrey on the 13th day of March, in the year 1681. Her father was a younger brother of a good family in Nottinghamshire, her mother of a lower degree, and indeed she had little to boast of her birth.

(On the Death of Mrs. Johnson)

In the preface to his scholarly and invaluable biography, *Mr. Swift and his contemporaries*, (Vol. I) Professor Ehrenpreis states : *I have been less concerned to add than to eliminate fables . . . . Here, neither Swift nor Stella is made a bastard.*

Complete disregard of a large body of evidence, both for and against a circumstance which would have obviously greatly influenced the lives of both Swift and Stella, is not justified. A considerable part of Swift's bitter grudge against his fate might be accounted for by a knowledge of his own illegitimacy; his unsatisfactory relationship with Stella may well have been bedevilled by his knowledge of her irregular birth. It is important, therefore, to examine the existing evidence that Stella was the child of Sir William Temple, a theory which was already widely current during her lifetime.

In July, 1723, several years before her death, the Bishop of Meath described her as *a natural daughter of Sir William Temple, a very good woman.* Presumably the Bishop, enemy though he was to Swift, would not have dared to write such an unqualified statement to the Archbishop of Canterbury, unless he believed that he had good grounds for it. Certainly, such stories were circulating during her lifetime; Lord Orrery noted that Mrs. Fenton (the Dean's sister) used to contradict the *aspersion of her being Sir William Temple's daughter,* whenever she heard it made. The rumours about her paternity were strengthened by the curious circumstances of her childhood, and by the fact that Sir William, who was by no means a wealthy man, left her a very substantial legacy. They were also given considerable weight by an article, which appeared in *The Gentleman's and London Magazine,* of November, 1757.

This article, which is ponderously — and infuriatingly — anonymous, is signed C.M.P.G.N.S.T.N.S., and was written to correct statements made by Lord Orrery in his *Remarks on the Life and Writings of Dr. Jonathan Swift*. The alphabetical disguise has never yet been penetrated, and, for that reason, the value of its information is lessened. But, even when allowance has been made for inaccuracies in the article, the fact remains that it does give the local views of the inhabitants of Farnham, the small Surrey town where so many of the leading characters of the Swift-Johnson-Temple drama played their parts. Since this article is not easily accessible, it is given here in full :

As the lives of eminent persons are the most instructive parts of history and are more read, perhaps, than any other compositions; so there are very few pieces that are more justly censured for partiality; for they are generally the works of persons interested in the praise or censure of the heroes of their history. Wisely, therefore, have the sovereign pontiffs decreed, that no person shall receive the honour of being sainted before the expiration of a complete century after their decease; in order to take off, by length of time, all sense of favour, or resentment, in such parties as might have connections with the friends or enemies of the future saint, which might otherwise have influenced their evidence in the examination which always precedes the making of a new saint.

These reflections naturally occur upon reading any of our modern lives; and they occurred to me, on my reading, a few days since, the life of Dean Swift, in one of the London Magazines, for the year 1755, extracted from Lord Orrery; the critic upon his Lordship; and the memoirs published by Deane Swift, Esq.; in which, though very concise, the writer has inserted most of the errors of the preceding works; and as the Dean's charity, his tenderness, and even his humanity have been impeached, in consequence of his hitherto unaccountable behaviour to his Stella, and of his long resentment shown to his sister; and as no person has yet thought proper to redeem that extraordinary genius from these imputations of cruelty and pride, by shewing his connections with Stella in their true light; although I think there are still some living, who have it in their power, from authentic materials, I flatter myself that I shall not be censured for endeavouring to do this justice to his memory myself.

At the place from whence I write, I have neither Ld. Orrery's works, Deane Swift's, nor the Critic upon his Lordship; so I am obliged to make use of the Magazine only : if, therefore, any of his quotations are false, I beg that the error be laid at the right door.

It is said that Swift made an acquaintance with Mrs. Johnson (the lady celebrated by the name of Stella) at Sir William Temple's : that she was the daughter of Sir William's steward; and that Sir William, in his last will left her 1,000 1. as an acknowledgement of her father's faithful services; and that she married the Dean in 1716; and his never owning her for his wife is imputed, by Ld. Orrery, to his pride, which made him disdain an alliance with one descended from so mean a family; though others impute it to the common rumour of her being Sir William's natural daughter, as Swift was said to be his son. She died (says the Magazine writer from Ld. Orrery) absolutely destroyed by the peculiarity of her fate. He quotes his Lordship's authority likewise, when he declares Swift's pride to have been such as to have induced him to refuse all reconciliation with his sister, for having married a tradesman, tho' in good circumstances, and with the approbation of her uncle or relations.

But I am certain Ld. Orrery will be pleased to be convinced that these accusations are false; Dr. Swift would have laid down his life could it have preserved his Stella, who was no otherwise related to Sir William Temple's steward than by her mother's marriage with him, many years after the death of Sir William. And as for his cruelty to his sister, it is well known that he maintained Mrs. Fenton many years, when a widow, and that she used to shew his picture to her visitants with expressions of highest gratitude and affection. That I may, however, leave no room for doubt, permit me to oppose to these imputations the true history of Mrs. Johnson, better known to the world by the name of Stella.

When Sir William left Sheen to reside at Moore Park in Surrey, he brought down with him, one summer, a gentlewoman in the character of a housekeeper, whose name was Johnson. She was a person of a surprizing genius; few women ever exceeded her in the extent of her reading; none in the charms of conversation. She had seen the world; her address and behaviour were truly polite; and whoever had the pleasure of conversing with her for a quarter of an hour, were convinced that she had known a more genteel walk in life than her present situation confined her to. She was not so happy

13

in her person as in her mind; for she was low of stature, and rather fat and thick than well-shaped; yet the imperfection of her shape was fully compensated by a set of fine features, and an excellent complexion, animated by eyes that perfectly described the brightness of her genius. She was, in a few words, the same among women that Sir William was among men. Is it surprising then, that such similar perfections should attract each other's notice?

This gentlewoman was the widow (as she always averred) of one Johnson, a merchant, who having been unfortunate in trade, afterwards became master of a trading sloop, which ran between England and Holland, and there died. He left her, as she said, three children; the eldest, a daughter, was brought up in London and there married one Filby, a baker, by whom she had 18 or 19 children; and living in a genteel manner, he was soon ruined, and was sent by their friends into the West of England, as a salt officer, whither she accompanied him, with such of her children as lived. The second of her children was a son, Edward Johnson, who was put to school at Farnham; and when of a proper age was sent abroad, in order to qualify him for trade; but he died there young. The third and last was her daughter Esther, who only, of all her children, was permitted to reside with her at Moore Park, where she was educated; and her appearance and dress so far exceeded the rank and fortune of her mother, and the rest of the children, that the world soon declared Miss Johnson to be Sir William's daughter. But had dress shown no distinction between her and the rest of her mother's children, nature had already distinguished her sufficiently. Her mother and brother were both fair; her sister is said to have been the same. The boy was said to be like his father; he, therefore, must be fair too, as the boy was so to an uncommon degree; yet Esther's, or, as she was usually called in the family, Miss Hetty's, eyes and hair were of a most beautiful black; and all the rest of her features bore so strong a resemblance to those of Sir W. Temple that no one could be at a loss to determine what relation she had to that gentleman. And could the striking resemblance be overlooked, Sir William's uncommon regard for her, and his attention to her education, must have convinced every unprejudiced person that Miss Hetty Johnson was the daughter of one who moved in a higher sphere than a Dutch trader. The respect which Sir

William affected to shew the child induced his family to copy his example and the neighbouring families behaving in the same manner, she early lost all that servility that must have tinged her manners and behaviour, had she been brought up in dependence, and without any knowledge of her real condition. When or where Sir William thought proper to acquaint her with the history of her birth, we profess not to know; but that he did inform her of the secret, we have reason to presume, from the following circumstances. As soon as she was woman enough to be entrusted with her own conduct, she left her mother and Moore Park, and went to Ireland to reside by the order of Sir William who was yet alive. She was conducted thither by Swift, but of this I am not so positive as I am that her mother parted from her as one who was never to see her again.

Here let me leave the daughter and return to Mrs. Johnson her mother, who continued to live at Moore Park till the death of Sir William, soon after she resided with Lady Giffard, sister to Sir William, and his great favourite, as her woman or housekeeper or perhaps in both capacities. Upon Lady Giffard's death she retired to Farnham, and boarded with one Filby, a brother of her daughter's husband and sometime after intermarried with Mr. Ralph Mose, a person who had for a long series of years been entrusted, as steward, with the affairs of the family, and had successively served Sir William Temple, Lady Giffard and Mr. Temple. He was a widower, and his first wife had been cook to Sir William Temple. Upon the death of Mr. Mose she went to board with Mrs. Mayne of Farnham, a gentlewoman, who had a particular esteem for her and at length retired to Mr. Filby's again and there died, not long after the year 1743. I saw her myself in the autumn of 1742, and although far advanced in years she still preserved the remains of a very fine face.

The reader may wonder, as numbers have done before, that a woman of her refined sentiments and exquisite taste should marry such a man as Mose : many have been the conjectures upon the occasion : perhaps her eldest daughter's distress might make her desirous of relieving her with the spoils of the old steward; or Mose might be privy to certain secrets that she was unwilling to have divulged, and therefore she might not dare to reject his proposals

15

for fear of drawing his resentment upon her. It was certainly a match of policy and the most refined sensibility in her was sacrificed to one who had not the least idea of delicacy. The lady to whom I am obliged for many of these anecdotes assured me that she had heard Mrs. Mose, in her freer hours, declare that she was obliged by indispensible necessity to marry the man, whose servile manners her soul despised; but that religion taught her to fulfil every duty that could possibly be expected from the most affectionate of wives. She had frequently rejected his offers, but was compelled at length to acquiesce.

Were I to attempt to describe her at full length, I might be thought guilty of the highest adulation, so extraordinary was the woman that was destined to please Sir Wm. Temple. Pomfret, in his little poem called "The Choice", is said to have given an exact description of Moore Park; to have delineated Sir William in the account of his own fancy and taste; and to have taken his picture of the female friend and companion from Mrs. Johnson; to that piece therefore do I recommend my reader.

While the mother thus spent her hours under the most painful restraint at Farnham, the daughter made surprising advances towards perfection under the tuition of Dr. Swift. In her poem, dated November 30, 1721, entitled "Stella to Dr. Swift on his birthday", we see that she attributes all that was excellent in her to his instructions. It is not surprising that her affection towards the Dean should be so great when we recollect that it commenced from her earliest age, at a time when she thought that affection entirely innocent; that it was increased by Sir William's often recommending her tender innocence to the protection of Swift, as she had no declared male relation that could be her defender. It was from Sir William's own lessons, that she received the first rules for her future conduct, which were afterwards continued by the Dean; and that the world may know what was the result of the joint efforts of these two exalted geniuses I shall relate a little anecdote for which I have undoubted authority:

When Stella, or Miss Johnson, resided in Dublin, her noble air, her genteel appearance, and the visits of many persons of distinction soon gave rise to a report that she had a large fortune, and that she kept in her lodgings cash, jewels and furniture to a very great value.

Such a report in Ireland could not fail of attracting the notice of indigent villainy. Stella had no male servant in the house, and no resistance could be expected from a few timorous women. On the night destined to deprive the world of one of its most distinguished ornaments, (for robbery and murder are terms synonimous there) Stella dismissed her women for the night, and not finding an inclination to sleep, she took a book and read for some time, being all undressed, with only a wrapping-gown over her. When she had read a while, she removed the candle to its place for the night as she always kept a light burning; and kneeling by her bed-side, she was more than once disturbed by a noise at her window; she performed her devotions however with great calmness and attention, a duty that she never omitted; and then arising, and advancing towards the place from which the sound proceeded, she saw, thro' the sash, a man who seemed to stand upon a ladder and to be waiting for her putting out the candle to begin his enterprise. The sex in general, upon such an occasion, would have fainted, scream'd out, or attempted to have run out of the chamber. Not so the daughter of Sir William Temple; she knew the cruel temper of the vulgar Irish, and took not the least apparent notice of the thief, but went directly to her closet, from which she returned immediately, and throwing up the sash with her left hand, and drawing out a pistol from under her loose wrapping-gown with her right, she fired at the villain, who immediately dropped from the ladder. She then called up the family, and the Watch coming soon after at the noise of the pistol, his confederates were obliged to fly, and never afterwards attempted to disturb her. In this case, providence seems to have assisted her in an extraordinary manner, for had she gone to bed at her usual time, or had she not employed an hour or two in reading, the censorious world would never have had it in their power to attribute her death to the pride of Dean Swift.

Ld. Orrery thinks this accomplished lady to have fallen a sacrifice to the peculiarity of her fate. I cannot oppose this opinion of his Lordship; a person of her delicate sensibility might be greatly affected by her frequent reflections on her disagreeable situation; but was it in Swift's power to prevent it?

When Stella went to Ireland, a marriage between her and the Dean could not be foreseen; but when she thought proper to com-

17

municate to her friends the Dean's proposal and her approbation of it, it was then become absolutely necessary for that person, who alone knew the secret history of the parties concerned, to reveal what otherwise might have been buried in oblivion. But was the Dean to blame, because he was ignorant of his natural relation to Stella? Or can he be justly censured because it was not made known before the day of marriage? He admired her, he loved her, he pitied her; and when fate had placed the everlasting barrier between them, their affection became a true platonic love, if not something yet more exalted. I do not deny but that she might lament the particular oddness of her fate; nor do I deny but that Swift's natural temper might acquire an additional severity and moroseness from hence, and that he might vent his passion, and revenge himself on the rest of mankind. But his affection for Stella became truly paternal; and whenever she lamented her unhappy situation, the friend, the tutor, the husband all in one, mingled his sympathetic tears with hers, and soothed the sharpness of her anxiety and sorrow. But he despised her family: Was Swift's reputed father then so noble? And to whom did the Dean declare the secret of his soul?

We are sometimes told that, upon the Hanoverian family's succeeding to the throne of Great Britain, Swift renounced all hopes of farther preferment; and that his temper became more morose and more intollerable every year. I acknowledge the fact in part, but it was not the loss of his hopes that sower'd Swift alone; this was the unlucky epocha of that discovery, that convinced the Dean that the only woman in the world, who could make him happy as a wife, was the only woman in the world, who could not be that wife. Could so turbulent a temper be easy under such a mortification? Let those judge who have been so happy as to have seen this Stella, this Hetty Johnson; and let those who have not judge from the following description.

Her shape was perfectly easy and elegant; her complexion exquisitely fine, her features were regular, with the addition of that nameless something, that so often exceeds the most exact beauty, and which never fails to add to it, when they meet together. Her teeth were beyond comparison; her eyebrows and hair of the most glossy black; and her eyes — but those I pretend not to describe; her mien and air were equal to the rest of the piece. Such was her exterior appearance; her mind was yet more beautiful than her person, and her accomplishments were such as to do honour to the man who was so happy as to call her daughter.

Can we wonder, after reflection upon the foregoing passages, that the Dean and Stella always took care to converse before witnesses, or at least a third person, from that time when they received the proper notice of the secrets of the family, even though they had never taken such precautions before. Can we wonder that they should spend one day in the year in fasting, praying and tears, from this period to her death? Might it not be the anniversary of their marriage? But it would be unnecessary to say more, since every unprejudiced person must be convinced from the preceding circumstances, that Hetty Johnson was neither daughter to Sir William Temple's steward, nor could Sir William leave her 1,000 l. as a reward for her father's faithful execution of his office, when that steward was not married to her mother till long after the decease of Sir William. He must be convinced also that Swift had more forcible reasons for not owning Stella for his wife than his Lordship has allowed; and that it was not his behaviour but her own unhappy situation, that might perhaps shorten her days.

I have yet a word to say with respect to Mrs. Fenton, the Dean's sister; he is said by Ld. Orrery to have refused all reconciliation with her on account of her marriage. But why should he have resented her marriage with a tradesman, any more than her going to service? She lived many years with Lady Giffard as her woman; and although it is probable that the Dean might disapprove of the match, as her husband, Fenton, was an extravagant careless fellow, and a notorious drunkard; yet after her husband's and Lady Giffard's death, she retired to Farnham and boarded with Mrs. Mayne, Mrs. Mose boarding there at the same time, with whom she lived in the greatest intimacy; and as she had not enough to maintain her, the Dean paid her an annuity as long as she lived; neither was that annuity a trifle.

If these anecdotes prove agreeable to the public, or they incite any other persons, who are possessed of proper materials, to throw a new light on these transactions, hitherto so extremely misrepresented, I shall think myself fortunate in having contributed something towards so generous an attempt as that of acquitting the innocent

19

from the imputation of guilt.

Yours etc.,

C.M.P.G.N.S.T.N.S.

Before examining some of the details of this statement, it may be useful to give a short account of the man, who is said to have introduced the *surprizing genius,* Mrs. Bridget Johnson, into his establishment at Moor Park, Farnham, Surrey.

William Temple was a son of Sir John Temple, Master of the Rolls in Ireland; his courtship and marriage to the celebrated Dorothy Osborne in 1654, was one of the great romances of 17th Century England. After the Restoration, he entered the Diplomatic Service and his distinguished career was rewarded with a baronetcy. Most of his service was in the Low Countries, where, for long periods, he was separated from his wife and family. His portraits prove that he was an extremely handsome man, and he had a reputation as a gallant.

Lady Giffard, his adoring sister (widowed after a week's marriage), lived with him most of his life. She has written:

He gave liberty only to those passions which he did not think it worth the care and pains it must cost to restrain them.

But the *Monthly Review,* November 1751, was more explicit:

It is well known that Sir William Temple was a very amorous man, and much addicted to intrigue with various women; and it is not improbable that such a man as Sir William should take uncommon precautions to provide well for his natural children, without letting the public, or even themselves, know that they were such.

And, finally, there is the entry, in the Diary of Laurence Hyde, recording a visit he paid in January 1677 to Sir William, who was then English Ambassador in Holland:

He held me a great long hour of things most relating to himself, which were never without vanity; but this most especially full of it, some stories of his amours and extraordinary abilities that way, which had once upon a time nearly killed him.

The extract provides a vivid little picture of the young English traveller, listening with bored respect to the middle-aged Ambassador's boastful tales of his sexual exploits. It also furnishes an appropriate background for the arrival at Moor Park of the elegant and mysterious *widow, as she always averred,* Mrs. Bridget Johnson,

20

who had *seen the world* and *known a more genteel walk in life.*

A couple of years after Sir William had warned young Mr. Hyde of the perils of Love, the Ambassador left Holland, refused the King's offer of a high office in England and returned to his country seat in Richmond. Within weeks of his return, in March, 1679, his much-loved little daughter died of small pox.[1]

Diana was the sixth of his children to die, and all Sir William's hopes and ambitions now centred on John, his sole remaining child. For a short time, Sir William represented Cambridge University in Parliament; after that he retired into private life, only leaving his country estate when forced out by such events as the Williamite invasion of England, or his son's tragic suicide. According to Lady Giffard, Sir William was :

Sensible extremely to good air and good smells, which gave him so great an aversion to Towne that he once passed five years at Sheen without seeing it.

The sensibility which made the stinks of the 17th Century London abhorrent to Sir William, did not hamper him in other ways, as shown by his own account of a dinner party he attended in Holland,

---

1. Shortly after her death in 1679, Sir William left his house in Richmond, Surrey, (where he had lived between his missions abroad since about 1654) and moved to Compton Hall, a small property which he renamed Moor Park, in memory of another Moor Park in Hertfordshire, where he had spent his honeymoon. The new Temple home stood close to the river Wey, about a mile from the pleasant Surrey town of Farnham. To-day, the ghostly tracings of the famous gardens, laid out by Sir William, are still faintly visible, and his heart in its silver case, lies, as he directed, beneath the central sundial. These gardens were the chief interest of his later years, and much of his enthusiasm and money must have been absorbed by them. Swift's lifelong devotion to gardening certainly began in the beautiful grounds of Moor Park, and his much loved "canal" at Laracor was a humble trickle from the imposing canal which reflected the glories of the Temple terraces.

Sir William made improvements in the early Seventeenth Century house, when he bought it from the Clarke family, but the impressive three-storied mansion which exists to-day would have been almost unrecognisable to Swift. The third storey, the imposing staircase, the fine bow-windows which add size and dignity to the otherwise modest reception-rooms, and various other major additions have changed the character and appearance of Moor Park. The house was progressively enlarged after Sir William's death, by succeeding owners, from the very modest mansion which Swift knew. Indeed, the various small houses on the estate must have been necessary to help to accommodate members of the Temple household, and the tradition that Mrs. Bridget Johnson and Stella lived in one is probably correct.

21

while he was *suffering from a great cold*. Each time he spat on the dining-room floor, he was greatly embarrassed because *a handsome wench that stood in the room with a clean cloth was presently down on the floor to wipe it up and scrub the boards clean. Someone speaking at table of my cold, I said the most trouble it gave me was to see the poor wench take so much trouble about it. My host told me it was well I escaped so lightly, and that if his wife were at home, even though I was an Ambassador she would have turned me out of door for fouling her house.*

How excessively house-proud could 17th Century Dutch ladies be! Sir William obviously considered so high a standard of hygiene absurd, else he would not have told the story.

But whatever his table manners, he was a highly cultured English gentleman, whose wide interests varied from Literature to Medicine. His fame as an author is established; less well known are his medical prescriptions. He strongly advocated :

. . . powdered centipedes, made up in little balls of fresh butter. I have never known it to fail of curing a sore throat; it must lie at the root of the tongue and melt down at leisure upon going to bed.

Sir William was also a man of resources; during *the Fanatic Times,* he produced a prayer, suitable for use by his politically divided household :

. . . when our servants were of so many different Sects, and I composed it that all might join in it.

And so an Ecumenical Service was contrived in which all the household — Episcopalians or Dissenters — might peacefully share.

So tactful a gentleman would doubtless cope with marital as well as theological problems with equal facility.

In April, 1689, the Temple family suffered a shattering blow. King William had appointed young John Temple his Secretary at War, partly, no doubt, because of the esteem in which the King held Sir William Temple. His future seemed assured; he had married a wealthy young Frenchwoman; he had two small daughters. A man, much trusted and recommended by John Temple, defected to the Jacobites in Ireland, and, for some reason, the young Secretary at War regarded this as an irredeemable personal disaster. Sir John Revesly reports in his *Travels and Memoirs:*

A very sad accident happened, which, for a while, was the dis-

course of the whole town. Mr. Temple, son to Sir William Temple
. . . . . a sedate and accomplished young gentleman, who had lately
by King William been made Secretary at War, took a pair of oars,
and drawing near the Bridge leapt into the Thames and drowned
himself, leaving a note behind him in the boat, to this effect : My
folly in undertaking what I could not perform, whereby some mis-
fortunes have befallen the King's service is the cause of my putting
myself to this sudden end. I wish him success in all his undertakings,
and a better servant.

Pennant, in his *Account of London* adds :

The unhappy suicide loaded his pockets with stones to destroy all
chance of safety : his father's false and profane reflection on the
occasion was "that a wise man might dispose of himself, and make
his life as short as he pleased".

There is something very moving in this picture of the heartbroken
father defending his dead son's right to his spectacular death,
against *the discourse of the whole town.* The distracted parents took
the young widow and her little daughters to Moor Park. The Crown
sympathetically refrained from confiscating the suicide's property,
as was its right, and the stricken Temples, in the words of Lady
Giffard :

. . . . all our hearts oppressed we returned with Sir William and
his desolate family to Moor Park.

Possibly it was Sir William's devoted sister, Lady Giffard, who
decided that her brother's despair at the loss of the last of his six
children might be lightened by the introduction to his house of the
pretty child, then living at nearby Richmond. Certainly, the
arrangements made for Mrs. Bridget Johnson's arrival at Moor Park
clearly show that little Esther was the pivot on which the situation
revolved. Her younger sister and brother — presumably the lawful
progeny of Mr. Johnson — were conveniently disposed of. Anne
was sent to be reared in London, where she subsequently married,
in July, 1700; Edward was probably fostered until old enough to be
put to school in Farnham. Later he was sent abroad, where he died
young. Only Esther arrived at Moor Park.

It has sometimes been suggested that the introduction of Esther
Johnson to the Temple household was solely due to Sir William's
love of the company of children; it should therefore be remembered

that her arrival at Moor Park coincided almost exactly with the introduction to the household of the widowed Mrs. Temple and her two small daughters. Two granddaughters would surely have been sufficient, if all that Sir William needed were children in his house.

Prior to the arrival of Bridget Johnson and her small daughter at Moor Park, nothing is known about her, not even her maiden name. There is no record of her marriage, nor of the death of her husband. Presumably she had lived at Richmond for at least eight years, as the Parish Register gives the dates of the baptisms of her three children :

> Esther Johnson — 20th March, 1681.
> Anne Johnson — 12th April, 1683.
> Edward Johnson — 8th July, 1688.

It will be noted that the correspondent of *The Gentleman's Magazine* had not seen the Richmond Register and has placed the children in wrong order.

Since Bridget Johnson was living in Richmond very shortly after Sir William's return there from Holland, it is at least possible that this handsome gentlewoman of *wide reading* and *charming conversation,* who *had seen the world* and *known a more genteel walk in life than her present situation* had enjoyed all these advantages in Sir William's ambassadorial establishment abroad. If so, it would be reasonable to suggest that, when she became pregnant in 1680, Sir William would have followed the royal example set by Charles II and accepted by many of his loyal subjects by providing a suitable husband for his mistress. And what more suitable than a man, who, it is stated, was master of a ship, trading with the Low Countries where Sir William had been ambassador for so many years? There is no record of the marriage, but the eldest child, Esther, was duly baptised in March, 1681, as *Johnson*.

Nothing is known for certain about this elusive man, but since the other two children — Anne born eighteen months after Esther, and Edward, seven years later — received no special favours from Sir William, it may be concluded that they were both the legitimate offspring of Bridget Johnson's husband. His faint ghost makes an occasional appearance as *Sir William Temple's steward,* which he certainly was not; as *a confidential servant of Sir William's,* for which there is not the slightest evidence; as *a cadet of a good old*

Nottinghamshire family, which has never been identified; and as *a distant relation of Lady Temple,* a wide shot into a very thick fog, by an optimistic biographer.

Lady Temple's reaction to the introduction of Mrs. Johnson and her child to Moor Park may account for her increasing absence in London. From about this time, she lived largely in her house in Pall Mall, where she could devote herself to Queen Mary, whose close friend she remained until the Queen's death in December, 1694. The establishment at Moor Park was taken over by Lady Giffard, who supervised her brother's household, as she had already done, on several previous occasions while he was on diplomatic service on the Continent, where she had accompanied him. When Lady Temple died shortly after her friend, the Queen, Lady Giffard remained at Moor Park, and looked after Sir William till his death.

Swift's account of Esther Johnson's parents would appear to be gratuitously insulting in his description of her witty, intelligent and fascinating mother. The uncalled for statement that Esther Johnson had *little to boast of her birth* can only be pardoned if Swift intended it as a rebuttal of current gossip that his dear friend, who had only died a few hours previously, was of ignobly noble birth.[2]

It is difficult to reconcile Swift's description of Bridget Johnson with that of the writer of the article in the *Gentleman's Magazine.* The statement that the Moor Park menage was the inspiration of the Rev. Mr. Pomfret's poem, *The Choice,* brings to mind Swift's curiously splenetic outburst against the author :

At a bookseller's shop some time ago, I saw a book with the title: "Poems by the Author of The Choice". Not enduring to read a dozen lines, I asked the company with me whether they had ever seen the book, or heard of the poem, whence the author denominated himself; they were all as ignorant as I. But I find it common with these small dealers in wit or learning to give themselves a title from their first adventure. This arises from that great importance which every man supposes himself to be of.

---

2. Swift had himself contributed to such gossip. It is impossible to disregard the statement of Dr. Delany that he had read a letter written to Sheridan by Swift, dated 2nd September, 1727, in which he stated that Esther Johnson was a relative of Sir William Temple.

When the Rev. Mr. Pomfret published *The Choice,* in 1700, he rocketed to fame overnight. The poem ran at once into a dozen editions.

Dr. Johnson has said : *Perhaps no poem in the English language has been so often perused as "The Choice".*

It is impossible to believe that Swift was unaware of the poem and its wide fame; it is reasonable to conclude that its subject had caused him annoyance, and that his contemptuous reference was the measure of that annoyance.[3]

The anonymous correspondent was evidently quite familiar with the personal appearances of Bridget Johnson, her daughter Esther and her son Edward, which are all described with some detail. Since the boy died young, the acquaintance evidently went back to their early days at Farnham. The writer apparently never saw Anne, who seems to have been sent by her mother *to be brought up in London.*

---

3. These circumstances give some interest to the poem, in which the author declares his ideal way of life.

> "Near some fair Town I'd have a private Seat
> Built uniform, not Little, nor too Great."

In these surroundings, Mr. Pomfret would have his household in the charge of "some kind Relation (for I'd have no wife.)"

> "— — — I'd choose
> Near some obliging modest Fair to live;
> For there's that Sweetness in a Female Mind
> Which in a Man's we cannot hope to find:
> That by a Secret but a pow'rful Art
> Winds up the Springs of Life, and does impart
> Fresh vital Heat to the transported Heart.
> I'd have her Reason all her Passions sway;
> Easy in Company in private gay,
> Coy to a Fop to the Deserving free,
> Still constant to herself and just to me . . .
> I'd have th' Expression of her thoughts be such
> She might not seem reserv'd nor talk too much . . .
> To this fair Creature I'd sometimes retire;
> Her Conversation would new Joys inspire,
> Give Life an Edge so Keen no surly Care
> Would venture to assault the soul or dare
> Near my Retreat to hide one secret Snare
> But so divine, so noble a Repast
> I'd seldom and with moderation taste,
> For highest Cordials all their Virtue loose
> By a too frequent and too bold a Use,
> And what wou'd cheer the Spirit in distress
> Ruines our Health, when taken to Excess."

In September, 1710, there is an entry in the *Journal,* from which it might be assumed that Swift had only then met Anne, for the first time :

This morning, Stella's sister came to me with a letter from Stella's mother, who is at Sheen — Your sister looked very well and seems a good, modest sort of girl ...

The information the correspondent of the *Gentleman's Magazine* gives about Anne's marriage to Filbey — whose family also came from Farnham — is corroborated by Swift, when he wrote to Stella in February 1712-13, reporting, somewhat contemptuously, that he was trying to get Filbey undeserved promotion in the Salt Office.

On the other hand, the article is wrong in stating that Stella left Moor Park before Sir William's death; but then the writer frankly confesses, *of this I am not positive.* Stella and Rebecca Dingley were certainly still at Moor Park when he died in January, 1699, and probably remained there until Swift persuaded them both to move to Ireland a couple of years later.

The detailed information about the insuperable obstacle to marriage between Swift and Stella was based on the widespread rumour — which may very well have originated in Farnham — that Swift, too, was a child of Sir William. In Denis Johnston's, *In search of Swift,* he has turned an acute legal mind to the problem of Swift's paternity, and has successfully proved that he was *not* the son of Sir William Temple; but he has produced a great deal of evidence that he *was* the son of Sir William's father, Sir John Temple, Master of the Rolls in Ireland.[4]

The relationship — uncle and niece — would have been a sufficient barrier to marriage, had it been contemplated. That question will be discussed later.

The minute description of Stella's appearance tallies with Swift's own constant allusions to his *Black Lady.* The reference to her teeth as being *beyond Comparison* was rather gruesomely verified in 1835, when the remains of the Dean and Stella were temporarily

---

4. For further evidence that an unacknowledged elder brother, Thomas Swift (buried in the Church of St. Andrew, Northborough, Northampton, England, on the 3rd December, 1737, as "brother of Jonathan Swift, Dean of St. Patrick's, Dublin") as well as Jane and Jonathan were all three children of Sir John Temple, see *Cadenus:* Sybil Le Brocquy, The Dolmen Press, Dublin.

disinterred in St. Patrick's Cathedral, Dublin, when work on the flooding river Poddle was in progress. Sir William Wilde reports the comment of someone who had handled the skull :

The teeth, which for their whiteness and regularity were in life, the theme of admiration were perhaps the most perfect ever witnessed in a skull.

The Gentleman's Magazine refers at length to the relationship between Swift and his sister, Jane Fenton. From her recently discovered will, it is obvious that she was not in straitened circumstances and that the annual allowance came, almost certainly, from the Temple estate and was merely paid through her brother, the Dean. Mrs. Fenton did not live with Mrs. Mayne, but with her stepchildren, Joseph Fenton's children by a previous marriage. With them, she died in Guilford, Surrey, England, in 1736.[5]

Bridget Johnson remained at Moor Park during Sir William's life. Her position in the menage is obscure. Very soon after her arrival, Sir William signed a document acknowledging his debt to her of £140. On this sum, she drew annual interest, and some years later she withdrew £20 of the capital. In Sir William's will, made in March 1694-5, he left :

. . . for legacy to Bridget Johnson, Ralph Mose, and Leonard Robinson £20 apiece, with half a year's wages to them and to all my other servants . . .

A codicil gave :

. . . another £100 to Mr. Jonathan Swift now dwelling with me.

Sir William was by no means a wealthy man, but one of the largest legacies was a property in Co. Wicklow, Ireland, which he left to Esther Johnson, *servant to my sister Giffard.* There is no mention whatever of the legacy being — as is often stated — a reward for her father's services as steward.

Bridget Johnson remained mysterious to the end. On the 25th October, 1711, she created further complications by marrying Ralph Mose, Sir William's steward, thereby starting the rumour that Stella's father had occupied that position. She also gave rise to much speculation as to why so fine a lady should have married such a man, a bare six months after the death of the first Mrs. Mose, the

---

5. See *Cadenus*, Sybil Le Brocquy, The Dolmen Press, Dublin.

Temple's cook. Bridget Johnson certainly did not spread the news of her marriage; at that time, Swift in London and Stella in Dublin were writing to each other almost daily, but there is not the smallest hint in the *Journal* that they knew anything of the marriage of Stella's mother.

From Lady Giffard's account book, it would seem that Swift's sister, Jane Fenton — who had left her unsatisfactory husband — replaced the new Mrs. Mose[6] in Lady Giffard's household. An entry records the arrival of *Fenton,* on the 11th September, 1711, and notes that her salary was £10 a year.

In a letter from her London house to Mrs. Temple at Moor Park, Lady Giffard wrote :

23rd July, 1715

Mrs. Mose has prevailed upon her husband to let her pass so many days here, once in three years; she could tell me no news from Moor Park, which would have made her more welcome.

Lady Giffard had already given over Moor Park to her nephew, John Temple, who would inherit it on her death, and Mr. Mose was still the steward there. Apparently, Mr. Mose did not easily allow his wife to leave him. Lady Giffard was probably anxious to have any available news of her late neighbour, the Duke of Ormond, who had escaped to France to throw in his lot with the exiled Stuarts, with a price of £5,000 on his ducal head. Meanwhile, his home, Richmond Lodge, had been confiscated and occupied by the Prince of Wales, which must have been a source of much gossip at the nearby Moor Park.

Lady Giffard remained on friendly terms with Stella's mother, until her death. In her will dated 1721 — that is ten years after Bridget Mose had left her employment—Lady Giffard bequeathed her :

. . . £20 with my largest silver saucepan, the bed in the largest room at Sheen with the largest chair of my own work.

She also acknowledged in her will that she owed £50 to Mrs. Mose, as well as £400 to Stella and £100 to Rebecca Dingley.[7]

6. The difficulty in distinguishing between the letters "r" and "s" in contemporary script has sometimes led to the confusing of Mose and More.
7. This £100 may well be the mysterious note which Swift gave to Rebecca Dingley in 1723, which she never spent, and which she eventually bequeathed to her executor, the Rev. John Lyon, many years later.

The article in the *Gentleman's Magazine* contains a great deal of information which is undoubtedly accurate. It was written by someone sufficiently sure of the facts to challenge contradiction by :

. . . any other persons, who are possessed of proper materials to throw a new light on these transactions, hitherto so extremely misrepresented.

The writer adds, provocatively :

. . . I think there are still some living, who have it in their power.

There were certainly friends and relatives alive in 1757, but no one came forward to challenge any of the statements made by C.M.P.G.N.S.T.N.S.

CHAPTER III

*I knew her from six years old and had some share in her educa-
tion, by directing what books she should read, and perpetually
instructing her in the principles of honour and virtue; from which
she never swerved in any one action or moment of her life.*

(On the Death of Mrs. Johnson)

Swift was always inaccurate about dates. When he first joined the
Temple household, in the Summer of 1689, the little girl was eight.
At the beginning of that year he had been forced to leave Trinity
College, Dublin, where he had been studying for a degree. The
struggle for the throne of England between James II and his Dutch
son-in-law had produced violent repercussions in the sister-kingdom
of Ireland. The Viceroy, Tyrconnell, had thrown in his lot with the
Catholic King, thereby causing well founded fears amongst the
Anglo-Irish, who were backing the Protestant Prince. By the end of
the year 1688, the only safety, for many Dublin citizens, lay in
England, and an exodus had begun, which became a panic flight as
the immediate result of a rumour.[1] To quote James Bonnell, who
was then Accountant-General of Ireland :

*Dublin: 9th December, 1688. Last Thursday, the Letter threaten-
ing a Massacre of all the English on this Day came to Town: and
People not receiving such Satisfaction from the Lord-Deputy as they
expected, began to think of England, and Multitudes flock'd away.
I went myself to Rings-end, thinking if there were any Alarm I was
nearer to take Shipping . . . Whilst I waited at Rings-end uncertain
in my Resolutions, I remembered a Verse of the first Lesson at last
Night's Prayers, which I then took notice of, but forgot in the Hurry
of going away . . . I thought, therefore, I would return and put
myself in His Hands.*

---

1. Many of the refugees halted their flight at Chester, and there was born Martha,
daughter of Swift's Uncle Adam. Long after, when she had been twice widowed,
Martha Whiteway played an important part in Swift's last years. Of her, the
Rev. Mr. Lyon noted:
*Mrs. Whiteway came from her own house at the other end of Dublin, three days of each
week to read and chat with him, after Stella's death, being ye principal female that frequented
his table for many years while his memory remained.*

31

Unlike thousands, whose faith was less serene and who crowded the sands of Ringsend, waiting for the rescuing ships, Mr. Bonnell's genuine sanctity kept him faithfully at his Dublin post; and it is pleasant to remember that, not only did he find safety there, but that he also earned the respect of the temporarily victorious Jacobites, who left him undisturbed in his high office.

Swift did not join the Dublin refugees in Chester. All his life, he cherished a fanatical belief in the value of walking, both as a physical and a financial panacea; he travelled on foot to Leicester, where his mother had been living since she had left Dublin and her infant son, some twenty years previously. It is doubtful whether Swift even knew his mother's appearance, when he arrived on her doorstep. He remained in Leicester long enough to alarm her by his flirtation with a local girl — an affair which had faint echoes some thirty years later. Perhaps his departure from Leicester was speeded because, as he related :

My prudent mother was afraid I should be in love; or perhaps because his *prudent* parent — herself existing on an annuity of £20 a year — decided that it was high time for her twenty-two year old son to earn some money. She certainly encouraged him to seek his fortune; and the words attributed to her, by Swift's biographer and cousin, Deane Swift, have a curiously fairy-story ring about them :

I really cannot tell in your present Circumstances what Advice to give you, but suppose you would apply yourself to Sir William Temple, who is both a good and a wise man? I cannot but think he would at least give you some Directions, and perhaps, if he were acquainted with your uncomfortable Situation, would recommend you to some kind of Employment either in Church or State. His Lady you know is a relation of ours, and besides his Father, Sir John Temple, had a Regard and Friendship for your Father, and for your Uncles until his last Hour. Go your Ways in the name of God to Sir William Temple and upon asking his Advice, you will immediately perceive what Encouragement or Preferment you are likely to expect from his Friendship.

This allegedly verbatim report of Abigail Swift's advice to her departing son first introduces the Temples into his story. Deane Swift, when writing his cousin's biography many years later, was much concerned with the social status of the Swift family, and even more concerned with the widespread rumours that the Great Dean wasn't a Swift at all, but the son of a Temple. His suggestion that Swift looked for Temple patronage because of a relationship with Lady Temple finds no outside corroboration. Swift, when writing his autobiography, makes no such claim — which he would have been extremely proud to do — but merely states that Sir John Temple, (Master of the Rolls in Ireland,) *had been a great Friend to the Family.*

Whatever be the correct version of Abigail Swift's parting words to her son, he certainly left Leicester and his first love behind him, and made his way, probably on foot, to the household of the *good and wise* Sir William, arriving there in the Summer of 1689.

Sir William's *Advice* to the young man is not recorded; nor is it known what hope of *Encouragement or Preferment* Swift was able to deduce from it, or from Sir William's *Friendship.* It is reasonable to believe that his services at Moor Park were not considered invaluable since, in less than a year, Sir William wrote to a friend, Sir Robert Southwell, who was just off to a warring Ireland, suggesting that he take young Swift with him. In the letter, Swift's position at Moor Park, was made very clear :

He has lived in my house, read to me, writ for me, and kept all accounts as far as my small occasions required. He has Latin and Greek, some French, writes a good and current hand, is very honest and diligent, and has good friends, though they have for the present lost their fortunes, in Ireland, and his whole family having been long known to me obliged me thus far to take care of him. If you please to take him into your service, either as a gentleman to wait on you, or as a clerk to write under you, and either to use him so if you like his service, or upon any establishment of the College, to recommend him to a fellowship there, which he has just pretence to, I shall acknowledge it as a great obligation to me as well as to him.

There is no suggestion here that Swift is any connection by marriage of the Temples; and his position at Moor Park appears to have been unimportant. Obviously, Sir William did not know anything about Swift's very unsatisfactory career as a student at Trinity College, when he suggested the possibility of his being appointed a Fellow, as soon as the deserted College was functioning again.

It is interesting to consult Swift's own account of this, his first stay at Moor Park:

He was received by Sir William Temple . . . where he continued about two years. For he happened, before twenty years old, by a surfeit of Fruit to contract a Giddiness and coldness of Stomach, that almost brought him to the Grave; and this Disorder pursued him, with Intermissions of two or three years, to the End of his Life. Upon this Occasion, he returned to Ireland, by advice of Physicians, who weakly imagined that his native Air might be of some use to revive his health.

As usual, Swift's dates are undependable; his first term of employment at Moor Park lasted less than a year. His stressing of his ill-health (to which Sir William had made no reference whatever, when recommending Swift's services to Sir Robert Southwell), gives the impression that he was using his illness as an excuse for the loss of his position at Moor Park.

In 1689, Swift went to Ireland, in Southwell's train. The latter had recently been appointed Secretary of State in attendance on the new King, during William III's Irish Campaign. Since nothing is known of Swift's career during those troubled days, it may be assumed that he took no part in the Campaign, and that he did not know of King William's narrow escape from death, on the eve of the Battle of the Boyne, when he was struck on the shoulder by a fragment of a cannonball. Indeed, the only faint echo of that fateful battle was the youthful Swift's eulogistic *Ode to King William on his successes in Ireland,* in which the poet pays this tribute to the victor of the Boyne:

> *Britannia stripp'd of her sole guard the laws,*
> *Ready to fall Rome's bloody sacrifice,*
> *You straight stepp'd in, and from the Monster's jaws*
> *Did bravely snatch the lovely, helpless prize . . .*

and Dean Swift's indignation, many years later, when the Duke of Schomberg's relatives refused to pay for a memorial to the gallant octogenarian General, who died on the banks of the Boyne.

All that is known with certainty about young Mr. Swift is that he did *not* become a Fellow of Trinity College, and that Sir Robert Southwell did not continue to employ him. Inside a year, he was back again at Moor Park for the second time. On his return journey, he once again visited his mother at Leicester and once again he alarmed her by embarking on yet another love-affair.

Swift's statement *that he had some share in her education,* is certainly an understatement. In a letter to his friend, Rev. James Stopford, he said of Stella :

This was a person of my own rearing and instructing from childhood.

He acted as her tutor, and to certain degree remained in that capacity for the rest of her life. Her handwriting so much resembled his as to be indistinguishable, and when she was a woman in her thirties, he was still correcting her misspellings and advising her on her reading.

There is a very wide divergence in the evidence about his position in the Temple household. His cousin and biographer, Deane Swift, asserts boldly :

It amounts to somewhat more than a bare moral impossibility that so great and wise a Statesman as Sir William Temple . . . should not immediately perceive what a Treasure was offered to his Friendship by this amazing and exalted young Genius, whose Abilities had been employed for seven Years in all the noblest Researches both of Greek and Roman Literature.

In contrast to that eulogy, Samuel Richardson wrote :

Mr. Temple, nephew of Sir William Temple . . . declared to a friend of mine, that Sir William hired Swift, at his first entrance into the world, to read to him, and sometimes to be his amanuensis, at the rate of £20 a year, which was then high preferment to him; but that Sir William never favoured him with his conversation, because of his ill-qualities, nor allowed him to sit down at table with him.

Probably, the truth lies somewhere between Deane Swift's picture of Sir William, sunning himself in the brilliance of *this amazing and exalted young Genius* and Richardson's account of Sir William refusing to speak to one . . . *whose bitterness, satire and moroseness made him insufferable to his equals and inferiors and unsafe for his superiors to countenance.*

The last description fits, only too exactly, the unhappy, frustrated man of whom the humiliated boy in Moor Park was to become the father.

It is probable that Swift may have been on a very different footing at Moor Park, when, at Sir William's invitation, he returned there for the third and last period and so there may have been a certain amount of truth in *both* descriptions of his position in the household. Many years later, when the Dean was addressing the Butler in his *Directions to Servants,* he included this very revealing paragraph :

If a humble companion, a chaplain, a tutor or a dependent cousin happen to be at table, whom you find to be little regarded by the master and company (which nobody is readier to discover and observe than we servants,) it must be the business of you and the footman to follow the example of your betters, by treating him many degrees worse than any of the rest; and you cannot please your master better, or at least your lady.

Here is assembled the entire *dramatis personae* of the Moor Park comedy :

The Humble Companion	Esther Johnson
The Chaplain	
The Tutor	Jonathan Swift
The Dependent Cousin	Rebecca Dingley
The Master	Sir William Temple
The Lady	Lady Giffard

So autobiographical does Swift become that he first inadvertently includes himself amongst the servants, and then, dropping the other victims, becomes the sole object of the menials' spite, with the occasional ill-will of Sir William Temple and the constant malice of Lady Giffard to contend with.

When Swift stressed his instructions of Stella in all *the principles of honour and virtue, from which she never swerved in any one action or moment of her life,* it rang out like a challenge to those who had dared to question the dead woman's truth or chastity. There is evidence that Dublin gossip buzzed loudly about a young orphan boy, Bryan M'Loghlin, whom Stella had adopted some years before her death, and to whom she left a legacy in her will.[2]

---

2. See "*Cadenus*": Sybil Le Brocquy, Dolmen Press, Dublin.

CHAPTER IV

She was sickly from her childhood until about the age of fifteen; but then grew into perfect health and was looked upon as one of the most beautiful, graceful and agreeable young women in London, only a little too fat. Her hair was blacker than a raven and every feature of her face in perfection. She lived, generally, in the country, with a family where she contracted an intimate friendship with another lady of more advanced years.

(On the Death of Mrs. Johnson)

Esther Johnson had some very serious illness in her early girlhood, and presumably Swift was referring to it when he wrote in the *Journal* in 1711 :

The Nurse asked me whether I thought it possible that he (Sir Andrew Fontaine) *could live, for the doctors said not. I said I believed that he would live; for I found the seeds of life in him, which I observe seldom fail. And I found them in poor dearest Stella, when she was ill many years ago.*

Whether Stella made a complete recovery from that illness or not, she was certainly in a delicate state, during the years (September, 1710—June, 1713) covered by the *Journal*. In it Swift constantly enquired for, and sympathised with her acute eye-trouble, blinding headaches and severe pain and numbing in her neck and shoulders. She was a complete invalid for several years before her death, and her extreme emaciation must have provided a painful reminder to Swift of the far-away days when she was *a little too fat.*

Swift's allusion to her fame as a London beauty is interesting. The girl had grown up in the Temple household in Surrey, sharing the quiet life of a country family, which, presumably, avoided London, as did Sir William for years on end. It is true that he owned a town house in Pall Mall, close by the present Marlborough House, and, after Lady Temple's death, the Moor Park household may well have made occasional prolonged visits to the capital, on business or pleasure. But it is difficult to picture young Stella as an acknowledged London Toast, in a society where competition amongst beauties was extremely keen.

One such lengthy stay may probably have taken place after the

Peace of Ryswyck, when King William's triumphant return to London from the Continent was made an occasion of public rejoicings. Sir William and Lady Giffard may well have decided to come to town to take part in the celebrations, which ranged from bonfires and fireworks to the first public service in St. Paul's Cathedral since it had been rebuilt, after the Great Fire.

A very early letter from Swift was written from Moor Park, and according to Deane Swift, was addressed to his sister, Jane, who was a temporary member of the Temple household in London. Swift, apparently, had been left behind, with Mr. Mose, the steward, the cook — presumably Mrs. Mose — and a skeleton staff.

I received your kind letter from Robert, by word of mouth, and think it a vast condescention in you to think of us, in your greatness; now we shall hear nothing from you for five months but "We courtiers". Loory is well and presents his humble duty to my Lady, and love to his fellow servants : but he is the miserablest creature in the world; eternally in his melancholy note, whatever I do; and if his finger do but ake, I am in such a fright you would wonder at it. I pray return my service to Mrs. Kilby in payment of hers by Robert.

Nothing grows better by your absence but my Lady's chamber-floor, and Tumble-down-Dick. Here are three letters for you, and Molly will not send one of them; she says you ordered her to the contrary. Mr. Mose and I desire you will remember our love to the King, and let us know how he looks.

Robert says the Czar is there, and is fallen in love with you and designs to carry you to Muscovy; pray provide yourself with muffs and sable tippets etc.

Aeolus has made a strange revolution in the rooks' nests; but I say no more, for it is dangerous to meddle with things above us.

I desire your absence heartily; for now I live in great state, and the cook comes in to know what I please to have for dinner; I ask, very gravely, what is in the house, and accordingly give orders for a dish of pigeons, or etc. You shall have no more ale here, unless you send us a letter. Here is a great bundle, and a letter for you; both came together from London. We keep home like so many cats.

The letter is dated 1696, which means that it was written shortly after Swift returned to Moor Park, for his last period in Temple's service. He had left Sir William's household, for reasons unspecified, in May, 1694. Some months later, having found that it was impossible to be ordained without a certificate of good character from his last employer, he wrote a letter to Sir William . . . a letter which was afterwards endorsed by one of Temple's relations, "Swift's penitential letter" . . .

I entreat your Honour . . . to send me some certificate of my behaviour during almost three years in your family, wherein I shall stand in need of your goodness to excuse my many weaknesses and follies and oversights, much more to say anything to my advantage. The particulars expected of me are what relate to morals and learning, and the reasons of quitting your Honour's family; that is, whether the last was occasioned by any ill actions. They are all entirely left to your Honour's mercy, though in the first I think I cannot reproach myself any farther than for infirmities. This is all I dare beg at present from your Honour . . . .

What were the moral "infirmities" in Swift's life in Moor Park, which he feared might deprive him of Sir William's testimonial of good conduct is not known. Sir William certainly relented; sent him the recommendation required by Archbishop Marsh, and Swift was ordained in Dublin, in January, 1695. He was given a living in Northern Ireland, where he found himself surrounded by Dissenters, whom he always loathed.

But he beguiled his time by falling in love, once again. This time his object was a highly suitable young lady, daughter of Archdeacon Waring, and he did his utmost to persuade her to marry him. *Varina,* as he called her, was reluctant to risk marriage with so poor a suitor, in spite of Swift's passionately eloquent letters. Nevertheless, when he was invited by Sir William to return to Moor Park, *Varina* was still unofficially engaged to the Rev. Jonathan Swift.

Although this letter is dated 1696, the allusion to Peter the Great's spectacular visit to England would appear to place it in 1698, unless, of course, the mistake is caused by Swift's delight in nicknames. The *Czar* may not necessarily mean the ruler of Russia, since *Tumble-down-Dick* certainly does not mean the late Lord-Protector, Richard Cromwell. All Swift's life he played with words; nicknames for his friends and enemies, puns in Latin and English and Greek, anagrams, secret codes and riddles. He wove mysteries so assiduously that, when writing his account of Stella, presumably for eventual circulation amongst her closest friends, he could not bring himself to name the family with whom she had spent most of her life, nor to state that the friend, *with whom she contracted an intimate friendship,* was the Temple's cousin, Rebecca Dingley.

It would seem that, when Swift wrote this letter (in reply to verbal greetings brought him by Robert from the Temple household in London), Lady Giffard and Sir William were again moving in Court circles. The widowed King had been intimate with them both in Holland, and they had fostered the scheme for his marriage with the Princess Mary. It is quite likely that the young women of the Temple ménage would have been welcomed into the Palace precincts and may have joined the curious crowds, which daily watched the King dine. Hence, perhaps, Swift's facetious remarks about *we courtiers,* and the risks of being carried off by the Czar.

The Canaletto pictures of London, painted some thirty years later than the visit of the Temple household, give a good idea of the great palaces of the nobility, the magnificent public buildings, the fine houses of the citizens and the charming rural scenery of Whitehall and the unbanked river. As late as May 1711, Swift tells Stella that *we are mowing already and haymaking, in Chelsea, and it smells so sweet as we walk through the flowery meads.* But he goes on to complain :

The haymaking nymphs are perfect drabs, nothing so clean and pretty as farther in the country.

The Canaletto pictures give no inkling of the filth and squalor which made the capital intolerable to Sir William Temple — and to King William. The Fleet river — known as the Ditch — had long been degraded into a foul sewer, into which the local citizens threw every form of refuse, exactly as their mediaeval ancestors had done before them. Later, it was to be celebrated by Pope :

> *Fleet Ditch, with disemboguing streams*
> *Rolls the large tribute of dead dogs to Thames*
> *The King of Dykes! Than whom no sluice of mud*
> *With deeper sable blots the silver flood . . .*

The disemboguing streams carried their grim quotas from the multitude of knackers'-yards, slaughter-houses, tanneries and fishmongers, to combine with a city's sewage and make the Thames an offence to nose and eye. The direction of the wind was a matter of deep concern to the inhabitants of the various London districts. After a very short experience of life in the Palace of Whitehall, King William hastily removed himself and his asthma to the purer air of Kensington.

It is astounding to remember that, for many a long year afterwards, the Thames continued to supply most of London's drinking-water. Since the entire population did not perish in one enormous epidemic, it would seem as if modern science perhaps exaggerates the importance of a pure water supply![1]

Swift, who was far beyond most of his contemporaries in his standards of personal cleanliness, records various bathes he had enjoyed in the murky, sewage-laden water of the Thames.

About the end of the Seventeenth Century, when the Temple household were visiting London, a Frenchman, M. de Misson, published a book, for the benefit of his fellow-countrymen, because, as he says:

England is a very famous country, but extremely little has been written about it.

He describes at length the magnificence of the great Hall of Westminster, where, some years previously, he had seen the splendid Coronation Banquet of the new sovereigns, William and Mary; he justifies the enormous trouble and expense incurred, centuries earlier, by Richard II, in bringing the oaken beams from Ireland, because it was recognised that any wood grown in that country was immune to spiders and other noxious insects — an extension of his power of banning snakes which St. Patrick never anticipated! He pictures the glories of Whitehall, built by James I and sanctified by the blood of his son, *Saint Charles the Martyr;* he describes the great Abbey of Westminster, where he had seen the Coronation of the new King and Queen — and her burial. He had been present at

---

1. The river reached its peak of horror in the Summer of 1858, when London suffered what was known as *The Great Stink*. On that occasion, the unfortunate citizens were almost suffocated by the noxious fumes which poisoned the atmosphere to such an extent that the window-curtains of the Houses of Parliament had to be kept soaked in chloride of lime, to enable the Members to breathe! For a supply of clean drinking water, London had to wait until well into the Nineteenth Century.

Hampton Court where, shortly before his death at the Battle of the Boyne, the Rev. Dr. Walker, defender of Derry, had received the grateful thanks of his Sovereigns, together with a £5,000 reward. He eulogises many of the London services, including the *Penny Post*, by which letters were safely delivered twice daily, as far as the suburbs; he describes London's glory, *The Bridge* — surprisingly the only one which spanned the Thames until nearly fifty years later. The ancient structure provided not only a street, lined with fine, lofty houses, but also a disused Chapel and a large variety of shops, while the *Might and Majesty of the Law* was afforded wide publicity by the grim rows of heads decaying above its towered gate. M. de Misson explains to his French readers the curious English habit of using coal as a fuel, and describes at length the method of lighting a coal fire; he admits that, once alight, it provides warmth, but he laments the smoke and sulphurous smells it caused in the streets, just as John Evelyn had lamented, thirty years earlier, when the newly restored Charles II attempted, vainly, to deal with the London *Smog*. De Misson methodically lists the lusty amusements of the city crowds — that *mobile,* whose corruption to *mob* Swift so angrily resented; the bull and bear-baiting, the cock-fighting, the pelting of the pilloried, the eager thronging to Tyburn gallows to compare the varying standards of criminal oratory, courage and costume. The nobility and gentry, while not above sharing these simple pleasures, added the excitements of duelling, of staking fortunes on the gambling tables of the Court and the Club, and of abducting heiresses when financial crises arose. For the *élite,* there were the amusements and tediums of the Court, and they shared the news and gossip of the Coffee-houses with the less distinguished strata of society. Beneath the social stream ran a strong political current, which could very easily trap and carry to destruction the unwary adventurer. Jacobite supporters of the exiled Stuarts might well distress their friends by the sight of their spiked heads and mangled quarters at Temple Bar or London Bridge.

Towards the end of the Seventeenth Century, *the Toasts*,[2] (as the

---

2. The use of the word *Toast* to describe an accepted beauty is believed to be derived from an episode in the reign of Charles II, when it was customary to put a piece of well-toasted bread in the winecup to add flavour to the wine.

fashionable beauties were known) were critically appraised in Court and Club; it is difficult to accept Swift's statement that Stella was *looked upon as one of the most beautiful, graceful and agreeable young women in London,* except perhaps by Dr. Swift — who was still unofficially betrothed to Miss Waring of Belfast.

A celebrated beauty is said to have been taking the cure in the Roman baths, in Bath, watched by a circle of fashionable admirers, one of whom, with excessive gallantry, took a glass of the bath-water to drink the fair lady's health. Another gentleman, not to be outdone, *offered to jump in, saying that though he liked not the Liquor, he would have the Toast.* His less wine-fuddled friends restrained the impetuous admirer, but, later, when they drank the Lady's health, they called her *The Toast*, and the custom soon became widespread.

CHAPTER V

"I was then, to my mortification, settled in Ireland; and about a year after, going to visit my friends in England, I found she was a little uneasy upon the death of a person, upon whom she had some dependence. Her fortune at that time was in all not above £1,500; the interest upon which was a scanty maintenance in so dear a country, for one of her spirit. Under this consideration and, indeed, very much for my own satisfaction who had few friends or acquaintances in Ireland, I prevailed upon her and her dear friend and companion, the other lady, to draw what money they had into Ireland, a great part of their fortune being in annuities upon funds. Money was then ten per cent in Ireland, besides the advantage of returning it and all necessaries of life at half price. They complied with my advice and soon after came over; but I happened to continue some time longer in England, they were much discouraged to live in Dublin, where they were wholly strangers. She was at that time about nineteen years old, and her person was soon distinguished. But the adventure looked so like a frolic, the censure held for some time, as if there were a secret history in such a removal; which, however, soon blew off by her excellent conduct. She came over with her friend in the year . . . and they both lived together until this day when death removed her from us.

(On the Death of Mrs. Johnson)

When Sir William Temple, *the person upon whom she had some dependence,* died in January, 1699, Swift made a note in his diary :
He dyed at 1 o'clock in the morning, and with him all that was great and good among men.

Later, he expanded his sentiments into an even more extravagant statement :
He was a person of the greatest wisdom, justice, liberality, politeness and eloquence of his age and nation; the truest lover of his country, and one that deserved more from it, by his eminent public services, than any man before or since; besides his great deserving by the commonwealth of learning; having been esteemed the most accomplished writer of his time.

It is tempting to speculate why Swift should have made such

45

extravagant claims for the dead man, claims which Swift would have been quick to describe as fulsome and absurd, had they been written by another hand. Circumstances probably provide the answer. The recent death of Sir William was a catastrophe for the little dependent group at Moor Park; he was the sun around which the comfortable regularity of their lives revolved — his fine mansion with its woodlands and river-stretch, his gardens that won Evelyn's praise and where Temple willed his heart to lie, these offered shelter and stability. His death threatened to disrupt that good life unless his heartbroken sister, who had inherited a life-tenancy of Moor Park, should piously decide to keep everything unaltered, as Sir William had left it. The eulogy of her adored brother was probably intended, in the first place, for the eye and heart of Lady Giffard. It was not unreasonable for Swift to hope that the household would continue its pleasant routine; Sir William, in his will, had appointed him editor of his papers, and where could that work be done as suitably and conveniently as in Sir William's library, at Moor Park?

Swift had never liked Lady Giffard, who was a woman of strong character. As editor of Sir William's papers, he incurred her blazing enmity, by publishing documents which she considered hurtful to her friends.[1]

Undoubtedly, Lady Giffard and Lady Giffard's good-will were of paramount importance at Moor Park immediately after her brother's death, and the household must have hung in anxious anticipation of her intentions. When she made it clear that she did not intend to maintain Moor Park indefinitely; in fact, that she proposed eventually handing over the estate to her nephew, John Temple (who would, in any case, inherit it on her death), all hope vanished. Swift only remained there long enough to help in winding up Sir William's affairs — paying the funeral expenses, listing the debts — before he left Moor Park, his home for so many years, for the last time. The Rev. Dr. Swift hurried to London with his legacy of £100, and urgently sought a living.

---

1. One of these friends was the Duchess of Somerset, (a favourite of Queen Anne), who wrote to Lady Giffard:
Dr. Swift . . . is a man of noe principle, neither of honour nor religion.
Many years later, the Duchess and Swift were still carrying on a fierce vendetta, and her influence may well have deprived him of his life's ambition, an English bishopric.

According to Swift, King William had once promised Sir William Temple that he would provide Swift with a Prebendary in Canterbury or in Westminster. Swift hopefully sent a petition to the King, but it remained either undelivered or unacknowledged, and royal promises proved as unreliable as less exalted pledges. By the summer of 1699, Swift was glad to accept the chaplaincy from the Earl of Berkeley, recently appointed a Lord Justice. Reluctantly, Swift accompanied the new ruler back again to Dublin. After Swift had served the Earl there as chaplain for some months, he failed in his efforts to become Dean of Derry, and had to be content with a poor living in Co. Meath. In the Spring of 1701, he returned with the Earl to England, and it seems very likely that he then *went to visit my friends in England, and found she was a little uneasy upon the death of a person upon whom she had some dependence.*

Life for Stella may well have become very different, now that Sir William had been dead a couple of years, and his sister ruled Moor Park in his stead. All that is certain is that both Stella and Rebecca Dingley were quite prepared to face the difficulties and dangers of emigrating to Ireland (which was still in a very disturbed state), when Swift suggested it. While it is possible that the ladies' decision was influenced by the high rate of interest, as he relates, it is very much more likely that Stella was willing to overlook the disadvantages of leaving her native country in the hope of sharing the life of Jonathan Swift.

The article in *The Gentleman's Magazine* states that some person, who knew the secret of their common Temple blood, was forced to disclose their true relationship — one which forever barred marriage between them as criminal. It also states that this disclosure was necessary because, on some unspecified date, a secret marriage had actually taken place. Such a story may very well have originated in Farnham, when their mutual friends and acquaintances had exhausted every other possible explanation of the continued celibacy of Swift and Stella. Only some such insuperable barrier, Farnham may well have argued, could possibly have kept them apart, since Stella made no secret of her devotion, and Swift openly displayed his warm affection for the girl.

It is reasonable to believe that Swift would not have persuaded Stella to leave England, unless he had intended to marry her, in the more or less immediate future. That he was extremely fond of her no one can doubt who has read the *Journal to Stella;* a warm, amused, semi-tutorial affection is evident in almost every line. She was a highly intelligent girl, whose mind he had moulded from childhood, a girl, moreover, who for years had shared his interests, his friends, his intimate surroundings. With her, he could be on an easy footing; she knew his every mood. She was handsome[2] and well-bred — on this Swift and the correspondent of *the Gentleman's Magazine* agree. Thanks to Sir William Temple's legacy, she now possessed a fortune fully competent for a clergyman's wife. In Swift's eyes, she must have appeared an ideal choice, after his two embarrassing experiences with the Leicestershire girls and his recent unsuccessful suit of *Varina.*

It is significant, too, that about this time rumours had reached Miss Waring that she had a rival in Swift's affections. In May, 1700, he wrote her a letter, in reply to one from her which no longer exists. She had made some allusion, it would seem, to a very cool letter Swift had written to her :

The other thing you would know is whether this change of style be owing to thoughts of a new mistress. I declare, upon the word of a Christian and a gentleman it is not.

Incidentally, this last existing letter to *Varina* ended Swift's connection with Miss Waring with a brutal frankness seldom exceeded.

It is unreasonable to believe that Swift had given up all thoughts of matrimony in 1701; it is impossible to imagine a situation in which, having brought his dear friend, Stella, to live beside him in Dublin, he could have married any other girl. The question naturally arises, why then did he not marry Stella, shortly after her arrival? Swift admits that her presence there, even with Rebecca Dingley's chaperonage, caused a minor scandal in Dublin. He attributes that to the fact that he, himself, had to remain in England, for some time after the Ladies reached Dublin, where they were *wholly strangers.* Swift curiously does not remember the date of

---

2. With the exception of a sketch done by her friend Archdeacon Parnell, there is no portrait of Stella, which can be identified as authentic. Paintings have been indiscriminately labelled *Stella,* or *Vanessa,* the unfortunate rival for Swift's later love.

their uprooting, but it seems likely that they arrived in Ireland in the early summer of 1701 — perhaps in time for the Civic junketings which accompanied the erection of a statue of William III in College Green.

Swift says that Stella was *about nineteen;* in that summer, she would have been about twenty. In the spring of that year, Swift had accompanied the Earl of Berkeley back to England, and Swift's return to Dublin had been delayed until the autumn. Meanwhile, the presence in Dublin of two unknown young Englishwomen was, according to Swift, regarded there as a *frolic,* which was frowned upon by Dublin society and caused *a censure,* which was only removed, after some time, by the *excellent conduct* of Stella and Rebecca Dingley.

One interesting question is provoked by that journey. In the early days of the Eighteenth Century — and indeed very much later — the journey from Surrey to Ireland was both difficult and dangerous. Travel by stage-coach was liable to all kinds of perils, including highway robbery; wayside inns offered the most primitive lodgings, and, for unescorted young gentlewomen, the sleeping accommodation would — at best — be highly embarrassing. The long sea-journey, from Chester or Holyhead daunted much more experienced travellers than Stella and her companion, who had probably never set foot on a sailing boat before, but who would certainly have heard of the constant dangers and shipwrecks in the Irish Sea.

It is difficult to believe that the ladies, accustomed to the dignified comfort and security of life at Moor Park, would ever have dared to make such a journey unescorted.

Another puzzle arises. Why were the young women *wholly strangers* in Dublin? The city was full of prosperous Swifts, with their numerous families and friends; Jonathan Swift himself had, up to very recently, been acting as Chaplain at the Viceregal Court, and must have had plenty of friends and acquaintances in Dublin, where he had previously spent many years in the University. Surely, a few letters from him would have been sufficient to open many Dublin doors to the friendless and suspect Ladies?

CHAPTER VI

For some years past, she had been visited with continual ill health;
and several times, within these last two years, her life was despaired
of. But, for this twelve month past, she never had a day's health,
and properly speaking, she has been dying six months but kept alive,
almost against nature, by the generous kindness of two physicians,
and the care of her friends.
(Thus far I writ the same night, between eleven and twelve).
(On the Death of Mrs. Johnson)

Stella's health seems never to have been good, but beyond Swift's
allusion to her early critical illness, little information is available as to
the cause of her ill-health. In early passages of the *Journal*, there
are several mentions of *Palsy Water*, which Stella's mother sent her;
but *Palsy*, in the Eighteenth Century, was an indefinite term. Some
authorities have assumed that she suffered from asthma; she certainly was the victim of devastating headaches, eye-trouble and
acute neuritis, which would account for the symptoms mentioned
by Swift in the *Journal*. She shared the current belief that healing
was to be found in the waters of the fashionable Spas; she and
Rebecca Dingley visited several in Ireland and sometimes discussed
the advisability of going to *The Bath*, then the Mecca of the English
invalid.

The physicians, who attended her so generously and devotedly,
were probably Dr. Helsham and Dr. James Grattan, both members
of Swift's circle. Mrs. Whiteway has stated that Stella and her
friend spent the last months of her life in Lady Eustace's house,
Harbour Hill, near the Phoenix Park.

A few weeks before her death, Stella made her will. She left the
interest on the bulk of her small fortune to her mother and sister for
their lives, the capital to revert to Dr. Steeven's Hospital, Dublin, for
the support of a chaplain. To Swift, she left a strong-box and all
her papers. He was not one of her executors. The most curious
legacy has been unnoticed :

I bequeath to Bryan M'Loghlin (a child who now lives with me
and whom I keep on charity) twenty-five pounds, to bind him out
apprentice as my executors and the survivor of them shall think fit.

51

In 1727, £25 was a fairly considerable sum of money. (Swift's mother was said to have lived comfortably on an annuity of £20 in her widowhood.) The fee then paid for apprenticing a boy, by a Dublin parish school, was £3 *and a suit of clothes*. The boy, Bryan, had been living for some time in Stella's household, as is proved by the humorous prologue to a poem Swift wrote on the death of one of Mrs. Dingley's numerous lap-dogs. It runs :

> *Elegy upon Tyger,*
> *Her dear Lady's joy and comfort*
> *Who departed this Life*
> *The last day of March 1727*
> *To the great joy of Bryan*
> *That his antagonist is gone.*

It is distinctly odd that Stella, who had been in dire ill-health for several years, should have taken a young boy into her household; and there is an accretion of evidence that Bryan may have been the son of the Dean and the unhappy Vanessa, who had died a few years previously.[1] It is perfectly in keeping with the courageous, upright character of Stella that she would have taken charge of this child, after his mother's death, in spite of the danger of scandal. It is also likely that the insertion of the curious phrase *whom I keep on charity*, was a last effort of defence against the current slander that Bryan was her own child by Swift.

Here, the Dean of St. Patrick's, having written some six hundred words laid down his weary pen, on the night of Stella's death . . .

Thus far I writ between eleven and twelve.

---

1. See "*Cadenus*", Sybil Le Brocquy, Dolmen Press. 1963.

CHAPTER VII

29th January

Never was any of her sex born with better gifts of the mind, or who so improved them by reading and conversation. Yet her memory was not of the best, and was impaired in the latter years of her life. But I cannot call to mind that I ever once heard her make a wrong judgment of persons, books or affairs. Her advice was always the best, and with the greatest freedom mixed with the greatest decency. She had a gracefulness, somewhat more than human, in every motion, word and action. Never was so happy a conjunction of civility, freedom, easiness and sincerity. There seemed to be a combination among all who knew her to treat her with a dignity much beyond her rank. Yet people of all sorts were never more easy, than in her company. Mr. Addison, when he was in Ireland, being introduced to her immediately found her out; and if he had not soon after left the Kingdom, assured me he would have used all endeavours to cultivate her friendship. A rude and conceited coxcomb passed his time very ill upon the least breach of respect: for in such a case she had no mercy but was sure to expose him to the contempt of the passersby; yet in such a manner as he was ashamed to complain, and durst not resent. All of us who had the happiness of her friendship agreed unanimously that, in an afternoon or evening's conversation, she never failed before we parted of delivering the best thing that was said in the company. Some of us have written down several of her sayings, or what the French call 'bons mots', wherein she excelled beyond belief. She never mistook the understanding of others; nor ever said a severe word, but where a much severer was deserved. Her servants loved and almost adored her at the same time. She would upon occasions treat them with freedom; yet her demeanour was so awful that they durst not fail in the least point of respect. She chid them seldom, but it was with severity which had an effect upon them for a long time after. (My head aches and I can write no more).

(On the Death of Mrs. Johnson)

When the Dean continued to write his memories of Stella, the day after her death, he dealt with her social life in Dublin and her position in the circle of their mutual friends. This is of interest, since it may be reasonably assumed that he had been visiting the house where she lay dead; that he had met and talked to her closest friends, and that to a large extent, he is repeating what they had said to him about the dead lady, and certainly what *he* had said to *them*.

When he records Addison's opinion of Stella's worth, it is because one section of Swift's mind had never entirely divorced itself from his early reverence for *the Great,* no matter how much he disclaimed this weakness. Addison had long ceased to be his dear friend; the rasp of English politics had broken the tie between them. Nevertheless in Swift's mind, Addison's testimony carried weight, although his acquaintance with Stella can only have been extremely slight. His stay in Ireland had been very short, after he accompanied the Lord Lieutenant, Lord Wharton, as Chief Secretary to Dublin. Addison did most of his work at his London office, a procedure which was quite normal at that period, when neither the Lord-Lieutenant nor other high officers of the Irish Establishment spent much time in Ireland. Since Addison was perfectly aware of the close friendship between Stella and the Dean, he would certainly have lauded her and regretted the lost opportunity of getting to know her better. The significant fact is that Swift, after some twenty years, should bother to record Addison's opinion.

That Stella could be merciless where she disliked is illustrated by some of the *Bons Mots,* so carefully, and presumably admiringly, recorded by Swift :

A Lady of my intimate acquaintance both in England and Ireland in which Kingdom she lived from the eighteenth year of her age twenty six years, had the most and finest accomplishments of any person I ever knew, of either sex . . . A gentleman who had been very silly and pert in her company, at last began to grieve at remembering the loss of a child, lately dead . . . A bishop sitting by comforted him, that he should be easy, because the child had gone to Heaven. "No, my Lord", said she, "that it is which grieves him, because he is sure never to see his child there"!

This picture of a man, attempting to cover his grief for his child's loss with a froth of folly, and his poor pretence being speared by Stella's theological wit, is not an attractive one. Nor, indeed is another specimen of her *Bons Mots* :

A very dirty clergyman of her acquaintance, who affected smart-ness and repartees, was asked by some of the company how his nails came to be so dirty. He was at a loss, but she solved the difficulty by saying "The Doctor's nails grew dirty by scratching himself".

Swift's obvious appreciation of the last anecdote lends some creditability to the otherwise incredible story, told by Theophilus Swift, about the *trial* of the wretched Dr. Sheridan, which the Dean is said to have organised at a houseparty in Co. Meath.[1]

Swift very markedly includes himself amongst *those who had the happiness of her friendship.* That he should do so at such a solemn moment should have been enough to silence for ever the suggestion that the Dean and Stella were, in reality, secretly married. Even had people been prepared to doubt Swift's honesty, nothing in Stella's character suggested that she would have been capable of carrying such a deceit to the verge of her grave. Shortly before her death she made her will; dying, she signed it *Esther Johnson: Spinster.*

Stella had a large circle of friends, who treated her with a dignity *much beyond her rank.* One reason for that may have been that her companion-chaperone, Rebecca Dingley, *was* a close relative of the Temple family. It was a curious situation where a member of that proud, noble family was content to act, in such a capacity, to the ostensible daughter of a sea-captain and a waiting-woman. The Dublin friends probably drew their own conclusions, and *conspired* to treat Stella as a Temple.

Mrs. Dingley (to give that spinster lady her honorary Eighteenth Century title), was the Martha of the household where Stella shone. She appears to have been a good-natured, fussy, absent-minded creature. Swift wrote a verse for her birthday in 1726 :

> *. . . Then who says care will kill a cat?*
> *Rebecca shews they're out in that.*
> *For she, tho' overrun with care*
> *Continues healthy, fat and fair.*

Together, the Ladies went the rounds of their card-playing orange-toasting, claret-drinking Dublin friends. Their entertain-ments figure large in the *Journal.* The gossip and the fun at the

---

1. See Swiftiana; Vol. II (Richard Phillips 1804).

various houses give Swift the contrast to his own more serious and socially-elevated London rounds. Together Stella and Dingley visited the Stoytes at their imposing Castle at Donnybrook; Dean Sterne, whose dinners were better than his wine; Swift's cousins, the Swantons; the Walls; the Grattans; the Jacksons. Everywhere, they played cards. Swift poked fun at their social round, magnifying their card losses and the endless gossip of the ladies. Together they paid country visits, which Mrs. Dingley heartily disliked. They went as far as Trim, and to stay with the Raymonds; they spent months at Wood Park, a fine mansion near Dublin, where life was luxurious. They also spent months at Dr. Sheridan's country house in Cavan, which was most uncomfortable.[2]

The Rev. Thomas Sheridan was a devoted friend to Stella. She must have had confidence in that odd, irresponsible character since she appointed him an executor of her will. During her long illness, he was constantly at her side and he attended her on her death-bed. Stella was fond of *the merry little grig, good natured but silly,* as a fellow-clergyman described him. Swift on the other hand, when in a good humour, treated the little clergyman as a Prince might a favourite Jester. In his evil moods, he made Sheridan the butt of his savage wit. Although Swift undoubtedly used his influence on many occasions on Sheridan's behalf, yet there was always an atmosphere, at best of condescension, at worst of contempt, in the relationship. Early in their acquaintance, Sheridan made the fatal mistake of writing verses which made fun at Swift's expense. It is doubtful whether Sheridan was ever completely forgiven for his blunder. He was one of those superficially brilliant people, who never quite grow

---

2. The Quilca house which Swift knew may well have dated from the early XVII century. It was a long, thatched building, near the beautiful lake. In or about 1724, it appears to have become so dilapidated that Dr. Sheridan began to rebuild it. Towards the middle of the XVIII century, Quilca was owned by his second son, Thomas, the biographer of Swift, the father of Richard Brinsley Sheridan. During Thomas Swift's occupancy, the house was a scene of much hospitality, and London celebrities, such as Peg Woffington, were entertained in rooms painted by Lewis, an English stage-decorator, with portraits of Swift, Milton, Shakespeare and the host himself. The refurbishing of Quilca must have added considerably to Thomas Sheridan's load of debt. On his death, in 1788, Quilca passed into the possession of the le Fanu family, relatives of the Sheridans. The house was owned until some twenty-five years ago by Mr. Peter O'Farrell, when it was demolished and replaced by a farm house.

up, and who have a genius for stumbling into awkward predicaments. One of his more notorious blunders was a sermon he preached, on the anniversary of the death of Queen Anne and the accession of George I. Sheridan's choice of the text *Sufficient unto the day is the evil thereof* was more than sufficient to blight all further hopes of Viceregal patronage.

He also blundered in the choice of a wife. Elizabeth McFadden made his life miserable, and was extremely unpopular with his friends. Swift described the lady as :

. . . The most disagreeable beast in Europe. Her person is detestably disagreeable; a most filthy slut.

Although the Dean was apt to run to extremes of eulogy of his friends and abuse of his enemies, Elizabeth Sheridan appears to have been an unpleasant woman ! It was through his marriage that Sheridan became owner of the Quilca estate, in Co. Cavan. There, a large part of *Gulliver* seems to have been written by the Dean and copied out by Stella. A mound opposite the site of the Seventeenth Century house is still known locally as *Stella's Bower.*[3]

Swift seems to have made constant use of Quilca, using and abusing it at will. In April, 1724, he listed the *Blunders, Deficiencies, Distresses and Misfortunes of Quilca,* and, even allowing for exaggeration, they add up to an extremity of discomfort :

. . . the dean's bed threatening every night to fall under him . . . the kitchen perpetually crowded with savages . . . an egregious want of all the most common necessary utensils . . . not a sod of turf this cold weather, and Mrs. Johnson and the Dean in person, with all their servants, forced to assist at the bog, gathering up wet bottoms of old clamps . . . a great hole in the floor of the Ladies' chamber,

---

3. Not far from Quilca is a tiny township, in Westmeath, called Lilliput, and it contains a small church named Laputa. It is tempting to believe that the author of *Gulliver's Travels* found these curious names locally, but there seems very little doubt that, during Swift's lifetime, the townland was known as "the Nure"—a corruption of the Irish word which means Yew-Tree. The earliest use of the word Lilliput which this writer has found, appears in a Deed of Sale between the Hon. Robert Rochfort and another, in 1786, where there is an entry describing "the lands of the Nure (called Lilliput)." The appearance of the name Rochfort probably gives the clue to the puzzle since that family was closely associated with the Dean, and may well have changed the name of the tiny township, in humorous memory of *Gulliver's Travels.*

*every hour hazarding a broken leg . . . Mrs. Dingley full of cares for
herself and blunders and negligence for her friends . . . Mrs. Johnson sick and helpless . . . The Dean deaf and fretting . . . Robin and
the nurse the two great and only supports of the family.*

Obviously everything and everybody had got thoroughly on the
Dean's nerves! Yet conditions at Quilca cannot have always been
so dire, for the following year Swift insisted that a stay there was
absolutely necessary as :

A receipt to restore Stella's youth.

After a long preamble, in which he unpoetically compares the
Lady to a famished cow, he proceeds :

> *. . . for you have fasted*
> *So long, till all your flesh is wasted,*
> *And must against the warmer days*
> *Be sent to Quilca down to graze,*
> *Where mirth, and exercise, and air*
> *Will soon your appetite repair.*

To-day, only the rusting gates and broken pillars guard the deserted avenue, lined with ancient trees. Beyond lies the unchanging
lake and the footpath through the fields, where Stella took her
prescribed *exercise and air,* under the Dean's stern and watchful
eye.

The Sheridan family had been landowners in Co. Cavan since
the reign of Elizabeth I. Thomas Sheridan's grandfather, the Rev.
Denis Sheridan, was an eminent scholar, who assisted his close
friend, Bishop Bedell, to translate the Bible into Irish, in the hope
of converting the reluctant natives to the Reformed Church of their
conquerors. Denis Sheridan's eldest son, William—a god-son of
Bishop Bedell—became Bishop of Kilmore in 1682. After the Revolution, he refused to take the Oath of Allegiance to William and
Mary, was deprived of his bishopric in 1691, and died in London in
1711. The third son of the Rev. Denis Sheridan, another Thomas,
became very wealthy as Collector of Customs in Cork; he further
demonstrated the family's Jacobite sympathies by marrying a reputed daughter of King James II. The fourth son, James — father of
Dr. Thomas Sheridan — was a scholar of Trinity College, Dublin,
in 1665, when he bought the small estate of Quilca, which was near
the family property of Togher, Co. Cavan. There, his son Thomas

was born in 1687, so that he was exactly twenty years younger than his friend, Dean Swift.

When the Bishop of Kilmore was deprived of his bishopric in 1691, his brother, the Collector of Customs, with his semi-royal wife fled to France, to the Court of the exiled King, James II; as a result of the family disaffection, all their estates in Ireland were confiscated. Quilca was acquired by a wealthy neighbour, Charles McFadden, and some twenty years later, in 1710, Thomas Sheridan recovered Quilca by marrying Elizabeth McFadden, Charles McFadden's daughter. After his marriage, he took the degrees of B.A., M.A., and D.D at Trinity College, and he is believed to have been helped to do so by his cousin, the Bishop of Cloyne.

Sheridan's uncle, Thomas, had two children by his semi-regal alliance; a son, Sir Thomas Sheridan, who eventually became tutor and trusted counsellor to his illustrious relative, the Pretender, accompanied him on the disastrous *Forty-five,* and with the Prince, escaped narrowly from the slaughter at Culloden; a daughter who apparently did not share the Jacobite sentiments of her family, as she married a Colonel Guillaume, who became *aide-de-camp* to King William III.

Possibly a subconscious resentment of Sheridan's family background—semi-royal connections, landed gentry and related bishops, all social adornments which the class-conscious Swift would have gladly shared—may have influenced his curious relationship with his friend.

By an accident, the names of Stella's last servants have survived, as Swift recorded them in a jingle which he wrote, unkindly celebrating the death of one of the numerous Dingley dogs, *Elegy upon Tyger.*

N.B. *She died in Puppy and left two helpless infants behind. And that Mrs. Sally and Jane and Robin cryed three days for.*

Robin is, presumably, one of *the great and only supports of the family* referred to in Swift's Quilca diatribe, and, with Mrs. Sally and Jane formed Stella's last household servants, *that loved and almost adored her at the same time.* It is ironic that, where so many important pieces in the Swift-Stella puzzle have been lost, or deliberately destroyed, the names of her last servants should have survived.

CHAPTER VIII

"January 30th Tuesday.
This is the night of the funeral, which my sickness would not suffer
me to attend. It is now nine at night; and I am removed into
another apartment that I may not see the lights in the church,
which is just over against the window of my bedchamber.

With all the softness of temper that became a lady she had the
personal courage of a hero. She and her friend having removed their
lodgings to a new house which stood solitary, a parcel of rogues,
armed, attempted the house, where there was only one boy. She was
then about four-and-twenty; and having been warned to apprehend
such an attempt she learned the management of a pistol; and the
other women and servants being half dead with fear, she stole off
softly to her diningroom window, put a black hood to prevent being
seen, primed the pistol fresh and gently lifted up the sash; and tak-
ing her aim with the greatest presence of mind, discharged the pistol
loaden with bullets into the body of the villain who stood the fairest
mark. The fellow, mortally wounded, was carried off by the rest,
and died the next morning; but his companions could not be found.
The Duke of Ormond had often drunk her health to me upon that
account and had always a high esteem for her".

(On the Death of Mrs. Johnson)

Swift continued his Memoir, driven from his usual writing place
by the flickering torch-lights in the windows of his Cathedral, where
Stella's friends were mourning around the newly-opened pavement
of the great church. He himself, as he states, was too ill to join those
friends who paid her that last courtesy, although he was well enough
to write some thirteen hundred words while the sad ceremony was
in progress. Presumably it was not sickness which kept him away,
nor, indeed, uncontrollable grief, to judge from the content of what
he wrote that night, while the Deanery walls echoed back the funeral
bell, and Stella's body was lowered into the clammy clay of *St.*
Patrick's Great Isle,[1] where she had directed that she be laid.

---

1. Over centuries, the periodic flooding of the low-lying Cathedral by the river
Poddle had been a constant problem. Swift himself directed that he be buried
there *in a dry place*. Nevertheless, when his remains were temporarily disinterred
in 1835, his coffin was found to be lying in wet mud and *largely filled with water*.

The first outstanding episode in Stella's life that comes to Swift's memory is one already related by the writer in the *Gentleman's Magazine,* and it is interesting to compare the accounts. In the Farnham version of Stella's adventure, there is much more detail, presumably supplied by a Dublin correspondent; the attendant woman, the night-light, the insomnia, the late-night reading, the prolonged night-prayers, the robber on the ladder, the calm, efficient shooting. In all these, Stella figures as a solitary heroine, who only alarms the household when danger is over and the rescuing Watch outside. Swift's account is much less detailed and the episode appears to gain its real importance from the approbation it elicited from the Duke of Ormond, and his Grace's habit of toasting the heroine of the alarming adventure. The Viceroy may well have heard the story and drunk to Stella's health, but there is no evidence that he ever met her, nor, from references in the *Journal,* that she knew any of his family. If the Duke *had often drank her health to me,* as Swift says, his Grace must have assumed that there was an understanding, if not an actual engagement between her and Swift, which is of interest.

The Ladies' lodgings, *in a new house which stood solitary,* were in William Street, then a daringly isolated suburban development, named after William III, by the grateful citizens of Dublin. The street was well outside the safer city area. If Swift is correct in describing Stella as about *four-and-twenty,* this adventure took place about 1705, a date which may well have some bearing on her later story.

> *She was indeed under some apprehensions of going in a boat after some danger she had narrowly escaped by water; but she was reasoned thoroughly out of it.*
>
> *(On the Death of Mrs. Johnson)*

So far as is definitely known, Stella was only three times on the sea; the first was when she and Rebecca Dingley came to live in Ireland about 1701; the second, when they both spent some time in England in 1707-8. Swift gives no clue about the date of the *danger,* but the fact that she had to be *reasoned thoroughly out of it* would seem to show that her narrow escape was during the first voyage to

Ireland, and that she had required considerable encouragement to risk the crossing to England, in 1707.

Apart from her natural fears of a journey, dangerous enough to daunt braver women than the Ladies, it is interesting to speculate why—and when—they broke up their Irish home, some six years after their arrival in Dublin. Nowadays, such journeys are taken very much for granted, but that was not the case in the Eighteenth Century, when even Viceroys avoided visiting Ireland, unless official duties made the sea-crossing absolutely necessary.

It is also important to remember that travelling was expensive and the Ladies were poor—how poor, becomes evident shortly. Although it is not known how long they remained in England, their visit certainly lasted several months, and the expense of lodgings would have been high and, for them, prohibitive.

The only actual evidence of this visit is in two letters written by Swift, then himself in London. The first is to Archdeacon Walls, who, with his wife, was a member of the Ladies' close circle of intimate Dublin friends:

London, January 22 1707-8.
. . . The Ladies of St. Mary's are well and talk of going to Ireland in the Spring . . . They desired me to give you their service when I writ.

The other allusion is in a letter from Swift to Dean Stearne, another close friend of the Ladies:

London, April 15th, 1708.
. . . Pug[2] is very well and likes London wonderfully, but Greenwich better, where we could hardly keep him from hunting down the deer.

There is no evidence of the date when the Ladies left St. Mary's Parish for England, but they certainly did *not* travel with Swift when he made the crossing in November, 1707. He accompanied Earl Pembroke, as the Viceregal Chaplain, on the Viceregal yacht to Parkgate, the port of Chester. There, the Viceroy was delayed, and Swift took the opportunity of visiting his mother in Leicester. Travelling thence to London, he stayed at an inn in Dunstable, where, amongst his fellow travellers, he met a charming, well-to-do

---

2. Elrington Ball very reasonably assumes that *Pug* was one of the long succession of Rebecca Dingley's adored dogs.

widow, Mrs. Van Homrigh, who was permanently removing her young family from Dublin to the gayer life of London. Something happened during the short stay in the Dunstable inn, which radically altered the lives of Swift, Stella and the youthful Esther Van Homrigh, to whom, under the name of *Vanessa,* Swift has ensured a melancholy and mysterious fame.

A reasonable explanation of the Ladies' journey to England and protracted stay there is found in a letter written by Lady Giffard to her niece, the Countess of Portland. The Countess was the elder daughter of Lady Giffard's brother, Sir John Temple, who had succeeded his father as Attorney-General in Ireland. In 1707, she was at the Hague with her husband, who was English Ambassador there; in July of that year, her younger sister, Lady Berkeley of Stretton, died suddenly, leaving seven young children and a distracted widower. To the Countess, Lady Giffard, wrote from her London house :

Dover Street: 18th July, 1707
For the Countess of Portland at the Hague

. . . I know your thoughts and mine have agreed so well upon all cruel accidents of this kind we have gone through that you will endeavour to turn them, as I am trying to do, wholly to the care of the desolate family that is left, and such as is the kindest way of remembering what we have lost. My Lord Berkeley is now with me and I am going with them tonight with my nephew and niece to leave him my house, very sorry that I cannot be in it with him, but he seems to like it much better than anything else that was proposed to him, till he can return to his own. Yet I was glad it came into my head to make him the offer, . . . I have been little from him since I came to town, and he seems never better pleased than in seeing any of her friends . . . He is extremely reasonable and disposed entirely to what I have begged of him, to turn his thoughts to the business and care of his family, and while you are away, to find he has little help, and that I am fast growing so useless a creature that should like nothing so much as that it were in my power to serve him. The difficulty now is to resolve whether he shall remove his family to the country . . . It would be a great thing to be out of the melancholy scene, in good air, and to have the children out of the town that begins to grow very sickly. The great want is somebody in the house

*to have some care of the children and be sometimes with him. If I
were younger and had better health I would offer myself and
Bridget for the little time he will be there this summer. However, I
will go to Moor Park at the same time, and be with them as often
as I can. I had great hopes of Mrs. Garraway, but that cannot be,
and Mrs. Ann Berkeley is in the country. Can you think of anyone
else?*

Had Lady Giffard been, as she said, *younger and in better health,*
she would have taken over the supervision of the desolate family,
with the aid of her waiting-woman, Bridget—Stella's mother—the
other relatives being unable to help in the emergency. At some stage
in the crisis, either the Countess in Holland, or Lady Giffard in
Surrey, must have thankfully remembered the Ladies in Dublin.
Who could have been more suitable *to be in the house and have
some care of the children* than Esther Johnson and Rebecca Dingley, who had both known the family intimately during the years in
Moor Park? And what more reasonable explanation of their journey from Ireland in 1707, and their long stay in England than that
it was undertaken at Lord Berkeley's expense? Perhaps, too, the fact
that the Irish interest of 10%, had just fallen to 8% may have had
some bearing, as Swift's later statements will show.

It should be remembered, also, that Swift's violent quarrel with
Lady Giffard only erupted in 1709, when, against her wishes, he
published the last of Sir William Temple's papers. Had Lady
Berkeley's death occurred at that time, it is very doubtful whether
even Swift's desire to free the Ladies from their load of Dublin
debts, would have been strong enough to overcome his objections
to their assisting Lady Giffard in her trouble. By then, she had become *that old beast,* as he described her in the *Journal.*

All that is certain about this visit—the last they ever made to their
native land—is that they visited Greenwich, in company with Swift,
that Mrs. Dingley brought her dog on the outing and that *Pug*
chased the deer in the Park. They may well have inspected Wren's
newly finished Hospital and admired the Great Hall, where James
Thornhill was then painting the ceiling. It is pleasant to imagine
Stella and Dingley obediently craning their necks, while Swift ex-
pounds the vast design overhead—Apollo driving his luminous
chariot across the sky, where William and Mary reign, triumphant,

65

in canopied state, attended by chubby cherubs and decorative Divinities. Swift, in his tutorial capacity, can scarcely have resisted the opportunity of taking the Ladies to the nearby Observatory, where, apart from other attractions, an excellent view could be had of London town, and of Blackheath, that notorious haunt of highwaymen, where, nevertheless, a century earlier the first Golf Club in the world had been founded by James I. (In spite of Swift's fanatical dedication to exercise, it is, somehow, difficult to imagine him playing Golf!).

There is one other faint echo of the Ladies' visit to England. In the *Journal,* in 1713, Swift reminds them of :

. . . The house in King Street, between St. James's Street and St. James's Square, where DD's brother bought the sweet-bread, when I lodged there, and MD came to see me.

Presumably the Ladies were off duty for the day and spending their time in London with Dr. Swift.

It is not known when they returned to Dublin, but they had come back before 9th November, 1708, when Swift's list of postal charges includes a letter to *MD.* Averaging the time between his letters to them, as recorded in his meticulous notes, the Ladies probably returned about the Summer of 1708, after a stay of almost a year in England.

One significant fact should be noted : Swift had already formed a very close friendship with the Van Homrigh[3] family, but the Ladies do not appear ever to have met them, either in London or in Dublin.

---

3. The name is usually written incorrectly. The family invarably signed themselves Van Homrigh, as do the Dublin descendants of that Partington, who changed his name in order to inherit the property of Vanessa's brother, Bartholomew Van Homrigh.

CHAPTER IX

She was never known to cry out, or discover any fear in a coach or on horseback; or any uneasiness by those accidents with which most of her sex, either by weakness or affection, appear so much disordered.

(On the Death of Mrs. Johnson)

In the *Journal*, Swift gives an amusing, imaginary picture of Stella on horseback :

The horses are not come to the door; the fellow can't find the bridle; your stirrup is broken; where did you put the whips, Dingley? Margaret, where have you laid Mrs. Johnson's riband to tie about her? Reach me my mask; sup up this before you go. So, so, a gallop, a gallop: sit fast, sirrah, and don't ride hard upon the stones .....Oh, Madam Stella, welcome home; was it pleasant riding? Did your horse stumble? How often did the man light to settle your stirrup? Ride nine miles? — faith, you've galloped indeed.

Stella and her attendant groom rode many miles, egged on by Swift's conviction that good health was the reward of strenuous exercise. In the *Journal*, there are several allusions to her various horses. From Swift's letters to Vanessa, it is clear that she, too, was urged to ride; many of her journeys between her estate in Celbridge and her Dublin home in Turnstile Alley were probably made on horseback. Swift used to urge her, also, to improve the failing health of her sister and herself by riding around the countryside. There is no evidence to show how Swift became convinced of female lack of courage. In his poem *The Furniture of a Woman's Mind*, he refers to one accepted feminine weakness :

If chance a mouse creeps in her sight,
Can finely counterfeit a fright.
So sweetly screams, if it comes near her,
She ravishes all hearts to hear her.

But in the poem, *To Stella, visiting me in my sickness*, which he wrote a year before her death, he boasts that among her many other virtues :

She thinks that nature ne'er design'd
Courage to man alone confined:

> *Can cowardice the sex adorn*
> *Which most exposes ours to scorn?*
> *She wonders where the charm appears*
> *In Florimel's affected fears;*
> *For Stella never learn'd the art*
> *At proper times to scream and start;*
> *Nor calls up all the house at night*
> *And swears she saw a thing in white.*
> *Doll never flies to cut her lace,*
> *Or throw cold water in her face,*
> *Because she heard a sudden drum,*
> *Or found an earwig in a plum.*

Swift further expatiates on female cowardice in his remarkable letter of advice to young Miss Staunton, on her forthcoming marriage :

. . . There is indeed one Infirmity which is generally allowed you, I mean that of Cowardice. Yet there should seem to be something very capricious that when Women profess their Admiration for a Colonel or a Captain on account of his Valour, they should fancy it a very graceful and becoming Quality in themselves to be afraid of their own Shadows; to scream in a Barge, when the Weather is calmest, or in a Coach at the Ring; to run from a Cow at an hundred yards distance; to fall into Fits at the Sight of a Spider, an Earwig or a Frog.

In the course of Esther Johnson's life, she bravely faced trials and misfortunes far worse than *Spiders, Frogs,* or even an earwig-infested plum.

CHAPTER X

She never had the least absence of mind in conversation, or was given to interruption, or appeared eager to put in her word, by waiting impatiently until another had done. She spoke in a most agreeable voice, in the plainest words, never hesitating, except out of modesty before new faces, when she was somewhat reserved; nor among her nearest friends ever spoke much at a time. She was but little versed in the common topics of female chat; scandal, censure and detraction never came out of her mouth; yet among a few friends, in private conversation, she made little ceremony in discovering her contempt for a coxcomb, and describing his follies to the life; but the follies of her own sex she was rather inclined to extenuate or to pity.

When she was once convinced, by open facts, of any breach of truth or honour in a person of high station, especially in the Church, she could not conceal her indignation, nor hear them named without showing her displeasure in her countenance; particularly one or two of the latter sort, whom she had known and esteemed, but detested above all mankind when it was manifest that they had sacrificed those two precious virtues to their ambition; and would much sooner have forgiven them the commonest immoralities of the laity.

(On the Death of Mrs. Johnson)

In Swift's *Hints for an Essay upon Conversation,* he gives his views, at some length, upon what he describes as :

. . . so useful and innocent a pleasure, so fitted for any period and condition in life.

It is interesting to compare the maxims he there lays down with his account of Stella's behaviour in company.

Hints for an Essay upon Conversation

I was prompted to write my thoughts upon this subject by mere indignation to reflect that so useful and innocent a pleasure, so fitted to every period and condition in life, and so much in all men's power, should be so neglected and abused . . . I rarely remember to have seen five people together, where someone among them has not been predominant . . . to the great disgust of the rest . . . I have often observed two persons discover, by some accident, that they were bred together at the same school or university; after which the rest are condemned to silence, and to listen while these two are refreshing each other's memory with the arch tricks and passages of themselves and their comrades . . . There are some faults in conversation to which none are so subject as the men of wit . . . If they have opened their mouths without endeavouring to say a witty thing, they think it so many words lost. It is a torment to the hearers, as much as to themselves, to see them upon the rack of invention . . . There are two faults in conversation . . . an impatience to interrupt others, and the uneasiness of being interrupted ourselves. . . . The little decorum or politeness we have are finely forced by art, and so are ready to lapse into barbarity . . . This sort of wide familiarity seems to have been introduced among us by Cromwell, who, by preferring the scum of the people, made it a court entertainment, of which I have heard many particulars . . . If there were no other use in the conversation of ladies, it is sufficient that it would lay a restraint upon those odious topics of immodesty and indecencies into which the rudeness of our northern genius is so apt to fall . . . I say nothing here of those who are troubled by the disease called the wandering of the thoughts . . .

She transgressed none of his conversational rules; her attention never wandered; her *bons mots* were spontaneous; she countenanced no immodesty nor indecencies.

And yet the fact remains that, from very early, various editors of Swift's *Journal to Stella* considered it necessary to expurgate passages which *they* thought indecent; and at least one inferred joke of Stella's belongs to the schoolboy-lavatory type of wit.

In 1720, he dedicated verses *To Stella, who collected and transcribed his Poems,* and it is reasonable to suppose that she continued to act as his amanuensis. Although it was only after her death that Swift's most scabrous verses shocked his contemporaries, nevertheless Stella must have made copies of some of his material which was neither modest nor decent.

Her indignation at *any breach of truth or honour in a person of high station, especially in the Church* was probably a pale reflection of Swift's own *saeva indignatio,* which illuminated such a wide circle of offenders, lay and clerical, with its baleful glare. From his very early battles with his Cathedral Chapter (about which he was still

70

seeking Bishop Attenbury's advice in 1716) to the end of his life, Swift carried on bitter personal feuds with his enemies. It would be difficult to find more concentrated venom in verse than his *Legion Club*, which dealt with the deficiencies of the Irish Parliament, whose members were the Dean's close neighbours, whom he was liable to meet any day on any Dublin street.

Her frequent fits of sickness, in most parts of her life, had preven-
ted her from making that progress in reading which she would
otherwise have done. She was well versed in the Greek and Roman
story, and was not unskilled in that of France and England. She
spoke French perfectly, but forgot most of it by neglect and sickness.
(On the Death of Mrs. Johnson)

Twenty-four hours previously, Swift had recorded that :
She was sickly from her childhood until about the age of fifteen;
but then grew into perfect health.

But, in reality, she appears to have been always a delicate woman. His assertion that she spoke French perfectly is a reminder that, when she arrived at Moor Park, that household included the recently tragically widowed Mrs. John Temple and her mother, Madame du Plessis Rambouillet. It would seem likely that the only way in which Stella could ever have acquired perfect French would have been through the teaching of the French noblewoman, or her daughter. Swift's own knowledge of French was far from perfect. Although he sometimes wrote letters in that language to Vanessa, it was to lessen the danger of spying eyes—perhaps, indeed, to lessen the shock to his own, when he threw discretion to the winds and wrote such passages as :
. . . *Soyez assurée que jamais personne du monde a eté aimée,*
honorée, estimée, adorée par votre ami que vous . . . To have told the girl, in French or in English, that she was the only person on earth who has ever been loved, honoured, esteemed, adored by her friend,—and that in 1721, some five years after his supposed marriage to Stella—puts the Dean in either of two categories; an ardent lover, or a base philanderer.

She had carefully read all the best books of travels, which serve

71

to open and enlarge the mind. She understood the Platonic and Epicurean philosophy, and judged very well of the defects of the latter. She made very judicious abstracts of the best books she had read. She understood the nature of government, and could point out all the errors of Hobbes, both in that and religion. She had a good insight into physic, and knew somewhat of anatomy; in both of which she was instructed in her younger days by an eminent physician, who had her long under his care, and bore the highest esteem for her person and understanding. She had a true taste of wit and good sense, both in poetry and prose, and was a perfect good critic of style; neither was it easy to find a more proper or impartial judge, whose advice another might better rely on, if he intended to send a thing into the world, provided it was on a subject that came within the compass of her knowledge. Yet perhaps she was sometimes too severe, which is a safe and pardonable error. She preserved her wit, judgment and vivacity to the last, but often used to complain of her memory.

(On the Death of Mrs. Johnson)

This passage reads more like a testimonial for an excellent secretary, than the memories of a grief-stricken friend. Whatever may have been the standard of Stella's philosophical or medical knowledge, there is certainly evidence of *her true taste in poetry.* Two of her poems have survived. One, addressed by her :

To Dr. Swift on his birth-day, Nov. 30, 1721. was considered by W. B. Yeats to be superior to any verse written by the Dean :

> *St. Patrick's Dean, your country's pride,*
> *My early and my only guide,*
> *Let me among the rest attend,*
> *Your pupil and your humble friend,*
> *To celebrate in female strains*
> *The day that paid your mother's pains;*
> *Descend to take that tribute due*
> *In gratitude alone to you.*
> *When men began to call me fair,*
> *You interposed your timely care;*
> *You early taught me to despise*
> *The ogling of a coxcomb's eyes.*

Shew'd where my judgment was misplac'd;
Refin'd my fancy and my taste.
Behold that beauty just decay'd,
Invoking art to nature's aid;
Forsook by her admiring train,
She spreads her tatter'd nets in vain;
Short was her part upon the stage;
Went smoothly on for half a page;
Her bloom was gone, she wanted art
As the scene chang'd to change her part:
She, whom no lover could resist
Before the second act was hiss'd.
Such is the fate of female race
With no endowments but a face;
Before the thirtieth year of life,
A maid forlorn, or hated wife,
Stella to you, her tutor owes
That she has ne'er resembled those;
Nor was a bother to mankind
With half her course of years behind.
You taught how I might youth prolong
By knowing what was right and wrong;
How from my heart to bring supplies
Of lustre to my fading eyes;
How soon a beauteous mind repairs
The loss of chang'd or falling hairs:
Now wit and virtue from within
Send out a smoothness o'er the skin:
Your lectures could my fancy fix
And I can please at thirty six.
The sight of Chloe at fifteen
Coquetting, gives not me the spleen;
The idol now of every fool
Till time shall make their passions cool;
Then, tumbling down time's steepy hill,
While Stella holds her station still.
Oh! turn your precepts into laws,
Redeem the women's ruin'd cause,

> *Retrieve lost empire to our sex*
> *That men may bow their rebel-necks.*
> *Long be the day that gave you birth,*
> *Sacred to friendship, wit and mirth;*
> *Late dying may you cast a shred*
> *Of your rich mantle o'er my head,*
> *To bear with dignity my sorrow,*
> *One day alone, then die tomorrow.*

It may be deduced that Stella was thirty-six when she wrote this. In reality, she was forty, but it seems that she considered that a woman's life was virtually finished at thirty-six, unless, as in her own case, a wise friend had prepared her, well in advance, for this — to modern thinking — extremely premature old age. Indeed, Swift constantly armoured the unfortunate lady against vanity. Their habit of exchanging birthday poems offered an annual opportunity to the Dean. In March, 1718, he wrote :

> *Now this is Stella's case in fact,*
> *An angel's face, a little crack'd.*
> *(Could poets or could painters fix*
> *How angels look at thirty six?)*
> *And ev'ry virtue now supplies*
> *The fainting rays of Stella's eyes.*

And again, in 1724 :

> *But, Stella, say what evil tongue*
> *Reports you are no longer young;*
> *That Time sits with his scythe to mow*
> *Where erst sat Cupid with his bow;*
> *That half your locks are turned to gray;*
> *I'll ne'er believe a word they say.*
> *Tis true, but let it not be known,*
> *My eyes are somewhat dimish grown:*
> *For nature, always in the right,*
> *To your decay adapts my sight*
> *And wrinkles undistinguish'd pass*
> *For I'm ashamed to use a glass.*

Although Swift could be merciless towards any small vanity on Stella's part, he was less exacting towards his own weakness; it is

generally admitted that his refusal to wear spectacles added an unnecessary misery to his later years.

Stella's other surviving poem, according to her close friend and
fervent admirer, Dr. Delany, was written during the painful period
when she *was stung with jealousy* on account of the rumours which
were reaching her about Swift's intimate relationship with Vanessa.
Reading between Dr. Delany's maze of words, it is evident that
Stella, herself, showed the poem to him.

Jealousy

O shield me from his rage, celestial pow'rs,
This tyrant, that imbitters all my hours :
Ah, Love, you've poorly play'd the hero's part,
You conquer'd, but you can't defend my heart.
When first I bent beneath your gentle reign
I thought this monster banish'd from your train:
But you would raise him, to support your throne
And now he claims your empire for his own.
Or tell me tyrants, have you both agreed
That where one reigns, the other shall succeed?

No reasonable person reading that poem could maintain that
Stella's feelings for Swift were purely platonic, as late as 1723, when
the mysterious events occurred, which led to the death of Vanessa,
an open rupture between Swift and the Ladies, and his disappear-
ance from the Dublin scene for several months, *to give place to
obloquy*, as Dr. Delany put it.

Swift's claim for her quick wit is justified by a story told of her
last illness. Her doctor assured her that she had reached the bottom
of the hill, but that he would do his utmost to help her up again.
She replied :

*Doctor, I fear that I shall be completely out of breath, before I
get to the top.*

She is reported to have suffered from acute asthma which adds
poignancy to her gallant jest.

*Her fortune, with some accession, could not as I have heard say,
amount to much more than £2,000; whereof a great part fell with*

75

her life, having been placed upon annuities in England, and one in Ireland.

(On the Death of Mrs. Johnson)

Sir William Temple's legacy to Stella was a piece of land in Co. Wicklow, and that is the one certain information about her fortune. It is reported to have been worth some £1,000, so that she appears to have doubled her capital during her life in Ireland. There are records of her ownership of house property, and there is a belief that Swift made a secret allowance to herself and to Mrs. Dingley. During the years 1710-1713, there are frequent allusions in the *Journal* to many transactions on behalf of the Ladies. Swift appears to have received monies due to them for his own use in London, and to have repaid them from his parish funds in Dublin. Like so much of the Swift-Stella story, their finances are impossible to disentangle. In Swift's will, he left an annuity of £20 to Mrs. Dingley, so that he probably had made her an allowance, at least since Stella's death had removed the major parts of their joint income. In 1736, Swift wrote to Mrs. Dingley's cousin, John Temple, at Moor Park :

. . . Mrs. Dingley, your cousin, lodges in my neighbourhood . . . She is quite sunk with years and unwieldiness: as well as a very scanty support. I sometimes make her a small present as my abilities can reach . . . If you will be so good as to order some mark of your favour to Mrs. Dingley . . . I do not mean a pension, but a small sum to put her for once out of debt: and if I live any time, I shall see that she keep herself clear of the world : for she is a woman of as much piety and discretion as I have known.

Poor Dingley, elderly, overfat and still foolish about money . . . There is no record of her cousin Temple's reaction to Swift's letter. She died some years before Swift and, surprisingly, (in view of Swift's belief in her extreme poverty), she left her executor, the Rev. John Lyon, a note for £100 which she had possessed since 1723.

Stella made no provision in her will for her life-long friend, except a legacy of *my little watch and chain and twenty guineas;* she directed that all her plate, books, furniture and moveables be sold, so, presumably, breaking up any joint home the Ladies had shared. Perhaps there had been some sad weakening in their long

76

friendship. Many years earlier, there had been several allusions in the *Journal* to quarrels. Swift wrote to them :

Are you good company together? And don't you quarrel too often? Pray love one another, and kiss one another just now, as Dingley is reading this.

And again :

Be a good girl and I'll love you; and love one another and don't be quarrelling girls.

The affectionately adult attitude of Swift towards the *quarrelling girls* is remarkable when it is remembered that Stella was then well over thirty and her friend at least forty-five.

Stella's interminable illness may have proved too great a strain for her ageing friend. That *some* break had occurred may account for a curious passage in a letter, written by Swift to Dr. Sheridan, a short time before Stella's death :

I brought those friends over that they might be happy together, as long as God should please; the knot is broken, and the remaining person, as you know, has ill answered the end, and the other who is now to be lost, is all that was valuable.

Whatever be the reason, Stella left the life interest in her fortune to her mother and sister, neither of whom she had seen for more than twenty years. After their deaths, she directed that the capital should go to the newly erected Steeven's Hospital in Dublin, for the support of a chaplain. She specified that he be unmarried, and that, should he marry, he was to be dismissed. It would seem that Stella did not approve of married clergymen ! She also gave instructions that, should the Church of Ireland ever cease to be the State Church, the money should immediately revert to her nearest living relative. When the Protestant Church was disestablished in Ireland, in 1871, a search for any surviving relations proved fruitless, although her sister, Anne Filbey, is reported to have had nineteen children.

Besides other trifling legacies, including the curious bequest to the unexplained child already alluded to, Dean Swift was given her locked strong-box — which contained £150 — and all her papers. Her will was put into probate, in May 1728, by her executors : the Rev. Thomas Sheridan, the Rev. John Grattan, the Rev. Francis

77

Corbett and Mr. John Rochfort.[1] One of her most specific directions was, very oddly, ignored.

I desire that a decent monument of plain white marble may be fixed in the wall over the place of my burial not exceeding the value of £20 sterling.

Swift was always extremely interested in monuments. In 1711, he undertook to write a lengthy Latin epitaph for the recently deceased Lord Berkeley. Later, as Dean, he corresponded with various families about the upkeep of their ancestral tombs, and he had a bitter argument with the relatives of the Duke of Schomberg, in England, who had neglected to honour his grave in St. Patrick's. Failing to get satisfaction, Swift wrote a scathing epitaph, which annoyed the King, when it was repeated at the English Court. When one of his manservants died, the Dean erected a memorial slab in his Cathedral, with an inscription which does honour to both master and man. Finally, he wrote his own famous epitaph and left explicit instructions for the memorial marble. But for Stella, he wrote no word, nor was any memorial to her memory erected over her grave during all the long years that he survived her.

---

1. Irony is never far distant from Swift's story; two of Stella's good friends and executors, the Rev. John Grattan and Mr. John Rochfort, were amongst those who petitioned for an enquiry into Swift's mental condition, fourteen years after her death.

CHAPTER XI

*In a person so extraordinary, perhaps it may be pardonable to
mention some particulars, although of little moment, farther to set
forth her character. Some presents of gold pieces being often made
to her while she was still a girl, by her mother and other friends, on
a promise to keep them, she grew into such a promise of thrift, that
in about three years, they amounted to above £200. She used to
show them with boasting; but her mother, apprehending she would
be cheated of them, prevailed in some months and with great im-
portunities, to have them put out to interest; when the girl, losing
the pleasure of seeing and counting her gold, which she never failed
of doing many times in a day, and despairing of heaping up such
another treasure, her humour took quite a contrary turn; she grew
careless and squandering in every new acquisition, and so continued
until about two-and-twenty; when, by advice of some friends and
the fright of paying large bills of tradesmen, who enticed her into
their debt, she began to reflect upon her own folly, and was never
at rest until she had discharged all her shopbills, and refunded herself a considerable sum she had run out. After which, by the addition of a few years and a superior understanding, she became, and
continued all her life, a most prudent economist.*

(On the Death of Mrs. Johnson)

Within a stone's-throw of the room where Swift was writing, the
funeral of his *truest, most virtuous and valuable friend* was in progress. With her death, the unhappy man had lost most of the circumstances which had made his frustrated life tolerable. As he
allowed his memory to range widely over the long years of their
acquaintance, the most important events came into clearest focus.
Why then did he remember so vividly that Stella had once, as a
young girl, got into serious debt? She had just paid the ultimate debt
to Life : surely, at such a moment, the financial sins of her youth
might have been overlooked and their distant echoes drowned by
the nearby tolling of her funeral-bell? What inner compulsion
forced the Dean to give such prominence to a comparatively slight
misdemeanour, more than a quarter of a century old? These questions have never been raised, and so have never been answered. And

79

yet, they almost certainly provide the solution to the problem—Why did Swift not marry Stella?

When the Ladies were persuaded, by Swift, to leave their native land and spend their future lives in that politically insecure, far away colony which was Eighteenth Century Ireland, there is little doubt that all their friends expected that he would shortly marry Stella. His biographer, Deane Swift, had no doubt that :

. . . her Intent was to captivate the heart of Dr. Swift.

The Rev. Thomas Swift, Jonathan's cousin, enquired, in a jocose letter :

. . . whether Jonathan be married? Or whether he has been able to resist the Charms of both these Gentlewomen that marched quite from Moor Park (as they would have marched to the North, or anywhere else) with full Resolution to engage him?

Still more significant is the postscript of a letter written by Lady Giffard to her niece, the Countess of Portland, at the Hague.

Do you know that Hetty is to dance barefoot? Bridget came yes-terday from London, where she has been marrying her other daughter.

The letter is headed *July 14,* but from internal evidence it can be dated 1700, since, in it, Lady Giffard sends her condolence to Lord Portland on the death of his good friend *My Lord Privy Seal,* and she also refers to King William's absence in Holland. Viscount Lonsdale, who was Keeper of the Privy Seal, died on the 10th July, 1700, shortly after his appointment as one of the Lord Justices, who governed the Kingdom during King William's absence from England.

This postscript is of particular interest because, as Swift himself tells us, the phrase *to dance barefoot* was then used when a younger sister married before her elder. At the wedding festivities, the elder and presumably taller sister was supposed to disguise her age and hide her shame by dancing without shoes. So that in July, 1700, Stella's unmarried state was already a subject of family mirth at Moor Park, where Mrs. Bridget Johnson had recently returned from London after marrying her younger daughter, Anne, to Mr. Filbey. It is only reasonable to believe that, when Stella and her chaperone left the household at Moor Park a few months later at Swift's invitation, it was taken for granted by her mother and all concerned that the girl was very shortly going to marry Swift.

When the Ladies left their home in Moor Park, Stella was about twenty, her companion, Rebecca Dingley, considerably older. Both had shared the comfortable, well ordered life of the Temple establishments, and knew no other way of living until, for the first time in their lives, they set up an independent home in the strange city of Dublin. As Swift has recorded, they were regarded with suspicion by their neighbours. They were alone in a foreign city, and were probably living, on a miniature scale, the life to which they had always been accustomed at Moor Park. When Swift did finally follow them to Dublin, he remained there only a short time before returning to London in April, 1702, a few weeks after the death of William III and the accession of Queen Anne had rippled the political pond. So that the Ladies, starting their new life in Dublin, had little opportunity to consult their only friend, Dr. Swift.

When he accompanied the Earl of Berkeley to England, Swift did so as his official Chaplain. The Eighteenth Century chaplain did not necessarily command the same respect as he does to-day; he was a member of the household staff with ill-defined duties, one of which often included the reading aloud of prayers to his lady, through a half-open door, while she made her toilet in an adjoining room, with the assistance of her waiting-woman. Swift was certainly on friendly terms with the Earl's wife and daughter, but it would require a great deal of humiliation, on the part of his employer, to justify the brutally contemptuous verses which the Earl's Chaplain composed about that unfortunate nobleman. To quote Churton Collins :

He gibbeted his patron in a lampoon, distinguished even among his other lampoons by its scurrility and filth.

When Swift left Dublin, as the Earl of Berkeley's Chaplain in 1701, he did so as a relatively unknown clergyman, holder of a remote country parish, with very uncertain prospects. A wife with some money of her own was a distinctly desirable asset. Miss Waring, who had lately seemed to Swift to be a very suitable partner, had, for various reasons, not responded. Meanwhile, the death of Sir William Temple had provided Stella with an Irish property. From her early childhood, Swift had been very fond of her; they had long shared the same household; she was handsome, well bred in her manner and witty. Above all, she was openly devoted to

81

Jonathan Swift. What more natural than that she should now take Miss Waring's place in his scheme of life? What more obvious than that he should bring Stella, heavily chaperoned by Mrs. Dingley, to reside in his immediate neighbourhood, until the suitable time for marriage had arrived?

But things went wrong. In the Summer of 1701, a political treatise, *A Discourse of the Contests and Dissensions between the Nobles and the Commons in Athens* appeared anonymously in London. It was a powerful appeal to the Whigs to cease squabbling and close their ranks against their Tory enemies, and it caused a sensation and also a great deal of speculation as to the author. But, soon after Swift's arrival in London, the secret leaked out, and he found himself in immediate high favour with the leaders of the Whig party, who dazzled him with their promises of speedy preferment. So that when he returned that autumn to Dublin, Dr. Swift was already a personage, a very different man from the junior clergyman who had sailed for England six months earlier. His horizon had greatly widened, and with it his ambitions.

With the Ladies, unfortunately, things had not gone so well; after a year in Dublin they were heavily in debt and had no choice but to turn to Swift in their trouble.

To understand the enormous importance to Swift of such a confession, it is necessary to remember his attitude towards money. He had suffered in his youth from poverty, and he had very early decided that lack of funds equated lack of freedom and that debt represented humiliation and misery. All his life, Swift was extremely careful about money. His biographers agree upon that; the more critical expand *careful* into *miserly*. He kept his own accounts with extreme exactitude all his life; even his postal charges were duly entered. As he grew older this trait developed into a mania, as even his devoted friend and defender, Dr. Delany, admits in his reply to Lord Orrery's charges. All through the *Journal to Stella*, there runs a stream of constant admonitions to the Ladies to be careful about their household accounts; to keep out of debt; to avoid expensive lodgings — echoes of the financial tragedy of those earlier years.

No one can dispute that Swift was exceedingly fond of Stella, but all the ample evidence shows that his affection for her was that of a loving, humorous, devoted elder brother. In the *Journal,* his endearments are as often offered to Rebecca Dingley as to Stella — the composite *MD* embraced them both as his *impudent, saucy, dear-boxes,* his *dear little rogues,* his *saucy couple of sluttikins.* He wrote to them, jointly, almost daily and worried about their well-being. Nevertheless, Swift never wrote to Stella in the terms which he sometimes used to Vanessa — the passionate words of a man writing to a woman whom he desired :

You are the only one in the world whom your friend has ever loved, honoured, esteemed, adored . . . Coquetry, pretence, prudery are blemishes you have never had . . . What brutes in petticoats are all the women in the world, compared with you? What cruelty to make me despise so many people I could have tolerated were it not for you.

And this letter was signed by a dozen dashes, each one representing a word of love, according to the code invented by Swift and shared by him with Vanessa. These, and many similar passages of passionate love addressed by Swift to Vanessa, have been overlooked or ignored by those authorities with whose theories they do not fit in. Nevertheless, unless the Dean is to be regarded as a shameless liar, who, over many years, pretended to be the passionate lover of a young woman, they must be accepted at their face value.

But even passionate love was not sufficient to overcome the obstacles — some of them financial (since Vanessa never obtained control over her considerable fortune before her death in 1723) which stood between her and marriage with the Dean. How much more defenceless was Stella, when Swift discovered that the girl, with whom he proposed a comfortable, placid, married life, was not the reliable housekeeper, upon whose capacities he had built his future. She had committed the unpardonable crime — she was heavily in debt. Apart from his fears for their mutual Future, the Present provided problems which made immediate marriage out of the question : Stella had *run out of a considerable sum.*

By the advice of some friends . . . she began to reflect upon her own folly, and was never at rest until she had discharged all her shopbills, and refunded herself a considerable sum she had run out. After which, by the addition of a few years and a superior understanding, she became and continued all her life, a most prudent economist.

83

Unfortunately for Stella, *the addition of a few years,* (while she did penance for her folly by pinching and scraping to pay off her debts) brought Swift to a peak of political power, from which he saw his own future from a very different viewpoint. Stella's small fortune shrank in his eyes with every new marriage he reported to her in the *Journal:*

Lady Mary is to be married to Lord Ashburnham . . . twelve thousand pounds a year . . .

Sometimes the bride is not even mentioned by Swift :

I dined with Lord Abercorn, whose son Peasley will be married at Easter to ten thousand pounds.

In his last letter to Miss Waring, written in 1700, he says bluntly :

When I desired an account of your fortune, I had no such design as you pretend to imagine. I have told you many a time that in England it was in the power of any young fellow of common sense to get a larger fortune than ever you pretended to.

Where money was in question, Swift did not lack *common sense.* Stella's *superior understanding* must gradually have come to accept the new role which was to be her's until her life's end — *the truest, most devoted and valuable friend.*

The lodgings, in the outlying and dangerous area of William Street, were probably part of the Ladies' economy campaign, as was, almost certainly, the lengthy visit to England in 1707-8. Quite obviously, the debt-burthened Ladies could not have afforded such a luxury unaided.

Stella had one opportunity of breaking away from Swift's orbit. Towards the end of 1708, he had again returned to London to resume his familiarity with the powerful Whig Lords, Somers, Halifax and Sunderland. English politics were at boiling point and Swift was in his element. In a letter to his friend, the Rev. William Tisdall, Swift sends various humorous messages to the Ladies, who were apparently living close by him in William Street. Mr. Tisdall is exhorted to see that Stella reads improving books. A little later, Swift writes again, full of mock concern at Mr. Tisdall's relationship with his neighbours :

You seem to be mighty proud, as you have reason, if it be true, of the part you have in the Ladies' good grace, especially her you call the Party. I am very much concerned to know it; but since it is an evil I cannot remedy, I will tell you a story . . .

To prove his deep concern, he tells a smutty story, of which Elrington Ball expurgates the indecent climax. But the good humour had quite disappeared from a letter he wrote a few weeks later (in reply to one from Tisdall, asking Swift to approach Mrs. Johnson, on his behalf, for her daughter's hand). Swift, it seems, had raised obstacles, and Tisdall had suggested that Swift wanted to marry the girl himself, to which he replied :

. . . If my fortune and humour served me to think of that state, I should certainly, among all persons on earth, make your choice; because I never saw that person whose conversation I entirely valued but hers. This is the utmost I ever gave way to . . . The objection to your fortune being removed, I declare I have no other, nor shall any consideration of my own misfortune, of losing so good a friend and companion as her, prevail on me against her interest and settlement in the world, since it is held so necessary and convenient a thing for ladies to marry; and that time takes off the lustre of virgins, in all other eyes than mine . . .

It has been suggested that Stella encouraged her suitor in order to force Swift's hand. If so, the ruse failed, although he did hurry back from England ten days later. But he never forgave the Rev. William Tisdall for his temerity; years later, he still lost no opportunity of belittling him to Stella, even labouring the charge that his feet stank !

And so Swift continued to enjoy the young woman's valuable *conversation,* when he wasn't away in England, enjoying the conversation of the Great. Meanwhile, Stella was left to *reflect on her folly* and to pay off her debt to the Dublin shopkeepers. If the long stay in England in 1707-8 was the final effort to clear her financial muddle, it came just too late; in December that year, Swift had met Vanessa, with the Van Homrigh family party in an inn at Dunstable.

The fact that Swift almost certainly intended to marry Stella, soon after he persuaded the Ladies to move to Dublin, is a proof that he then had no idea of his own Temple connection. He must have had suspicions — if not complete assurance — that the girl was

85

Sir William's daughter. Although he was extremely tolerant of easy virtue in royal mistresses, and was close friends with both Lady Orkney and Mrs. Howard, he can have had no doubts about his mother. He was at Laracor when she died in Leicestershire, in 1710, and he made this note :

I have now lost my last barrier against death. God grant that I may be as well prepared for it as I confidently believe her to have been. If the way to Heaven be through piety, truth, justice and charity she is there . . .

When he wrote these words, Swift had no possible doubt of Abigail Swift's virtue. But there is a curious passage in the *Journal* : London, 17th July, 1711 :

I know nothing of the trunk being left or taken; so 'tis odd enough if the things in it were mine; and I think I was told there were some things for me that my mother left particularly for me.

Unfortunately, there is no further reference in the *Journal* to the missing trunk, which his mother, dying in Leicester, had destined for him; so it is a conjecture that, amongst its contents, *left particularly* for him, were papers revealing the paternity of Sir John Temple.[1] His dying mother might have been haunted by the fear of his eventually committing a criminal offence by marrying Stella, she may even have been *that person who alone knew the secret of the persons concerned, who revealed what otherwise might have been buried in oblivion,* to quote the writer in the *Gentleman's Magazine.*

It may also be significant that, according to his biographer, Deane Swift, *The Doctor was upon no terms of friendship with any of the Swift family, nor they with him, after his return to Ireland.* Whatever tenuous links had held him to his Dublin relatives were then completely broken, for many years.

But at the beginning of the Eighteenth Century, when Stella came to Ireland at Swift's invitation, no suspicions of their illegitimate kinship barred marriage between them. By the time that

---

1. In the Register of Trinity College, Dublin, there are no less than four attempts to fill in the name of Swift's father. First, *Jonathan* was entered and then erased, an indecipherable name being substituted, *Thomae* was then written in, scratched out again, and finally *Jonathan* was squeezed into the small remaining space.

knowledge of his Temple paternity may have reached Swift, in 1710, ambition had raised other obstacles to the union.

The addition of a few years, from 1701 to 1707, had drastically altered Swift's plans for his future career, and Stella no longer figured in them as an ideal wife. Her opportunity of marriage disappeared during her debt-burthened years, never to re-emerge. No wonder the painful episode loomed so large on the night of her burial. Swift must always have had a sense of guilt, where she was concerned. Stella had spent long, frustrated years *reflecting upon her own folly,* while Time inexorably removed the *lustre* from her virginity.

While there is much disagreement between authorities as to whether Swift eventually married Stella, it would appear certain that some crisis arose, about 1716, around which various theories have been built. The simplest solution offered is that Stella, alarmed and distressed by rumours of the Dean's intimacy with Esther Van Homrigh — then living on her Celbridge estate, but constantly visiting her Dublin house — insisted on marriage; that the Dean reluctantly consented, on condition that the marriage should never be made public and that it remained an empty formality. Seeing that the marriage was to be kept a close secret, it is difficult to see what possible protection it gave to Stella's reputation, damaged by Dublin's malicious tongues.

A curious episode took place, about this time, which would seem to have a direct bearing on this question. Swift's close friend, Dr. Delany, called to see the Archbishop, and was alarmed to meet a distraught Dean, rushing from the room. Dr. Delany found the Archbishop equally distressed and was told :

You have seen the most unhappy man on earth, but on the subject of his wretchedness you must never ask a question.

To understand the full significance of this episode (related by Dr. Delany's widow), it is necessary to remember that Dr. King was never a friend of Swift's. The Dean wrote to the Archbishop in May, 1727 :

. . . From the moment of the Queen's death, your Grace has thought fit to take every opportunity of giving me all sorts of uneasiness, without ever giving me, in my whole life, one single mark of your favour, beyond common civilities; and if it were not below

a man of spirit to make complaints, I could date them from six and twenty years past.

There was never any personal sympathy between the two men; their relationship was always that of a Dean reluctantly acknowledging his minimum duty towards his Archbishop.[2]

It is, therefore, interesting to know that Dr. Delany found the Archbishop in tears, at Swift's terrible predicament — whatever it may have been.

Stella had, at the time, been living in Dublin for many years; she had gradually become a close friend of many of the clerical circle, which revolved around the two Dublin Cathedrals. During the first years of her presence, when Swift made no secret that she was his very special protegée, speculation about the timing of their marriage must have been rife in Dublin society. As the years passed, gossip would have died away, but, nevertheless the ashes of scandal lay dormant, needing only the breath of an enemy to fan it to flame. Swift never lacked enemies, political or personal, and his ambiguous relationship with Stella must, from time to time, have provided welcome material for them. His situation became even more vulnerable from the end of 1714, when the rich and beautiful Miss Esther

---

2. In May, 1716, several years after Swift became Dean of St. Patrick's, Dr. King explained, in a letter to the Archbishop of Canterbury, that he had only agreed to Swift's appointment because "I thought a Dean could do less mischief than a bishop". Seven months later, Dr. King ended a letter to Swift with the scarcely veiled accusation that the Dean like his friend the exiled Lord Bolingbroke, had been plotting for restoration of the Pretender. "We have a strong report that my Lord Bolingbroke will return here and be pardoned; certainly it must not be for nothing. I hope he can tell no ill story of you". In his letter of reply, Swift indignantly refuted the Archbishop's suspicions; but he also hotly denied that prior to Queen Anne's death, Bolingbroke had plotted the return of the Pretender. Swift also exempted Lord Oxford from any such charge.

There is no doubt whatever that Bolingbroke conspired for a Stuart restoration; it is just possible that Swift was not aware of it, although he was on extremely familiar terms with the Tory Secretary of State. A recently found collection of letters provide valuable evidence of a plan by Oxford to restore the Pretender to the English throne on the death of Queen Anne. A number of these letters are from John Baptiste Colbert, Marquis de Torcy, Louis XIV's Secretary of State, to the Abbᴇ Francois Gaulier, who, between 1711 and 1714, was the French go-between in London. One is an unsigned letter from Colbert to "Vandenberg", who has been identified as Oxford. Lord Oxford was a most intimate friend of Swift, with whom he worked constantly. While it is possible that Swift might not have been aware of Bolingbroke's plotting, it is almost incredible that he could have been deceived successfully by his close friend, the Earl of Oxford.

Van Homrigh arrived in Ireland. Her close relationship with Swift had already lasted for some years. Quite certainly rumours of his constant visits to her London home had reached Dublin. The presence of both Swift's lady-friends in the same city must have set even his friends' tongues wagging; with such promising material to hand, his enemies must have done their utmost to embarrass the Dean of St. Patrick's.

With regard to Swift's visit to the Archbishop, it is important to remember that Dr. King was a trusted friend of the Van Homrigh family and had acted as adviser to Vanessa. Early in 1718, he wrote to George Tollet, an important Government official in London, reporting that he had recently had a number of consultations with Vanessa and her sister about their complicated legal affairs. So that the Archbishop must have been trebly concerned about any scandal-mongering which concerned two ladies of his acquaintance, as well as his principal Dean. It is a reasonable conjecture that some serious crisis had forced Dr. King, acting as Archbishop, to send for his Dean to question him as to the position between himself and the two ladies, and that Dr. Delany was witness to the ending of a most painful interview. What Swift had told the Archbishop, which justi-fied the description, *the most unhappy man on earth,* is not known, but had the Dean been forced to reveal his illegitimate relationship with Stella — through their Temple blood — which barred marriage between them, it would amply account for the emotional episode. Remembering Swift's fierce pride, the fact that scandal-mongers had given his Archbishop the right, as well as the duty, to catechise him would have amounted to an outrage. He must have bitterly resented the humiliation to which he had been exposed, and it is not without significance that, about the same time, Stella's tragic appearance was commented upon. Swift would not have spared even the most innocent contributor to his agonising dilemma.

That the Dean was highly susceptible to the dangers of Dublin gossip is proved in an undated letter—which may well have resulted from this crisis—that he wrote to Vanessa, in her house in Dublin :

. . . This morning a woman who does business for me told me she heard I was in love with ——, naming you, and many particulars; that little master and I visited you, and the A-B did so . . . . I ever feared the tattle of this nasty town and told you so; and that was

the reason why I said to you, long ago, that I would see you seldom when you were in Ireland. And I must beg you to be easy if for some time I visit you seldomer and not in a particular manner . . . . These are accidents in life that are necessary and must be submitted to; and tattle, by the help of discretion, will wear off.

There is no evidence as to the identity of the A-B but it was certainly not the Archbishop, as has been suggested. Even Dublin *tattle* could scarcely have regarded such visits as scandalous. *Little Master's* presence was obviously an occasion for gossip.

Swift's anecdote about the young girl's hoard of gold pieces is curious . . . *In about three years, her mother and other friends gave her over £200.* Considering that her mother's salary was some £10 a year and that she had two other children to provide for, it is difficult to believe that Bridget Johnson was able to contribute many gold pieces, or that any *friend* except Sir William Temple was in a position to have given so large a sum to young Miss Hetty Johnson.

CHAPTER XII

She had a strong bent to the liberal side, wherein she gratified her-self by avoiding all expense in clothes (which she ever despised) beyond what was merely decent. And although her frequent returns of sickness were very chargeable, except fees to physicians, of which she met with several so generous that she could force nothing on them (and indeed she must otherwise have been undone,) yet she never was without a considerable sum of ready money; in so much that upon her death, when her dearest friends thought her very bare, her executors found in her strong box £150 in gold.

(On the Death of Mrs. Johnson)

A few months before Stella's death, Swift wrote, from England, to Dr. Worrall, his Vicar and trusted agent :

Pray answer all calls of money in your power from Mrs. Dingley and desire her to ask for it.

Apparently, the Dean shared her friends' belief that Stella was very bare, and also their surprise when it was discovered that the strongbox she bequeathed to Swift, contained so considerable a sum in gold. Many years earlier in 1711, a strong-box figured in the *Journal*, when Swift indignantly wrote to Stella :

Twelve shillings for mending the strong-box; that is for putting a farthing's worth of iron on a hinge and gilding it. Give him six shillings and I'll pay it and never employ him again.

If the repaired strong-box had lasted seventeen years, the charge was not excessive.

A little later, Swift gives more details of Stella's economies :

She lamented the narrowness of her fortune in nothing so much as that it did not enable her to entertain her friends so often and in so hospitable a manner as she desired. Yet they were always wel-come; and, while she was in health to direct, were treated with neatness and elegance, so that the revenues of her and her companion passed for much more considerable than they really were. They lived always in lodgings, their domestics consisted of two maids and one man.

(On the Death of Mrs. Johnson)

In the *Journal,* Swift wrote to Stella in March, 1711 :

Mrs. Barton sent this morning to invite me to dinner; and there I dined, just in that genteel manner that MD used, when they would treat some better sort of body.

What Swift would designate entertainment in a *genteel manner* is described in his poem, *Stella at Wood-park.* She had taken refuge at Charles Ford's estate, some ten miles from Dublin, just before Vanessa's tragic death caused a mysterious and total break in Stella's relations with the Dean. This rupture lasted several months before a reconciliation took place, and Stella returned to her Dublin home. The return was celebrated in this poem, which gives some idea of the mode of living enjoyed in the household of a wealthy bachelor, Charles Ford, known to Swift and the Ladies as *Don Carlos.*

> *Don Carlos in a merry spight*
> *Did Stella to his house invite:*
> *He entertain'd her half a year*
> *With gen'rous wines and costly chear.*
> *Don Carlos made her chief director*
> *That she might o'er the servants hector.*
> *In half a week, the dame grew nice,*
> *Got all things at the highest price:*
> *Now at the table-head she sits*
> *Presented with the nicest bits:*
> *She look'd on partridges with scorn*
> *Except they tasted of the corn:*
> *A haunch of ven'son made her sweat*
> *Unless it had the right fumette.*
> *Don Carlos earnestly would beg;*
> *Dear Madam, try this pigeon's leg;*
> *Was happy when he could prevail*
> *To make her only taste a quail.*
> *Through candle-light she view'd the wine*
> *To see that every glass was fine.*

Swift goes on to describe the painful alteration in Stella's mode of living when the long visit ended and she returned to her lodgings at Ormond Quay :

> The coachman stopt; she look'd and swore
> The rascal had mistook the door:
> At coming in, you saw her stoop;
> The entry brush'd against her hoop;
> Each moment rising in her airs
> She curst the narrow winding stairs;
> Began a thousand faults to spy;
> The ceiling scarcely six feet high;
> The smutty wainscot full of cracks;
> And half the chairs with broken backs . . . .

After a painful adjustment had gradually taken place in the lodgings beside *Liffey's stinking tide,* Stella finally :

> *Fell back into her former scene,*
> *Small beer, a herring and the Dean.*

She kept an account of all the family expenses, from her arrival in Ireland to some months before her death; and she would often repine, when looking back upon the annals of her household bills, that everything necessary for life was double the price, while interest of money was sunk to almost one half; so that the addition to her fortune was indeed grown necessary.

(On the Death of Mrs. Johnson)

There is no indication as to how her fortune was largely increased, but there is evidence that she bought and sold house property. In March 1717, she bought a house in Trim from George Blakely, for £65. It had the imposing name of Talbot's Castle. A year later, she sold it to Swift, for £200. Lest it be thought that the enormously enhanced price was a delicate ruse on Swift's part to give her a present, it must be stated that the Dean sold the house again, a few months later, for £233.[1]

---

1. That Swift was an acute businessman is evident; added proof came recently into the present writer's hands.
To the Revernd the Petty cannons of the Cathedral Church of St. Patrick's Dublin
The Memorial of Dr. John Hawkshaw sheweth That the said John Hawkshaw's Grandfather did at his own expense after a tedious five yeares law suit (Wch amounted to the purchase of ye lands) recover unto the Petty Cannons the lands in Lucan wch he now holds from you by lease and that he has unexpired of his lease about forty two yeares.
That One now offers to improve on part of said land, viz on two or three acres, provided,

Here, having written some thirteen hundred words, the Dean laid down his quill. By then, Stella's funeral ceremonies would have ended, and the voices of the mourners may well have been sounding dully in his ears, as they made their way towards him, through the bleak darkness of the Cathedral Close to the bleaker darkness of the Deanery.

---

he can have the Encouragement of 60 yeares lease, without which he will not lay out any money for Improvements, which Improvements can be of no benefit to ye said Hawkeshaw these fifteen years his Tenant under Tenancy having a lease of fifteen yeares to come unexpired.

The sayd Hawkshaw offers as Fine for making his 42 yeares to come 60 the Summe of ten pounds str.

Jo. Hawkshaw.

At the bottom of Dr. Hawkshaw's Memorial, Dean Swift has written:

I agree that the Petti cannons should renew Doctor Hawkshaw's Lease on the following conditions:

First, that the said Doctor should immediately advance his Rent one Pound per ann.

Secondly, that after twenty years more of the present Lease shall be expired, the said Doctor shall advance two Pounds per ann more:

Thirdly, that upon the Expiration of the present Lease, the said Doctor shall pay twelve Pounds per ann, besides Receivers Fees, for the Remainder of the new Lease that shall be made to him.

Lastly that the said Doctor shall immediately pay twelve Pounds by way of Fine, in consideration of the new Lease.

Jonath. Swift.

Underneath, another hand has written:

This proposal made 1717 and rejected.

Dean Swift was giving no bargains to Dr. Hawkshaw! Perhaps he was still annoyed by Dr. Hawkshaw's handling of business affairs, which he criticised so warmly, time after time, in the *Journal to Stella*.

CHAPTER XIII

(I since writ as I found time)
But her charity to the poor was a duty not to be diminished and therefore became a tax upon those tradesmen who furnish the fopperies of other ladies. She bought clothes as seldom as possible, and those as plain and cheap as consisted with the situation she was in; and wore no lace for many years. Either her judgment or fortune was extraordinary in the choice of those on whom she bestowed her charity, for it went farther in doing good than double the sum from any other hand. And I have heard her say she always met with gratitude from the poor; which must be owing to her skill in distinguishing proper objects, as well as her gracious manner in relieving them.

(On the Death of Mrs. Johnson)

Swift's views on women's clothes were extreme, as indeed were his views on most objects, and he never hesitated to expound them, whether they were requested or not. A good specimen of his opinions on women's clothing—amongst other things—is his extraordinary *Letter to a Young Lady on her Marriage*, which he addressed to the daughter of his friend, Dr. Staunton, an eminent Dublin lawyer, on her marriage to John Rochfort, son of another of the Dean's friends, Chief Baron Rochfort. It is doubtful whether any unfortunate bride has ever received such a document!

It begins:

Madam, the Hurry and Impertinence of receiving and paying Visits on Account of your Marriage being now over, you are beginning to enter a Course of Life, where you will want much advice to divert you from falling into many Errors, Fopperies and Follies to which your Sex is subject . . . And beware of despising or neglecting my Instructions, whereon will depend not only your making a good Figure in the World, but your own real Happiness, as well as that of the Person who ought to be dearest to you.

The Dean then proceeds to lecture the bride:

I must likewise warn you strictly against the least Degree of Fondness to your Husband before any Witnesses whatever, even before your nearest Relations, or the very Maids in your Chamber.

This Proceeding is so extremely odious and disgustful to all who have either good Breeding or Good Sense, that they assign two very unamiable Reasons for it: the one is gross Hypocracy and the other hath too bad a Name to mention ...

After touching upon various other errors into which the girl is likely to fall, he reaches one of his favourite topics, which he had so often dinned into Stella's ears :

You have but a very few Years to be young and handsome in the Eyes of the World; and as few months to be so in the Eyes of a Husband, who is not a Fool; for I hope you do not still dream of Charms and Raptures, which Marriage ever did and ever will put a sudden End to. Besides, yours was a Match of Prudence and common good Likeing, without any Mixture of that ridiculous Passion which hath no Being but in Play-books and Romances.

This amazing letter was written in 1723, immediately after the rupture of his long relationship with Vanessa and shortly before her tragic death. It is difficult not to associate the Dean's venom towards happiness in marriage with his own total failure. Very probably, he had assisted at the Staunton-Rochfort wedding, and a psychiatrist might draw interesting conclusions from his obvious determination to destroy the bride's illusions about marriage.

Having declared love and passion anathema, he then proceeds to advise the girl how to make herself tolerable to her husband :

You must improve your Mind by closely pursuing such a Method of Study as I shall direct or approve of. You must get a Collection of History and Travels, which I will recommend you, and spend some Hours every Day in reading them, and making Extracts from them if your Memory be weak ... The Endowments of your Mind will even make your Person agreeable to your Husband.

It would have been very interesting to have watched the faces of the newly-married pair, while reading the Dean of St. Patrick's prescription for matrimony !

But worse was to come.

As little Respect as I have for the Generality of your Sex, it hath sometimes moved me to Pity to see the Lady of the House forced to withdraw immediately after Dinner; and this in Families where there is not much Drinking, as if it were an established Maxim that Women were incapable of Conversation. In a Room where both

*Sexes meet, if the Men are discoursing upon any general Subject,
the Ladies never think it their Business to partake in what passeth;
but in a separate Club to entertain each other with the Price and
Choice of Lace and Silk, and what Dresses they liked or disapproved
at the Church or the Play-house. And, when you are amongst your-
selves, how naturally, after the first Compliments, do you apply
your Hands to each others Lappets and Ruffles and Mantuas, as if
the whole Business of your Lives and the public Concern of the
whole world depended upon the Cut or Colour of your Petticoats!
. . . When I reflect upon this, I cannot conceive you to be human
Creatures, but a sort of Species hardly a Degree above a Monkey,
who hath more diverting tricks than any of you; is an Animal less
mischievous and expensive; might, in Time, be a tolerable Critick in
Velvet and Brocade; and, for ought I know, would equally become
them.*

The savagery of the last few lines echoes the hatreds of Gulliver.
The tirade against the behaviour of women, when secure from male
eyes, prompts the obvious query as to where the Dean got his information. Stella, he has recorded, avoided female entertainments, and
so did his other close contact, Vanessa.

Swift then proceeds to lecture the bride on her wardrobe :

*I would have you look upon Finery as a necessary Folly, which all
great Ladies did whom I have ever known: I do not desire you to be
out of the Fashion, but to be the last and least in it: I expect that
your Dress shall be one Degree lower than your Fortune can afford:
and in your own Heart I would wish you to be an utter Contemner
of all Distinctions which a finer Petticoat can give you; because it
will neither make you richer, handsomer, younger, better-natured,
more virtuous or wise than if it hung upon a Peg.*

His final remarks on the young lady's clothes are almost incredible, coming from the Dean who had set himself up as an authority
on Good Taste :

*You will perhaps be offended when I advise you to abate a little
of that violent Passion for fine Cloaths so predominant in your Sex.
It is somewhat hard that ours, for whose sake you wear them, are
not admitted to be of your Council. I may venture to assure you
that we will make an Abatement at any Time of four Pounds a yard
in a Brocade if the Ladies will but allow a suitable Addition of Care*

in the Cleanliness and Sweetness of their Persons. For the satyrical Part of Mankind will needs believe that it is not impossible to be very fine and very filthy; and that the Capacities of a Lady are sometimes apt to fall short in cultivating Cleanliness and Finery together. I shall only add, upon so tender a Subject, what a pleasant Gentleman said concerning a silly Woman of Quality: that nothing would make her supportable but cutting off her Head; for his Ears were offended by her Tongue, and his Nose by her Hair and Teeth.

Rumour has it that young Mrs. Rochfort *was* offended by this extraordinary *Epithalamium.*

So, Stella had little temptation to indulge in fine clothes and fopperies, even had she been inclined to such weaknesses. The Dean was very explicit in his belief that women adorned themselves solely for the sake of himself and his fellow-males, and that, moreover, such adornment was not appreciated by him. All that he, personally, required from the *Sex* was *Cleanliness.* More than twenty years earlier, when his burning passion for Miss Waring had cooled to grey ashes, he had written to her that he was quite indifferent as to whether her *person be beautiful,* since all he looked for from her was *Cleanliness.* So Stella wore plain, cheap clothes, unrelieved by lace, and, presumably, did as much washing as the meagre Dublin water-supply and other Eighteenth Century handicaps allowed.

Of her *charity,* all that is known is that, about the time when Swift was offering advice to young Mrs. Rochfort, Stella adopted a small boy. Much mystery surrounds this child, but there is a good deal of circumstantial evidence that he was the son of Vanessa and Swift, and that shortly after his mother's tragic death, Stella had taken him into her own keeping, thereby giving rise to scandalous rumours in Dublin, that she was herself the mother.

Monck-Berkeley recorded the statement of Swift's last servant, who had been at school with this child, that *he strongly resembled* the Dean, a circumstance which must have greatly added to Stella's embarrassment.

It is very significant that shortly before Stella's death Swift wrote a poem which could only have been intended to encourage her to ignore scandalmongers :

On Censure
Ye wise, instruct me to endure

An evil, which admits no cure.
Or how this evil can be borne
Which breeds at once both hate and scorn.
Bare innocence is no support
When you are tried in Scandal's court.
Stand high in honour, wealth or wit,
All others who inferior sit
Conceive themselves in conscience bound
To join and drag you to the ground.
Your altitude offends the eyes
Of those who want the power to rise.
The World a willing stander-by
Inclines to aid a specious lie,
Alas! they would not do you wrong,
But all appearances are strong.
Yet whence proceeds this weight we lay
On what detracting people say?
For let mankind discharge their tongues
In venom till they burst their lungs,
Their utmost malice cannot make
Your head, or tooth, or finger ache.
Nor spoil your shape, distort your face,
Or put one feature out of place.
Nor will you find your fortune sink
By what they speak or what they think;
Nor can ten hundred thousand lies
Make you less virtuous, learn'd, or wise.
The most effectual way to balk
Their malice is — to let them talk.

The boy, who went by the name of Bryan M'Loghlin, only survived Stella by a few years. He is probably the subject of that unique entry, in the Register of St. Patrick's Cathedral, where neither the name of the dead nor the place of burial is specified.[1]

Significantly, this is signed by Rev. Dr. Worrall, the Dean's close confidant and Vicar.

The conditions in which a large part of the Dublin population

---

1. See *Cadenus*: Sybil Le Brocquy.

existed, during Stella's life there, must have severely strained both the hearts and pockets of its charitable citizens. The poverty in which most of the inhabitants festered defies description. To quote John Churton Collins :

The condition of Ireland, between 1700 and 1750, was in truth such that no historian, who was not prepared to have his narrative laid aside with disgust and incredulity would venture to depict it. In a time of peace, the unhappy island suffered all the most terrible calamities, which follow in the train of war. Famine succeeding famine decimated the provincial villages and depopulated whole regions. Travellers have described how their way has lain through districts strewn like a battlefield with unburied corpses, which lay, some in ditches, some on the roadside, and some on heaps of offal, the prey of dogs and carrion-birds. "I have seen", says a writer quoted by Mr. Lecky, "the helpless orphan exposed on the dunghill and the hungry infant sucking at the breast of the already expired mother".

Whatever degree of culpability may attach itself to the inhabitants of Ireland, there can be no question that the English Government was, in the main, responsible for the existence of this hell. It requires very little sagacity to see that the miseries of Ireland flowed naturally and inevitably from the paralysis of national industry and the alienation of national revenue . . . Reference has already been made to the Statutes which annihilated the trade and industrial energy of the country. Equally iniquitous and oppressive was the alienation of the revenue. On that revenue had been quartered the parasites and mistresses of succeeding generations of English Kings.

In the *Journal to Stella,* in 1712, Swift records his first meeting with Lady Orkney :

. . . the late King's mistress, (who lives at a fine place called Cleveden) and I are grown mighty acquaintance. She is the wisest woman I ever saw . . .

Her wisdom in handling her Dutch lover had endowed her with the enormous income of £26,000 a year, taxed on the Irish Revenue. Swift can scarcely have been unaware of the source of her ill-gotten gains.

It is impossible to give here more than a brief account of the almost universal destitution amongst what was usually referred to as *the mere Irish*.

As early as 1660, the rapidly increasing prosperity of Irish trade had aroused bitter resentment in English commercial circles and, as a result, various enactments systematically destroyed the chief Irish export trades in cattle and wool. The immediate result was to throw thousands of able-bodied, industrious artisans on to public charity, and as Irish trade decayed the numbers of the workless grew in town and countryside.

Some twenty years later, when the Catholic King, James II, came to Ireland, looking for help against his invading son-in-law, the Prince of Orange, he was welcomed by the great part of his oppressed Irish subjects, who hoped for some relief if the King were victorious. But his defeat at the Battle of the Boyne ensured the ultimate disaster for his supporters. The English Government took a terrible revenge. A series of Penal Laws were enacted with the intention of reducing the Catholic Irish to a condition in which they could never again become a threat to England. They were to become for ever impotent *insignificant slaves, fit for nothing but to hew wood and draw water,* to quote from the definitive book on the Irish Famine.[2]

New Irish Penal Laws came into force in 1695; they barred Catholics — some 95% of the population—from the Law, the Army and Navy, from all Commerce or Civic office. No Catholic could vote, buy land, or be employed by the Crown. All Catholic estates, which were not immediately confiscated, were gradually dismembered by being compulsorily divided, on the owner's death, amongst all his sons, unless one of them chose to become a Protestant and so take the entire property. Catholics were forbidden to teach and Catholic children were not allowed to attend school, nor to be sent abroad for education. The practice of the Catholic religion was banned, and priests were hunted and, when captured, executed. (This identification in suffering of the Irish Clergy and laity created a bond between them which has lasted over centuries.)

Edmund Burke described the Irish Penal Code as :

---

2. *The Great Hunger*: Cecil Woodham-Smith (Hamish Hamilton, London).

. . . a machine as well fitted for the oppression and impoverish-
ment of human nature itself, as ever proceeded from the perverted
ingenuity of man.

Already during the first quarter of the Eighteenth Century, the
Penal Laws had produced their reasonably anticipated evils : dire
poverty and hatred of the oppressive forces of the Law.

To quote *The Great Hunger* :

During the long Penal period, dissimulation became a moral
necessity, and evasion of the Law the duty of every Godfearing
Catholic. To worship according to his Faith, the Catholic must
attend illegal meetings; to protect his priest, he must be secret and
cunning and a concealer of the truth.

In 1726, Swift wrote :

The whole Country, excepting the Scotch Plantation in the
North, is a Scene of Misery and Desolation scarcely to be matched
on this side of Lapland.

In the year of Stella's death, he wrote one of the most bitterly
savage satires ever penned :

A modest proposal for preventing the Children of the poor People
in Ireland from being a Burden to their Parents and Country; and
for making them beneficial to the Publick.

It begins :

It is a melancholy Object to those who walk through this great
Town . . . when they see the Street, the Roads and Cabin Doors
crowded with Beggars of the Female Sex, followed by three, four or
six Children, all in Rags and importuning every Passenger for an
Alms. These Mothers, instead of being able to work for their honest
livelihood, are forced to employ all their Time in strolling to get
Sustenance for their helpless Infants; who, as they grow up, either
turn Thieves for want of Work, or leave their dear Native Country
to fight for the Pretender in Spain, or sell themselves to the Bar-
badoes.

I think it is agreed, by all Parties, that this prodigious Number of
Children in Arms, or on the Backs, or at the Heels of their Mothers,
and frequently their Fathers, is, in the present deplorable State of
this Kingdom, a very great additional Grievance; and, therefore,

whoever could find out a fair, cheap and easy Method of making these Children sound and useful Members of the Commonwealth would deserve so well of the Publick as to have his Statue set up as a Preserver of the Nation.

Swift proposed to earn the public's gratitude and a Dublin statue by a most rational scheme for the planned propagation and careful processing of Irish infants, to be slaughtered for the market at one year old.

As to our City of Dublin, Shambles may be appointed for this Purpose in the most convenient Part of it; and Butchers, we may be assured, will not be wanting; although I rather recommend buying the Children alive and dressing them hot from the Knife, as we do roasting Pigs . . . I grant this Food will be somewhat dear, and therefore very proper for Landlords, who, as they have already devoured most of the Parents, seem to have the best Title to the Children . . . I desire those Politicians, who dislike my Overtures . . . that they will first ask the Parents . . . whether they would not at this Day, think it a great Happiness to have been sold for Food, at a Year old, and thereby have avoided such a perpetual Scene of Misfortune as they have since gone through, by the Oppression of Landlords, the Impossibility of paying Rent without Money or Trade, the Want of common Sustenance, with neither House nor Cloaths to cover them from the Inclemencies of the Weather; and the most inevitable Prospect of intailing the like, or greater Miseries upon their Breed for ever.

It is difficult to-day to read Swift's very lengthy and gruesomely detailed suggestions about the preparation of various dishes without being sickened.

There is nothing comparable he says :

. . . in Taste, or Magnificence to a well-grown, fat yearly Child; which, roasted whole, will make a considerable Figure at a Lord Mayor's Feast, or any other publick Entertainment.

It is almost incredible that these social conditions, which fired Swift's horror and rage, had come about in so short a time. To quote an eminent historian :

On February 8th, 1685, Charles II died and Ormond ceased to be Lord Lieutenant. Ireland was now in somewhat of the flourishing

103

condition she had been in 1640, and in the last twenty years, the Revenue had doubled itself.[3]

By the early years of the Eighteenth Century, the Irish Penal laws had done their deadly preparatory work and the Nineteenth Century Famines had become ghastly certainties. The survival of the Irish people is one of History's miracles, and Swift's prophecy of :

. . . the most inevitable prospect of intailing the like or greater miseries upon their breed, for ever . . .

must, in the year of Grace, 1728, have appeared a rational conclusion.

Dr. Delany gives a curious account of the Dean's own arrangements for dealing with beggars in the Liberty of St. Patrick's, where he ruled, independent of all Civic authority :

I never saw Poor so carefully and conscientiously attended to in my life, as those of his Cathedral; they were badged and never begged out of their own district . . There was no such thing as a vagrant or an unbadged beggar seen about his Cathedral. Not only the servants of his Church, but his own Poor also were obliged to drive them away at their peril; they knew they could not suffer any such to appear, but at the hazard of their employment and badges.

Some wretched beggars used to try to hide the badges, given them by the Dean as a licence to beg in the streets around the Cathedral. Delany quotes him — with approval — as saying :

If Beggary be not able to beat out Pride, it cannot deserve Charity.

Perhaps that instinct which prompted these derelicts to hide the Beggar's badge may have been one of those imponderables which helped a race to survive. Much humour has been expended on the Irishman's claim to kingly ancestors. When all other props to human dignity had been swept away in a dreadful Present, a legendary Past may have provided a refuge from the despair of reality.

---

3. *A History of Ireland*, Edmund Curtis, M.A.Litt.D. (Methuen).

CHAPTER XIV

But she had another quality that much delighted her, although it might be thought a kind of check upon her bounty; however, it was a pleasure she could not resist: I mean that of making agreeable presents; wherein I never knew her equal, although it be an affair of as delicate a nature as most in the course of life. She used to define a present, that it was a gift to a friend of something he wanted or was fond of, and which could not easily be gotten for money. I am confident that during my acquaintance with her, she has, on these and some other kinds of liberality, disposed of to the value of several hundred pounds. As to presents made to herself, she received them with great unwillingness, but especially from those to whom she had ever given any: being, on all occasions, the most disinterested mortal I ever knew or heard of.

(On the Death of Mrs. Johnson)

The nature of Stella's thoughtful and agreeable presents was not recorded by Swift, but she certainly gave books to the Dean, and significantly autographed them *Esther Johnson.* Swift also gave her presents of books, as he tells in the *Journal:* 4th Jan., 1710-11.

I went to Bateman's, the book-seller . . . and bought three little volumes of Lucian, in French, for our Stella.

The *other kinds of liberality,* to which Swift refers, must have included the provision for the child, Bryan M'Loghlin.

From her own disposition at least as much as from the frequent want of health, she seldom made any visits; but her own lodgings, from before twenty years old, were frequented by many persons of the grave sort, who all respected her highly upon her good sense, good manners and conversation. Among these were the late Primate Lindsay, Bishop Lloyd, Bishop Ashe, Bishop Brown, Bishop Sterne, Bishop Pulleyn and some others of later date; and indeed the greater number of her acquaintance was among the clergy.

(On the Death of Mrs. Johnson)

While Stella was probably acquainted with all these great clerics, with whom Swift so impressively surrounds her, her close friends were amongst the lesser ranks — the Walls, Stoytes, Grattans, Delanys, Ashes, Manleys and Sheridan.

Honour, truth, liberality, good nature and modesty were the virtues she chiefly possessed, and most valued in her acquaintance: and, where she found them, would be ready to allow for some defects: nor valued them less although they did not shine in learning or in wit; but would never give the least allowance for any failures in the former, even to those who made the greatest figure in either of the two latter.

(On the Death of Mrs. Johnson)

Stella never made the *least allowance* for a failure in *honour or truth,* which probably accounts for the complete break between herself and Swift, which lasted for over six months, in 1723. She then fled from Dublin to the refuge of Wood Park, where, according to Dr. Delany, she was greatly *shocked and distressed,* although he did his *utmost endeavour to relieve, support and amuse her, in her sad situation.* In the meanwhile, the Dean disappeared from his friends, *on a tour of the South of Ireland for about two months . . . to dissipate his thought and give place to obloquy.* No reasonable explanation has been put forward to account for the Dean's flight from Dublin's obloquy, following immediately on Vanessa's death; nor indeed for Stella's flight from Dublin, some weeks before it. There is enough circumstantial evidence to justify a theory that the dying Vanessa, believing that Stella was merely Swift's middle-aged friend of years, appealed to her to take charge of the boy, Bryan M'Loghlin, after her own imminent death. The shock to Stella of discovering the deception Swift had practised for so many years would have accounted for Stella's rupture of their friendship. Three months later, Dean Swift wrote to Sheridan :

Are the Ladies in town, or in the country? If I knew I would write to them. Are they in health?

After a friendship which had lasted some forty years, the break was then complete.

Stella's courage, *good nature and liberality* were amply proved by her adoption of Bryan M'Loghlin. At the time she was in very poor health and it must have been extremely inconvenient to house a young boy. It would seem from the evidence of Richard Brennan,

106

(Swift's last manservant) that the child was sometimes a boarder at the school belonging to St. Patrick's Cathedral, but his presence in Stella's household is proved by the introductory lines Swift wrote for his

Elegy upon Tyger
Her dear Lady's joy and comfort
Who departed this Life
The last day of March 1727
To the great joy of Bryan
That his antagonist is gone

Mrs. Dingley's pampered lap-dog may well have been unpopular with the twelve year old boy, who shared the household attention.

She had no use for any person's liberality, yet her detestation of covetous people made her uneasy if such a one was in her company; upon which she would say many things very entertaining and humourous. She never interrupted any person who spoke; she laughed at no mistakes they made, but helped them out with modesty; and if a good thing were spoken, she would not let it fall, but set it in the best light to those who were present. She listened to all that was said, and had never the least distraction or absence of thought.

(On the Death of Mrs. Johnson)

All this, Swift had previously written about Stella. Apparently, he did not re-read his earlier notes.

It was not safe, nor prudent, in her presence to offend in the least word against modesty; for she then gave full employment to her wit, her contempt and resentment, under which even stupidity and brutality were forced to sink into confusion; and the guilty person, by her future avoiding him like a bear or a satyr, was never in the way to transgress a second time. It happened one single coxcomb, of the pert kind, was in her company among several other ladies; and in his flippant way began to deliver some double meanings. The rest flapped their fans and used the other common expedients practised in such cases, of appearing not to mind or comprehend what was said. Her behaviour was very different, and perhaps

107

may be censured. She said thus to the man: "Sir, all these ladies and I understand your meaning very well, having, in spite of our care, too often met with those of your sex who wanted manners and good sense. But believe me, neither virtuous nor even vicious women love such kind of conversation. However, I will leave you, and report your behaviour; and whatever visit I make, I shall first inquire at the door whether you are in the house, that I may be sure to avoid you".

(On the Death of Mrs. Johnson)

It is easy to picture the other ladies flapping their fans in acute embarrassment, whilst Stella delivered her stern rebuke, with much the same deliberation with which she had shot the burglar in her youth. Here is the strong-minded woman, who seldom finds her way into the popular picture of Stella. It is interesting to contrast this picture with Thackeray's sample of sympathetic Victorian sentiment run riot :

Who hasn't in his mind the image of Stella? Who does not love her? Fair and tender creature; pure and affectionate of heart! Boots it to you now, that you have been at rest for a hundred and twenty years not divided in death from the cold heart which caused yours, whilst it beat, such painful pangs of love and grief . . . boots it to you now, that the whole world loves and deplores you? Scarce any man, I believe, ever thought of that grave, that did not cast a flower of pity on it, and wrote over it a sweet epitaph. Gentle lady, so lovely, so loving, so unhappy! You have had countless champions, millions of manly hearts mourning for you. From generation to generation we take up the fond tradition of your beauty; we watch and follow your tragedy, your bright morning love of purity, your constancy, your sweet martyrdom. We know your legend by heart. You are one of the saints of English story.

Against Thackeray's vision of the *gentle lady*, it is a useful corrective to place Swift's own list of Stella's shortcomings. In 1720, he dedicated verses :

To Stella, who collected and transcribed his poems.

In it, he acknowledges the good fortune of one whom Stella *chooses for a friend*, and emphasises the fact that his praise of her owes nothing to Stella's *beauty, dress, or paint, or youth.* The poem ends :

> *Stella, when you these lines transcribe*
> *Lest you should take them for a bribe,*
> *Resolv'd to mortify your pride,*
> *I'll here expose your weaker side.*
> *Your spirits kindle to a flame,*
> *Mov'd with the lightest touch of blame;*
> *And when a friend in kindness tries*
> *To show you where your error lies*
> *Conviction does but more incense;*
> *Perverseness is your whole defense;*
> *Truth, judgment, wit give place to spite*
> *Regardless both of wrong and right;*
> *Your virtues all suspended wait*
> *Till Time has open'd Reason's gate;*
> *And what is worse, your passion bends*
> *Its force against your nearest friends,*
> *Which manners, decency and pride*
> *Have taught you from the world to hide:*
> *In vain; for see your friend has brought*
> *To public light your only fault;*
> *And yet a fault we often find*
> *Mix'd in a noble generous mind;*
> *And may compare to Aetna's fire,*
> *Which, though with trembling, all admire*
> *The heat that makes the summit glow*
> *Enriching all the plains below.*
> *Those who in warmer climes complain*
> *From Phoebus' rays they suffer pain*
> *Must own that pain is largely paid*
> *By gen'rous wines beneath the shade.*
> *Yet, when I find your passions rise,*
> *And anger sparkling in your eyes*
> *I grieve those spirits should be spent*
> *For nobler ends by nature meant.*
> *One passion with a different turn*
> *Makes wit inflame, or anger burn.*

> *So the sun's heat with diff'rent pow'rs*
> *Ripens the grape, the liquor sours.*
> *Thus Ajax, when with rage possest*
> *By Pallas breath'd into his breast,*
> *His valour would no more employ*
> *Which might alone have conquered Troy;*
> *But, blinded by resentment, seeks*
> *For vengeance on his friends, the Greeks.*
> *You think this turbulence of blood*
> *From stagnation preserves the flood*
> *Which, thus fermenting, by degrees*
> *Exalts the spirits, sinks the lees.*
> *Stella, for once you reason wrong;*
> *For should this ferment last too long,*
> *By time subsiding, you may find*
> *Nothing but acid left behind:*
> *From passion you may then be freed,*
> *When peevishness and spleen succeed.*
> *Say Stella, when you copy next*
> *Will you keep strictly to the text?*
> *Dare you let these reproaches stand*
> *And to your failing set your hand?*
> *Or if these lines your anger fire*
> *Shall they in baser flames expire?*
> *Whene'er they burn, if, burn they must,*
> *They'll prove my accusation just.*

Possibly she burnt *her* copy, but Swift took the precaution of keeping another. He certainly published the verses before her death.

That the poem did not *in baser flames expire* suggests that Stella had a sense of humour. Nevertheless, when the poetic trimmings have been removed — the agricultural benefits of Etna's volcanic activities, as well as the disastrous effects of the rage of Ajax on the Trojan Wars — the stark fact remains that Stella is accused of a violent temper, which intimidated her nearest friends, including the indomitable Dean! Thackeray would not have recognised his meek and gentle martyr, but the *flippant coxcomb* would have added his testimony to Swift's, as the indignant lady flounced from his unpleasant company, *with anger sparkling in her eyes.*

110

In view of Swift's earlier statement that she had been instructed in physics by an eminent physician, it is interesting to find her excusing her bad temper on the medical ground that it produced a turbulence of blood, which prevented *stagnation* and its attendant evils. Swift refused to accept her theory, although some of his own views on medicine were decidedly odd. In 1711, he wrote to Stella :

I visited the Duchess of Ormond this morning .. I spoke to her to get a lad touched for the Evil, the son of a grocer in Capel Street . . . The poor fellow has been here, some months, with his boy. But the Queen has not been able to touch, and now it grows warm, I fear she will not touch at all.

Queen Anne was the last Sovereign who attempted to cure the King's Evil — scrofula — by her royal touch. The belief that the poor diseased lady had any pretensions to cure anybody of anything is proof of the strength of an age-old superstition, which even the mighty mind of Swift could not withstand. A few years earlier, Sir John Penicuik, one of the Commissioners who negotiated the Union of Scotland and England, described a visit to Queen Anne :

One day, I had occasion to observe the Calamities, which attend human Nature, even in the greatest Dignities of Life. Her Majesty was labouring under a fit of the Gout, and in extreme Pain and Agony; and on this Occasion everything about her was in much the same Disorder as the meanest of her Subjects. Her Face, which was red and spotted, was rendered something frightful by her negligent Dress, and the Foot affected was tied up in a Poultice and some nasty Bandages. I was much affected by this Sight, and the more when she had occasion to mention her People of Scotland. What are you, thought I, who talks in the style of a Sovereign!

Nevertheless, Doctor Swift was quite prepared to believe that Divine power to heal the sick Dublin child lay in her poor gouty hand. It is one example of the many conflicting characteristics of this extraordinary man.

By returning very few visits, she had not much company of her own sex, except those whom she most loved for their easiness, or esteemed for their good sense: and those, not insisting on ceremony, came often to her. But she rather chose men for her companions, the usual topic of ladies' discourse being such as she had little knowldege of, much less relish. Yet no man was upon the rack to entertain her, for she easily descended to anything that was innocent and diverting. News, politics, censure, family management, or town talk, she always diverted to something else, but these indeed seldom happened, for she chose her company better; and therefore many, who mistook her and themselves, having solicited her acquaintance and finding themselves disappointed, after a few visits dropped off; and she was never known to enquire into the reason, nor ask what was become of them.

(On the Death of Mrs. Johnson)

If Swift's picture of Stella's social life be true, she had altered very considerably since the days of the *Journal*. During those years, the Ladies' lives had revolved inside a circle of close Dublin friends, whose amusements were centred around the dining and card-tables — Sterne, then Dean of St. Patrick's; the wealthy Alderman Stoyte and his wife, who owned a fine mansion in Donnybrook; Archdeacon Walls and his wife; Mrs. Manley and her husband, who was Post-Master-General (and much suspected of tampering with letters!) The *Journal* is full of allusions to their dinners and card parties :

Pray dine with the Dean, but don't lose your money.

How goes Ombre? Does Mrs. Walls win constantly, as she used to do? and Mrs. Stoyte? . . . .

And so go to your gang of Deans and Stoytes and Walls, and lose your money . . . .

Rise tomorrow and walk to Donnybrook and lose your money with Stoyte and the Dean; do so, dear little rogues, and drink Presto's health sometimes with your Deans and your Stoytes and your Walls and your Manleys and your everybodies . . . . . So the Bishop of Clogher and his lady were your guests for a night or two. Why you have become a great gamester and company-keeper.

In their letters, the Ladies kept him well supplied with the Dublin gossip. During the latter part of her life, Stella appears to have earned local fame as a conversationalist, and Dr. Delany tells the story that :

An humorous but wrong-judging gentleman of her acquaintance took it into his head to set up the character of another lady, in rivalship to hers: and raised some awkward mirth to himself from Stella's sitting silent at a visit, where that lady displayed her talents.

Apparently, Stella's silence ended the contest. It also produced some mediocre verses from Dr. Delany entitled *The Linnet and the Jay*.

She was never positive in arguing; and she usually treated those who were so, in a manner which well enough gratified that unhappy disposition; yet in such a sort as made it very contemptible, and at the same time did some hurt to the owners. Whether this proceeded from her easiness in general, or from her indifference to persons, or from her despair of mending them, or from the same practice which she so much liked in Mr. Addison, I cannot determine; but when she saw any of the company very warm in a wrong opinion, she was more inclined to confirm them in it than oppose them. The excuse she commonly gave, when her friends asked the reason, was that it prevented noise and saved time. Yet I have known her very angry, with some whom she much esteemed, for sometimes falling into that infirmity.

(On the Death of Mrs. Johnson)

So Stella's hot temper was usually well enough under control to prevent her from arguing against the *wrong opinions* of her visitors, no matter how angry she might feel with those among *them whom she much esteemed*.

Not for the first time, those interested in Stella must deplore the fact that this remarkable woman apparently kept no diaries, or that, if she did, they have not survived. Her own account of her friends — and enemies — would have provided an invaluable light on Swift and the circle of acquaintances that they shared. In her will, she left all her papers, both inside and out of her locked box, to the Dean. Since he had, almost certainly, taken back all his letters to MD (which subsequently formed the *Journal to Stella*) shortly after his return to Ireland in 1714, when he used them as material for his historical memoirs, it is interesting, if futile, to speculate about the papers he inherited on her death.

When the MD letters came to light, many years after Swift's death, he had carefully deleted the more intimate passages; it is unlikely that he would have preserved her private papers, had any existed.

The history of the *MD* letters is curious. His cousin, Mrs. Whiteway, claimed that the Dean gave her forty letters, in 1738, in a *parcel of papers*, which she did not bother to open until some ten years after the Dean's death. The remaining twenty-five were found amongst Swift's papers, by the Rev. Dr. Lyon, who appears to have lived in the Deanery and taken charge of its inmate, after Swift had been declared insane in 1740. Dr. Lyon gave them to his friend Wilkes, who sold them to a bookseller. These letters were published in 1766, edited by Dr. Hawkesworth; the originals are in the British Museum. Mrs. Whiteway's *parcel of papers* were taken over by her son-in-law, Deane Swift, and published in 1768. The original letters have disappeared. In 1784 Thomas Sheridan combined all the letters in the *Journal to Stella* — a name Swift did not invent for her until many years after his long London sojourn, when the letters were written.

She loved Ireland much better than the generality of those who owe both their birth and riches to it; and having brought over all the fortune she had in money, left the reversion of the best part of it, £1,000, to Dr. Stephen's Hospital. She detested the tyranny and injustice of England in their treatment of this Kingdom. She had, indeed, reason to love a country, where she had the esteem and friendship of all who knew her, and the universal good report of all who ever heard of her, without one exception, if I am told the truth by those who keep general conversation. Which character is the more extraordinary in falling to a person of so much knowledge, wit and vivacity, qualities that are used to create envy, and consequently censure; and must be rather imputed to her great modesty, gentle behaviour, and inoffensiveness, than to her superior virtues.
(On the Death of Mrs. Johnson)

As previously stated, Stella's sole fortune was land in Co. Wicklow, left her by Sir William Temple; there is no evidence of any other property, which she *brought over* from England, unless, perhaps the £400 mentioned by Lady Giffard in her will, upon which she paid Stella interest until her death in 1722. This money may well have been the augmented collection of gold pieces, which Stella's mother had persuaded her to put out to interest, so reluctantly, in her early girlhood.

It is odd that Swift should have misspelled the name of Dr. Steevens, of whose Hospital he was a trustee.

Stella would certainly have reflected the Dean's detestation of *the tyranny and injustice* with which Ireland was treated by England. By the time of her death, it had become an obsession with Swift, who did everything in his power to expose and thwart the political corruption of his enemies, the Whigs, which had reduced the entire country to near beggary.

But it is well to make clear the limits inside which his *savage indignation* functioned. When he tiraded against the wrongs\of the Irish, he meant those people, whom he constantly described as the *English born in Ireland*. In a memorandum, written in 1726 to the Earl of Peterborough, to be passed on to Sir Robert Walpole, he complains :

That all persons born in Ireland are called and treated as Irishmen, although their fathers and grandfathers were born in England; and their predecessors, having been conquerors of Ireland, it is humbly conceived that they should be on as good a foot as subjects of Britain.

Having thus clearly defined the unhappy position of the English born in Ireland, who were being treated by the English Government as badly as if they were native Irishmen, he protests against the many abuses they were suffering : chiefly trade discriminations and the abominable custom of filling all lucrative positions, in Church or State, with Englishmen born in England. Again, in 1733, he addressed the Freemen of the City of Dublin :

As to the people of this Kingdom, they consist either of Irish Papists, who are as inconsiderable, in point of power, as women and children; or of English Protestants, who love their brethren of that Kingdom, although they may sometimes complain and think themselves hardly used.

And again :

We consist of two Parties; I do not mean Papist and Protestant, High and Low Church, Episcopal and Sectarian, Whig and Tory, but of these English who happen to be born in this Kingdom (whose

115

ancestors reduced the whole nation under the obedience of the English Crown) and the gentleman sent from the other side to possess most of the chief employments here.

Swift's indignation burned ever more fiercely on the arrival of each new Englishman, appointed to an Irish Deanery or Bishopric. He explained their subsequent misbehaviour by his theory that, naturally, only the most excellent persons were appointed by the English Sovereign, but that, by singularly bad luck, the new bishops were invariably waylaid by English highwaymen, who murdered the saintly men, stole their papers and wardrobes, and so disguised, usurped their high offices in Ireland!

In the Fourth Drapier Letter, Swift wrote :

A short paper, printed in Bristol and re-printed here, reports Mr. Wood to say that he wonders at the impudence and insolence of the Irish in refusing his coin . . . where, by the way, he is mistaken: for it is the true English people of Ireland who refuse it; although we take it for granted that the Irish will do so too, whenever they are asked.

There is not the slightest doubt that Swift always considered himself an Englishman, who happened to have been born in Ireland. His attitude towards his nationality could have been paralleled by any Englishman in the 18th Century, who was born in India. Swift had little sympathy with the vast, suffering Papist majority of Irish, whom he regarded as equally dangerous and misguided in their politics and their religion.

From time to time, the more liberal minds in England and Ireland attempted to have the Sacramental Test Act repealed. This Law provided that anyone seeking public office must take the Sacrament of the Established Church, and so it barred all Dissenters — Presbyterian, Quaker or Catholic — from all appointments in the State or Church. The liberals argued that, while such deprivation was reasonable and proper so far as Catholics were concerned, it was unwise to penalise fellow-Protestants, even though their consciences would not allow them to conform to the ceremonial of the State Church.

To Swift these views reeked of dangerous political heresy, which imperilled the very existence of the Established Church. In 1708, he propounded his detestation of such theories in :

116

A letter from a member of the House of Commons in Ireland.

We are told the Popish interest here is so formidable that all hands should be joined to keep it under; that the only names of distinctions among us ought to be those of Protestants and Papists, and that this expedient (the Repeal of the Test Act) *is the only means to unite all Protestants upon one common bottom. All of which is nothing but misrepresentation and mistake.*

If we were under any real fear of the Papists in this Kingdom, it would be hard to think us so stupid as not to be equally apprehensive with others, since we are likely to be the greatest and most immediate sufferers; but, on the contrary, we look upon them to be altogether as inconsiderable as women and children. Their lands are almost entirely taken from them, and they are rendered incapable of purchasing any more. And, for the little that remains, provision is made by the late Act against Popery, that it will daily crumble away; to prevent which, some of the most considerable among them are already turned Protestant. Then, the Popish priests are all registered, and without permission (which I hope will not be granted) they can have no successors; so that the Protestant clergy will find it, perhaps, no difficult matter to bring great numbers over to the Church. And, in the meantime, the common people, without leaders, without discipline, or natural courage, being little better than "hewers of wood and drawers of water", are out of all capacity of doing any mischief, if they were ever so well inclined . . . . . It is agreed among naturalists that a lion is a larger, stronger and more dangerous enemy than a cat; yet, if a man were to have his choice, either a lion at his foot, bound fast in three or four chains, his teeth drawn and his claws pared to the quick, or an angry cat, in full liberty at his throat, he would take no long time to determine.

Swift had neither fear nor favour for the maimed and shackled lion of Papacy, but all his life he dreaded the dissenting angry cat. It was an Age of intolerance, and he was a man of his Age.

Stella, on the other hand, though born in England, appears to have travelled some distance towards the point at which the earlier Norman invaders became *more Irish than the Irish themselves.* In the *Journal*, Swift makes jocose references :

I think I am civiller than I used to be, and have not used the

expression "You in Ireland", and "we in England", as I did when I
was here before, to your great indignation!

And a few weeks later :

Impudent sluts! Because I write "Dublin, Ireland", therefore you
must write "London, England": that is Stella's malice!

Stella spent the greater part of her forty-five years in Ireland, and
the most of that in her Mary Street lodgings, close to the Liffey —
hence Swift's title, the *Ladies of St. Mary's*. When they first came
to Dublin, the city had broken through its confining mediaeval
walls, which had contained little more than the seat of government,
the Castle; Christ Church Cathedral; (St. Patrick's Cathedral, a few
hundred yards away was outside the City walls) the Tholsel, head-
quarters of civic authority; and a maze of congested buildings in
narrow streets. (The Wide Street Commissioners had not yet begun
their grandiose plans for Dublin's Georgian future). The old University lay far outside the city. (It still commemorates its past isola-
tion by its present official address, *Trinity College, near Dublin*).
Close by the College stood Chichester House, an ancient and dela-
pidated mansion, which housed the Irish Houses of Lords and
Commons until 1727, when it was demolished and replaced by
Pearce's magnificent building. On one side of Chichester House ran
a narrow street, Turnstile Alley. There, Bartholomew Van Homrigh, a member of Parliament, had owned a convenient house. His
daughter inherited it, and used it constantly when she left her
Celbridge property to stay in Dublin. Swift's frequent visits to her
there cannot have passed unnoticed in a small community, and
during the nine years of the Dean's close association with Vanessa,
the buzz of Dublin gossip must often have reached Stella's ears, in
her nearby home.

Already in the Seventeenth Century, speculative builders had
erected some great mansions in St. Stephen's Green, notably the
Earl of Shelbourne's house, on the site where the Shelbourne Hotel
now stands. The tree-lined outer walks of the Green offered a gay
and fashionable parade, and its undrained central marsh provided
quantities of snipe and wild birds, during the Winter season. The
neighbouring Grafton Street was rapidly developing, and St.
Patrick's Well, at its northern end, was a place of constant pilgrim-
age. Even Dawson Street was beginning to attract the speculative

builder. Swift describes how :

The mason, the bricklayer, the carpenter, the slater, the glazier take a lot of ground, club to build one or more houses, unite their credit, their stock and their money, and when it is finished, sell it to the best advantage they can. But, as it often happens, and more every day, that their fund will not answer half their design, they are forced to undersell it at the first storey, and are all reduced to beggary. In so much that I knew a certain fanatic brewer, who is reported to have some hundreds of houses in this town and is said to have purchased the greater part of them at half value from ruined undertakers . . . .

The adjective *fanatic* in Swift's vocabulary meant a Dissenter. The brewer in question was Mr. Leeson, afterwards created Earl of Milltown, who, out of his enormous wealth, built Russborough House, one of the most magnificent mansions in the neighbourhood of Dublin.

The Ladies used to visit out as far as Donnybrook where they were constantly entertained by the wealthy Stoyte family, headed by Sir Francis Stoyte, Lord Mayor of Dublin. There they spent at least one Christmas holiday. To reach Donnybrook Castle, the un-bridged Dodder had to be crossed by a ford; nevertheless, Swift constantly exhorted the Ladies to walk there. (His belief in the curative value of exercise never faltered.)

Stella's friends were largely drawn from the circle of clergy attached to the two Cathedrals, and a group of comfortable citizens. There is no evidence that the Ladies were ever entertained in the great Vice-regal mansion, on the riverbank at Chapelizod, known as the King's House since William III held his court there, during his 1690 stay in Dublin. But they must have been familiar with the charming locality, from whence, legend asserts, another unhappy girl, Isolde, set out, with Sir Tristram for a new life in Cornwall. Stella's good friend, Mrs. Proby — whose husband was Surgeon-General to the Forces — lived there, as did Lady Eustace, in whose home Stella spent the last months of her life.

Outside Dublin, the Ladies spent time at Laracor, Co. Meath, when Swift was in residence in his parish there; a small house in the neighbourhood is still known as Stella's Cottage. They also paid periodic visits to Trim, staying either with the Bishop of Clogher, or

119

with the Raymonds. Quilca with all its discomforts, often was their home for months at a time, as was Wood Park, the home of Charles Ford. Stella's friends, the Swantons, had a house at Portrane, near Dublin, where she stayed one summer. There was an ancient Norman peeltower, apparently belonging to the local rectory; it was known locally as *Stella's Tower*. In her will, Stella left a legacy to one of the Swanton family — who were connections of Swift — so that the friendship lasted till her death.

Besides these purely social visits, the Ladies, sharing the common Eighteenth Century belief in the efficacy of spas, visited Wexford and Templeogue, where Stella drank the waters, and Dingley apparently did the housekeeping under extremely trying conditions, to judge by Swift's humorous references in the *Journal*.

Except for the solitary visit the Ladies paid to their native land in 1707-8, their lives were spent in a quiet Irish backwater. It is unlikely they ever dreamed that their relationship with the Dean of St. Patrick's would inexorably carry them, in his turbulent wake, into a wide, unsheltered sea.

CHAPTER XV

*Although her knowledge, from books and company, was much more
extensive than usually falls to the share of her sex, yet she was so far
from making a parade of it, that her female visitants, on their first
acquaintance, who expected to discover it by what they call hard
words and deep discourse, would be sometimes disappointed and say
they found she was like other women. But wise men, through all her
modesty, whatever they discoursed on, could easily observe that she
understood these very well, by the judgment shown in her observations, as well as her questions.*

(On the Death of Mrs. Johnson)

There is no indication as to when Swift finally ceased his reminis-
cences of Stella; they appear to have petered out, having become
repetitive. He was tired . . . a mainspring of energy, which had been
slackening during her long illness, had ceased to function. Stella was
gone . . . . .

During her last weeks, the Dean wrote two prayers, which, presumably, he recited at her bedside. In one of them he asked the *all-
powerful Being to pity us, the mournful friends of thy distressed servant, who sink under the weight of her present condition, and the
fear of losing the most valuable of our friends: restore her to us, O
Lord, if it be thy gracious will, or inspire us with constancy and
resignation to support ourselves under so heavy an affliction . . . .*

And then the prayer continues, unexpectedly :

*Restore her, O Lord, for the sake of those poor, who, by losing
her, will be desolate: and those sick, who will not only want her
bounty, but her care and tending; or else, in thy mercy, raise up
some other in her place, with equal disposition and better abilities . .*

If Stella were conscious and listening to Swift's request for a
superior replacement, she must have needed all the comfort her
sense of humour, or her philosophy could bring.

Among the many virtues with which Swift endowed her, he made
no claim for piety. She was not familiar with the Bible. In the
Journal, Swift wrote :

*Yes, Stella shall have a large printed Bible. I have put it down
among my commissions for M.D. I am glad you have taken the
fancy of intending to read the Bible.*

121

It is difficult to believe that Dean Swift, himself, was a pious man. His temperament and gifts were such that, no matter what profession he chose, he would probably have been successful. Had he accepted King William's offer of a commission in the Army, he would undoubtedly have been a magnificent officer—and successfully smothered his objections to a standing army! It is easiest to imagine him a lawyer. What an advocate he would have made—and what a judge! Had circumstances allowed him to continue his political career in England, there could have been few limits to his success. Of all professions, he was perhaps least temperamentally fitted for the Church; but, once ordained, he threw all his energies into the fight for its advancement, and all his venom on those he considered its enemies. He faithfully carried out his clerical duties; his Cathedral services were as near perfection as he could bring them. In this respect, Dr. Delany related one of his *particularities:*

. . . his singular attention to the style of every man that preached in his Church . . . As soon as anyone got up into the pulpit, he pulled out his pencil and a piece of paper, and carefully noted every wrong pronunciation or expression that fell from him . . . . These he never failed to admonish the preacher of, as soon as he came into the Chapter-house.

The most hardened orator must have quailed in the pulpit when the Dean produced his pencil and paper!

Swift heartily disliked music, but nevertheless gave great attention to his Cathedral choir. In London, he attended religious services regularly, but was in no way shocked at the custom of taking the Sacrament by *rakes,* who complied with the law, *not for piety, but for employments.*

In the *Journal,* Swift refers to Lent several times :

I wish you a merry Lent. I hate Lent. I hate the different diets, and furmity and butter, and herb porridge; and sour devout faces of people who put on religion for seven weeks.

I dined with Dr. Arbuthnot and had a true lenten dinner, not in point of victuals, but spleen; for his wife and a child or two were sick in the house, and that was full as mortifying as fish.

It is extremely difficult to discover how severe were the civil fasting regulations in the Eighteenth Century. An Act was passed in the reign of Edward VI :

For the encouragement of Fisheries and the increase of Cattle.
It was not repealed until the middle of the Nineteenth Century, and was still listed in *The Justice of the Peace and Parish Officer* in 1785, for the guidance of Magistrates.

This Law laid it down :

That no person shall eat any manner of flesh on any Friday or Saturday, or the Embring Days, or in Lent, or on any other day commonly reputed a fish-day, on pain of forfeiting 20 shillings or a month's imprisonment. And every person in whose house any flesh shall be eaten on fish days, and not disclosing the same to a public officer having authority to punish the same, shall forfeit 13s. and 4d.

After settling the rates of payment to "informers", the Act goes on to give the circumstances under which licences could be obtained to eat meat. An interesting light on the apparent scarcity of the *Roast Beef of Old England* is the stipulation that no licence entitled the owner to eat beef, during the forbidden seasons, nor veal between October and May. It was obligatory to serve a fish-dish for every licenced meat-dish.

If the Act were still being strictly enforced in the early Eighteenth Century, it is no wonder Swift complained of the *sour faces*.

In his *Thoughts on Religion*, he gives an interesting summary of his own doctrinal position :

I look upon myself, in the capacity of a clergyman, to be one appointed by providence for defending the post assigned to me and for gaining over as many enemies as I can.

If fate had made him a soldier, he would scarcely have had to alter a word of that statement.

Although I think my cause is just, yet one great motion is my submitting to the pleasure of Providence, and to the laws of my country. I am not answerable to God for the doubts that arise in my own breast, since they are the consequence of that reason which he hath planted in me, if I take care to conceal those doubts from others, if I use my best endeavours to subdue them, and, if they have no influence on the conduct of my life. Liberty of conscience, properly speaking, is no more than the liberty of possessing our thoughts and opinions, which every man enjoys without fear of the magistrate. But, how far he shall publicly act in pursuance of these opinions is to be regulated by the laws of the country.

No Martin Luther here! Doctrinal doubts were quite permissable so long as they were concealed from others, and no efforts were made to act upon them. No wonder Swift considered Irish Catholics dangerously irrational creatures; they could have released themselves and their families from the savage grip of the Penal Laws by a discreet silence, and an even more discreet public compliance *with the laws of the country.*

Swift approved — for once — of Oliver Cromwell's viewpoint:

Cromwell's notion upon this article was natural and right. When, upon the surrender of a town in Ireland, the Popish governor insisted upon the article for liberty of conscience, Cromwell said he meddled with no man's conscience, but, if by liberty of conscience the governor meant liberty of the Mass, he had express orders from the Parliament of England against absolutely admitting any such liberty.

If Swift fought for liberty, as he himself claimed in his epitaph, he would have been horrified at the suggestion that such liberty included religious toleration.

There is no evidence as to Stella's attitude, but it is difficult to believe that she would have differed greatly from opinions so sternly upheld by the Dean; nevertheless, there is a temptation to hope that a woman of her compassion may have sometimes weakened into unauthorised charity at the sight of the misery of some unbadged Papist, in the Liberty of St. Patrick's Cathedral.

*　　*　　*　　*　　*　　*

She was born at Richmond in Surrey, on the 13th day of March, in the year 1681 ...

This day being Sunday, January 28th 1727-8, about 8 o'clock at night a servant brought me a note with an account of the death of the truest, most virtuous and valuable friend that I, and perhaps any other person was ever blessed with ...

Between these dates lie the forty-six years of Esther Johnson's life, about which little is known except what Swift has set down. She spent most of her youth at Moor Park, where she lived the life and received the education of a member of the English aristocracy. She was lovely, witty and gay. On Sir William Temple's death, she received a legacy of land in Co. Wicklow. Shortly afterwards on

Swift's invitation, she came to live in Dublin, with Rebecca Dingley as companion and chaperone. Both ladies being inexperienced housekeepers, they ran into considerable debt with Dublin shopkeepers, and were debt-ridden for several years. Gradually, they made friends and, with the exception of one period in their native land, they spent the rest of their lives in Ireland, where they died.

Swift's account of Mrs. Johnson gives no detailed picture of this woman, whom he describes as perhaps the best friend who has ever existed. Even allowing for the emotional strain under which his words were written, it is difficult to account for his overwhelming gratitude to the dead lady. He had enjoyed her friendship and her company for the best part of forty years. She had nursed him through many illnesses in the Deanery — always under the chaperonage of Rebecca Dingley; she had entertained him in her Dublin house and acted as hostess in his; she had helped him with his writing — acting as copyist and critic. But these services do not justify Swift's excess of gratitude. What unstated claims had Stella to be the greatest of all friends?

That she loved him passionately and desired to marry him is beyond doubt. That he did not marry her can only be disputed by ignoring the evidence of a letter Swift wrote in July, 1721, to her unhappy rival for Swift's love, Vanessa. In that letter he said:

"I continue to esteem, love and value you above all things, and so will to do to the end of life . . . .

Soyez assurée que jamais personne du monde a ete aimée, honorée, estimée, adorée par votre ami que vous".

Had Swift been married to Stella in 1716, as has been suggested, this letter to Vanessa would convict the Dean of St. Patrick's of the vilest treachery to both women who loved him. Reason as well as Charity deny this marriage, for which Stella hoped so long. That she should have accepted his will, in this and many other circumstances of her life, certainly deserved his gratitude.

Less than two years after Swift had assured Vanessa that she was the only woman he adored, she died, after a complete rupture of her long relationship with the Dean — a rupture which has never been satisfactorily explained. At some unspecified date after Vanessa's death, Stella in her compassion took into her home a young boy, *who strongly resembled* the Dean, thereby sacrificing her good name to Dublin scandal-mongers. If this woman, who loved Swift and renounced a normal life of marriage in order to remain his friend, had taken into her charge the unacknowledged son of Dean Swift by another woman, then indeed with justice he described her as : *the truest, most virtuous and valuable friend that I, or perhaps any other person was ever blessed with.*

EPILOGUE

After Dean Swift's death on the 19th October, 1745, his manuscript *On the Death of Mrs. Johnson* was found among his papers. Possibly he had intended to expand these notes into a biography for circulation amongst her friends; had the Memoir been intended for no eyes but his own, he would scarcely have so discreetly omitted such details as the name of the Temple family. Discretion was obsessional with Swift; when he began to write his own autobiography, he did so in the third person.

It is said that, after Stella's death, her name never crossed his lips, so he may have found the task of elaborating his notes more than he could bear. She had become the one fixed point in his erratic, frustrated life; when she was no longer there, he swung away into a wild disorder which culminated in disaster.

Fourteen years after Stella's death, nineteen *honest and lawful men* were sworn to enquire as to whether the Dean was of *sound mind and memory.* They found that he was not, and that he *had not been capable of taking care of his person or fortune* for some months past. Amongst the men who sat in the Deanery to enquire into the Dean's sanity, there were four merchants, a chandler, a brewer, two carpenters, a jeweller, a currier and an alderman. There is no record of their sittings, nor any reason to believe that their verdict was wrong. Nevertheless, the *dramatis personae* and the scene might have been invented by Swift himself, in one of his ironic rages.

For more than three years, suffering varying degrees of physical and mental agony, Dean Swift continued to exist, under ward, in the Deanery, from which his pen had changed the flow of human thought. Few tragedies are not diminished by comparison with that of Jonathan Swift, Dean of St. Patrick's Cathedral Church, Dublin.

INDEX

relationship with Dr Sheridan, 56, 59

complaints about Quilca, 57-8

Stella's funeral, 61

meets Van Homrigh family, 36

rupture with Stella, 75

Will, 76, 113

writes no epitaph for Stella, 78

love-letters to Vanessa, 83

friendship with Royal mistresses, 86, 100

death of mother, 86

entry of father's name in T.C.D. Register, 86

relationship with Archbishop King, 87, 88, 89

views on women, 95, 96, 97, 98

A Modest Proposal, 102-3

mention of Bryan M'Loghlin, 107

M D letters, 114

attitude towards Catholics and Dissenters, 115, 116, 117, 124

Swift, Mrs. Abigail : 86

Swift, Thomas, 27

Temple, Sir John, 27, 32, 33, 64

Temple, John, 21, 22, 23

Temple, Sir William, 12, 13, 14, 15, 16, 17, 19, 20, 21, 22, 25, 26, 28, 32, 36, 37, 39, 40, 45, 47, 48, 76, 81, 90, 114, 125, 127

Tollet, George, 89

Van Homrigh, Esther (*Vanessa*), 64, 67, 75, 83, 87, 88, 89, 97, 106, 118, 125

Van Homrigh, Mrs. Esther, 64, 85

Van Homrigh, spelling of the name, 66

William III, 22, 34, 38, 41, 47, 49, 59, 80, 101, 119, 122

Yeats, W. B., 72